THE END OF THE HOLOCAUST

THE END
OF THE
HOLOCAUST

ALVIN H. ROSENFELD

INDIANA UNIVERSITY PRESS
Bloomington and Indianapolis

This book is a publication of

INDIANA UNIVERSITY PRESS
601 North Morton Street
Bloomington, Indiana 47404-3797 USA

iupress.indiana.edu

Telephone orders   800-842-6796
Fax orders   812-855-7931
Orders by e-mail   iuporder@indiana.edu

Manufactured in the United States of America

LIBRARY OF CONGRESS CATALOGING-IN-PUBLICATION DATA

Rosenfeld, Alvin H. (Alvin Hirsch), [date]
    The end of the Holocaust / Alvin H. Rosenfeld.
       p.   cm.
    Includes bibliographical references and index.
    ISBN 978-0-253-35643-7 (cloth : alk. paper)
       1. Holocaust, Jewish (1939–1945)—Historiography. 2. Holocaust, Jewish (1939–1945), in literature. 3. Holocaust, Jewish (1939–1945)—Influence. 4. Frank, Anne, 1929–1945—Influence. 5. Collective memory—United States. 6. Popular culture—United States. I. Title.
    D804.348.R65 2011
    940.53'1814—dc22   2010047849

1 2 3 4 5 16 15 14 13 12 11

This book is for my wife,

Erna Rosenfeld,

and our children and grandchildren

Gavriel and *Erika,*
Julia and *Benjamin*

Dalia and *Asher,*
Natan, Gidon, and *Adin*

CONTENTS

ACKNOWLEDGMENTS

Many friends, colleagues, former students, and family members have read portions of this manuscript and given me the benefits of their insights. While they bear no responsibility for the flaws that may remain in the final version of this book, their comments and criticisms proved helpful time and again. I am especially grateful to Edward Alexander, Ilan Avisar, Lisa Braverman, Dov-Ber Kerler, Myron Kolatch, Barbara Krawcowicz, Matthias Lehmann, Vivian Liska, Daniel and Gale Nichols, Cynthia Ozick, Aron Rodrigue, Dalia Rosenfeld, Erna Rosenfeld, Gavriel Rosenfeld, Sidney Rosenfeld, Tammi Rossman-Benjamin, John Schilb, David Semmel, David Singer, Eric Sundquist, Leona Toker, Jeffrey Veidlinger, and Elhanan Yakira. It is also a pleasure to acknowledge the assistance of Meghan Clark, who efficiently and cheerfully helped me prepare the manuscript of this book for publication.

I am grateful to Indiana University for awarding me a sabbatical research leave during the fall semester 2009 and to Andrea Ciccarelli, the director of the university's College Arts and Humanities Institute (CAHI), for a research fellowship during spring 2010. Both awards made it possible for me to read and write in a more focused way than otherwise would have been possible.

I thank the following for permission to reprint earlier versions of some of the material in this book:

The Jean and Samuel Frankel Center for Judaic Studies, of the University of Michigan, for permission to reprint an earlier version of "The Americanization of the Holocaust," which appeared as the David W. Belin Lecture in American Jewish Affairs.

The United States Holocaust Memorial Museum, for permission to reprint material from "Anne Frank and the Future of Holocaust Memory," the Joseph and Rebecca Meyerhoff Annual Lecture, available as an occasional paper from the Museum's Center for Advanced Holocaust Studies, copyright 2005 by the United States Holocaust Memorial Museum.

Northwestern University Press, for permission to reprint material from "Popularization and Memory: The Case of Anne Frank," from *Lessons and Legacies: The Meaning of the Holocaust in a Changing World*, edited by Peter Hayes (1991).

The American Jewish Committee, for permission to reprint material from "The Assault on Holocaust Memory," *American Jewish Year Book* (2001).

The American Labor Conference on International Affairs, Inc., for permission to reprint commentary on Imre Kertész and Elie Wiesel, which previously appeared in *The New Leader* (November/December 2004 and January/February 2009).

The Weekly Standard for permission to reprint material that originally appeared in "Exploiting Anne Frank," which was first published on June 23, 2008. For more information visit www .weeklystandard.com.

THE END OF THE HOLOCAUST

Introduction

This is a book about victims and survivors of the Holocaust. It reflects some of the ways we have come to think about such people and also about ourselves in relationship to them. Above and beyond these matters, my concern is with changing perceptions of the Holocaust within contemporary culture and with the impact of certain cultural pressures and values on our sense of this particular past. It is a gruesome past, yet also an unavoidable one. "Unavoidable" is not the same as "acceptable," however; and, as I shall argue, the history of the Holocaust becomes broadly acceptable only as its basic narrative undergoes change of a kind that enables large numbers of people to identify with it. At the core of this process of transformation and identification lies the fate of the victims and survivors—their memories, stories, and future status as imagined figures within a continually evolving narrative of the Nazi crimes against the Jews.

By referring to the victims and survivors as "imagined figures," I am aware that I run the risk of being misunderstood. Obviously, such people were and are real people, who were forced to undergo real and terrible suffering. None of that is at issue here. What is at issue are the sources of our knowledge of their suffering. In looking at these sources, especially in their more popular forms, attention inevitably is directed to the narrative potency of literature and other forms of cultural representation as readily as it is drawn to the documentary sources of most history writing. The emphasis on narrative — on the telling as much as on what is being told — is here by design, for only by acknowledging it can we hope to understand how the past reaches most of us at all. History, in this sense of it, therefore, implicates both the event and its representation. And its representation, as Yosef Yerushalmi has put it, is being shaped "not at the historian's anvil, but in the novelist's crucible."[1] The historian's role is and will remain crucial to uncovering the past, yet historical memory broadly conceived may depend less on the record of events drawn up by scholars than on the projection of these events by writers, filmmakers, artists, and others. Here is how Raul Hilberg, a scholar distinguished by his insistence on mastery of the essential historical documents, has described the situation I am seeking to clarify: "To portray the Holocaust, Claude Lanzmann once said to me, one has to create a work of art. . . . The artist usurps the actuality, substituting a text for a reality that is fast fading. The words that are thus written take the place of the past; these words, rather than the events themselves, will be remembered."[2] Imre Kertész, the Hungarian-Jewish writer and Nobel Prize winner, who personally suffered "the events" that Hilberg refers to, agrees: "The concentration camp is imaginable only and exclusively as literature, never as reality. (Not even — or, rather, least of all — when we have directly experienced it)."[3]

Following Yerushalmi, Hilberg, and Kertész, it is clear that anyone who writes about the Holocaust today, more than sixty-five years after the end of World War II and the liberation of the Nazi death camps, is likely to soon find himself pondering questions of a literary and cultural nature along with questions of a more purely historical kind. It is not that we know all that we need and want to know about the catastrophe itself. Far from it. Rather, because we have become acutely aware that knowledge of this past is transmitted to us by such a large and diverse body of materials, it is necessary to think about the nature and function

of these forms of mediation as well as about the kinds of historical information and interpretation they convey. For this reason,
studies of the literary representation of the past have come prominently to the fore in recent years as an essential part of study of
the Holocaust. For this reason as well, some are tempted to place
in quotation marks the very term that is commonly used to designate the Nazis' genocidal crimes against the Jews—"Holocaust"
instead of Holocaust—to indicate how essential it is to comprehend the constructed "story" of the event if one has any hopes of
preserving its history and memory in responsible ways. For most
people, in fact, the event is simply not accessible apart from its
representations. Because the latter have become so numerous
and so varied, it is important that one attend to how the story
of the Holocaust has been conveyed, who is conveying it, how
and by whom it is being received, within what particular cultural contexts, with what degree of measurable impact on individual and collective awareness, with what consequences for cultural memory, and so forth. These are complex matters, but they
require attention if we are to understand the place of this traumatic past within our lives today and the shapes it may assume
in the lives of those in generations to come. In the chapters that
follow, therefore, my primary aim will be to chart the evolving
terms of the Holocaust "story" rather than contribute anything
significantly new to the history of the event as such.

There was a time, not so long ago, when it was commonly
understood that this "story" was comprised of three main
groups—the victims, their murderers, and the great majority of
people in the surrounding societies who looked on or looked away
as the crime unfolded. The chief victims, most everyone knew
(even if not everyone was prepared to acknowledge it), were the
European Jews, although it has long been recognized that other
groups of people—including large numbers of Slavs, Gypsies, the
handicapped, homosexuals, and certain political and religious
groups—had also been targeted by the Nazis for mistreatment,

subjugation, enslavement, and, in some cases, death. Nevertheless, it was generally recognized that Hitler's obsessive fixation on the Jews was at the core of the cruelest and most broadly encompassing crimes of the Third Reich and that the Jews and the Jews alone had been singled out for total annihilation. That the genocide did not completely succeed was more a function of events outside of the perpetrators' control than outside of their murderous designs. To represent the extent of their gruesome achievement, the canonical number "Six Million" has been generally adopted to signify that the Jews, persecuted and slaughtered en masse, were the primary victims of the Holocaust.

As for the victimizers, or perpetrators, their identity was clear right from the start: they were the German followers of Hitler, both military and civilian, as well as members of other European groups who aided the Nazis in implementing their infamous "Final Solution of the Jewish Question in Europe." The trials of the postwar period exhibited to the public at large the names, faces, and alibis of a small number of the leading perpetrators. Some of the most notorious of the murderers, including Hitler himself, escaped justice through suicide, concealment, or escape to foreign countries. Most others remained in Germany, Austria, or their home countries elsewhere in Europe, chose to keep silent about their participation in the crimes of the Third Reich, and often faded into the obscurity of generally colorless, bourgeois lives. Nevertheless, while most of the names and specific deeds of the individual perpetrators were lost to public awareness, their collective identity as Nazi murderers remained firm and was reinforced from time to time by certain sensational acts of public exposure, such as the capture and trial of Adolf Eichmann and the search for, and trials of, other Nazi criminals.

As for the people in the surrounding societies—now commonly called the "bystanders"—they were those who did little to either help or hinder the "Final Solution" and instead chose to remain passive witnesses to it, thereby enabling it in some measure to proceed without check. This is a category that embraces broad and variegated populations of people, including the common citizenry of most of the countries of Nazi-occupied Europe and also major European institutions, such as the Christian churches, the Red Cross, universities, sections of commerce, industry, labor, law, the civil service, etc. In Raul Hilberg's formulation, the bystanders were those who "were not 'involved,' not willing to hurt the victims and not wishing to be hurt by the perpetrators."[4] Although some profited from the plight and disappearance of the Jews, most were guilty of no specific crimes; and while some aided their Jewish neighbors through small acts of decency and kindness, most won no honor for themselves through the commission of especially meritorious deeds. Neither heroes nor criminals, they were ordinary people who lived through hard times and looked on as others among them experienced even harder and much crueler times. In moral terms, the passivity of the bystanders came to be understood as a form of silent complicity, but their role was a muted one and evoked no feelings comparable to either the pity and horror evoked by the lot of the victims or the contempt, outrage, and revulsion awakened by the deeds of the perpetrators.

There are others who also fall within the compass of this story—most notably, those who actively fought against the Nazis and their allies and those who willingly and courageously helped to safeguard or rescue the Jews who had been targeted as victims; nevertheless, in the main, it has generally been understood that the story of the Holocaust is the story of the victims, perpetrators, and bystanders. In the years following the defeat of Nazi Germany and for a number of years thereafter, the core of the Holocaust narrative, comprised of these three groups, remained pretty clear; and, at least among the majority of those who thought and wrote about these events in a serious way, there has been a high degree of consensus about the nature of the catastrophe, even if not a full understanding of the motives of those who were responsible for creating it. Why genocide became a part of European history in the middle of the twentieth century is a question not easily answered, but that it occurred, how it occurred, who brought it about, and who its primary victims were—these have not been matters at issue.

For the most part, the major lines of the story sketched out above remain in place among serious students of the Nazi era. Over time, and in subtle and less subtle ways, however, there have been shifts of both definition and priority within the principal categories of the Holocaust narrative. Depending on a number of variables, the contours and meaning of the "Holocaust" have been susceptible to change. As a consequence of such change, for instance, the category of the "victims" is in the process of being enlarged to encompass people other than just the Jews; depending on certain readings, the category of the "perpetrators" may either minimize or elevate the role of "ordinary Germans" and, in certain extreme cases, may even include Jews themselves; and the "bystanders," some argue, should include not only the multitude of onlookers within the European countries under Nazi domination but the organizational elites of American and British Jewry as well as the political leadership of pre-state Palestine. Thus, while the principal actors in the Holocaust "story" remain the same—victims, perpetrators, bystanders—the categories themselves have taken on a new elasticity and may now embrace individuals and types not previously housed within them. In addition, some of those who had occupied relatively minor roles in this drama in the past—most notably, "survivors" and "rescuers"—have been repositioned within it and today enjoy a substantially heightened profile. There are others as well—types that have newly emerged, or are trying to emerge, or are being kept from emerging as part of the essential narrative. Within Germany, "resisters to the tyranny of Fascist rule" are being promoted by some, as are German victims of allied bombings, Soviet army pillages, rapes, expulsions, and the like.

In Poland, "martyrs of the Polish nation" are prominently honored. In Hungary, Romania, Ukraine, and the Baltic states, a new prominence, and also a new equivalence, is being given to the national victims of the "Double Genocide," honoring the "martyrs" of Soviet Communism together with (and in some cases instead of) the Jewish victims of Nazi tyranny. Within France, the Netherlands, and other West European countries, there is an ongoing struggle over the role of "collaborators." In Israel, "Jewish heroes" have long been honored by the nation at large, and within certain circles there is also an incipient interest in "Jewish avengers." In the United States, much public attention is bestowed upon "survivors" and "liberators." Throughout much of the Muslim world, the Nazi Holocaust is either denied altogether as a genocidal crime against the Jews or, through radical acts of distortion and inversion, is appropriated and reconfigured to indict Israeli Jews as "Nazis" guilty of "genocidal" crimes against Palestinian Arabs. Precisely how all of this typological ferment, competition, and change will sort itself out and how, over time, it may newly shape our sense of the past is impossible to say with any certainty, but I shall attempt to describe those changes that are already evident and explain some of their cultural causes and consequences.

At the least, I intend to show that the Holocaust "story," far from being fixed once and for all, is, in fact, very much in flux. Certainly on the popular level of mass culture, and, to some extent, also within the academic study of the subject, the Holocaust has become a volatile area of contending images, interpretations, historical claims and counter-claims. Some proponents of genocide studies, for instance, decry ongoing attention to the Holocaust as being too narrow, or too parochial, and argue that it is time to insert study of the Nazi crimes against the Jews into the broader comparative framework of their discipline. Others argue that Holocaust studies, by awarding supreme victim status to the Jews, deny it to other victim groups and thereby assign a "permanent privilege" to the Jews alone. Some even claim that such maneuvers are part of a "Zionist" scheme to make Israel the beneficiary of universal sympathy through an exclusive concentration on Jewish suffering during the Nazi era. In these and other cases, hermeneutical disputes about how the "story" should be told or not told, even about whose "story" it is and who, therefore, has the right to tell it, are not arcane matters but, in fact, issues of considerable cultural, political, and even national consequence. They tie in intimately with questions of personal and group identity; national responsibility, honor, and shame; religious and moral integrity; and fundamental political values. In all of these respects and others, the Holocaust solicits a kind of passionate attention that surpasses the attention evoked by most other events of the past century. Its representation now constitutes a language of its own, which is in wide circulation across all levels of our culture and is used and misused in manifold ways. While there is still much that we do not understand about the Holocaust in its time, there is no escaping its imaginative afterlife, or rhetorical presence, in our time. In the pages that follow, I hope to clarify some of the ways in which this presence — made manifest in the still developing story of the event — is kept alive before a large and receptive audience, which in some manner is changed by it and also changes it in turn. For reasons that will soon become clear, I will focus predominantly on images of "victims" and "survivors," the two groups that have received the most attention in recent years, although I will make more than passing allusion as well to "perpetrators," "rescuers," and others.

A word needs to be said about the nature of my engagement with these issues. As I understand the drift of change with respect to an evolving public memory of the Holocaust, especially within American culture, we may soon reach a point of surfeit regarding serious, ongoing attention to the Nazi assault against the Jews. In fact, in certain circles such a point has already been reached. With victims of new atrocities filling the news each day and only so much sympathy to go around, there are people who simply do not want to hear anymore about the Jews and their sorrows. There are other dead to be buried, they say, other losses to mourn. Enough, therefore, about Auschwitz and Treblinka. Elsewhere attention persists, but it can take odd forms, turning the murder of millions into programs of popular entertainment, political action strategies, new forms of theological and liturgical expression, or well-intended but often banal platforms for civic and moral education. If some of these tendencies continue, and it is likely that they will, one can imagine a time when the memory of the Jewish catastrophe under Hitler will be reduced to the status of a grisly horror show or a modern-day passion play, the immense historical and moral weight of the Nazi crimes whittled down into the familiar categories of a Sunday school sermon or conventional box-office spectacle. Indeed, as I will demonstrate, we are already in such a time, with everything that says about the diminution of historical memory and the coarsening of any moral sense that depends upon maintaining a clear-eyed view of the past.

It is this realization that accounts for the note of skepticism in the title of this book: *The End of the Holocaust*. Why, some will ask, call into question the vitality of a cultural phenomenon whose energy and reach are greater than ever? Each year, after all, witnesses the publication of new books and articles on the Holocaust, the production of new films and television programs, the establishment of new museums and resource centers, the development and implementation of new school curricula, the convening of more classes, conferences, public commemorative events, and so forth. The Association of Holocaust Organizations 2010 *Directory*, for instance, runs to 272 pages and lists some 250 institutions and organizations world-wide that, in one way or another, provide services, assemble resources, and conduct programs related to the Holocaust. With so much ongoing activity, the evidence clearly points in the opposite direction—to more and not less attention focused on the Holocaust. Why, then, speak about its "end"?

What I have in mind in employing this term will become clear as the chapters of this book unfold. My overall argument is more about the changing character of historical awareness and its attenuation than about historical periodization and precise moments of ending. It makes sense, for instance, to say that World War II in Europe ended in the spring of 1945, but it would not be sensible to say that the Holocaust also came to closure at the same time. For many survivors, indeed, the Holocaust has never ended and never will end until they themselves expire. At least its anguish is felt as never-ending. I think of Primo Levi, for instance, whose writings make painfully clear the continuing nature of what he called, with grace and characteristic understatement, "the offense." Liberated from Auschwitz, Levi returned to his native Italy only to find that the sufferings he had undergone in Auschwitz remained with him. He was home, surrounded by family and friends, but his dreams took him elsewhere: "Now everything has changed to chaos; I am alone in the center of a grey and turbid nothing, and now, I know what this thing means, and I also know that I have always known it; I am in the Lager once more, and nothing is true outside the Lager."[5] For Levi and for countless others like him who had been incarcerated in the Nazi camps, the nightmare is a recurring one, and closure is out of the question. For them, the Holocaust, far from ever reaching its "end," was and remains a continuing trauma.

What happens to such sufferings, though, when they are treated in less serious ways, exploited for political or commercial gain, turned into something that resembles their opposite? What happens to our sense of this horrific past when it is reprogrammed to suit popular tastes and made into award-winning entertainments about life being nothing short of beautiful? What happens when others lay claim to the language of the Holocaust, and the sorrows of the Jews become contested by other sorrows and embattled in ugly disputes about comparative victimization? What happens to public awareness about the past when the emphasis of concern suddenly shifts from reflections on the Nazi crimes to legal battles about Nazi gold? Or when some take pleasure in denying the historical basis of these crimes entirely and seek to convince the public that the Holocaust is nothing more than an elaborate hoax designed by "Jewish" or "Zionist" interests? What stage of historical consciousness have we reached when, as one is amazed to learn, children of Holocaust survivors can bring themselves to crack jokes like the following: "Why did Hitler commit suicide? Because he got the gas bill." "What's the difference between a loaf of bread and a Jew? A loaf of bread doesn't scream when you put it in the oven."[6]

What happens in the light of such developments is fairly predictable: as the mass murder of millions of innocent people is trivialized and vulgarized, a catastrophic history, bloody to its core, is lightened of its historical burden and gives up the sense of scandal that necessarily should attend it. The very success of the Holocaust's wide dissemination in the public sphere can work to undermine its gravity and render it a more familiar thing. The more successfully it enters the cultural mainstream, the more commonplace it becomes. A less taxing version of a tragic history begins to emerge—still full of suffering, to be sure, but a suffering relieved of many of its weightiest moral and intellectual demands and, consequently, easier to bear. Made increasingly familiar through repetition, it becomes normalized. And, before long, it turns into something else—a repository of "lessons" about "man's inhumanity to man," a metaphor for victimization in general, a rhetoric for partisan politics, a cinematic backdrop for domestic melodramas. In observing Hitler's war against the Jews undergo such transformations, one can, with good reason, grow properly skeptical and begin to anticipate something like an approaching "end of the Holocaust." To be sure, books, films, television programs, popular plays, commemorative services, and the like will continue to keep stories and images of the Nazi crimes before a vast and receptive public, but this wide exposure itself hardly guarantees the perpetuation of a historical memory of the Holocaust that will be faithful to the past and representative of its worst excesses. It is more likely, in fact, that the steady domestication of the Holocaust will blunt the horrors of this history and, over time, render them less outrageous, and, ultimately, less knowable. Imre Kertész captures the essence of this seeming paradox precisely: "The Holocaust appears to be ever more unintelligible the more people talk about it. . . . [It] recedes ever more into the distance, into history, the more memorials to it we construct. . . . The unbearable burden of the Holocaust has over time given rise to forms of language that appear to talk about the Holocaust, while never even touching the reality of it."[7]

To look on as these developments unfold is not easy, and to write about them dispassionately even less so. Nevertheless, I have tried to be both restrained and clarifying in my descriptions and analysis of the phenomena I address. Whether I have always succeeded is another matter. As will no doubt be apparent, there are certain tamperings with the memory of the dead that I find simply intolerable, and I feel compelled to say as much. At the same time, I do not favor overdramatizing this subject or writing about it in a hectoring prose style. Especially in considering authors who are themselves Holocaust survivors, I have tried to be as sober-minded as possible, for only in such a way can one come close to gleaning the important truths to which these writers dedicated themselves. One of these truths, memorably formulated by Jean Améry, sets a tone and a direction that I find inspiring and have tried to follow over the course of this book:

It is certainly true that moral indignation cannot hold its ground against the silently erosive and transformative effects of time. It is hopeless, even if not entirely unjustified, to demand that National Socialism be felt as an outrage with the same emotional intensity as in the years immediately following the Second World War. No doubt there exists something like historical entropy: the historical 'heat gradient' disappears. . . . But in viewing historical processes we should not foster this entropy; on the contrary, we should resist it with all our power.[8]

In tribute to the moral witness of Jean Améry, Primo Levi, Imre Kertész, Elie Wiesel, and others, I would like to think that, at least in a small way, this book might contribute to keeping some portion of the outrage alive.

ONE

Popular Culture and
the Politics of Memory

*Most people willingly deceive themselves with a doubly false
faith: they believe in eternal memory (of men, things, deeds,
peoples) and in rectification (of deeds, errors, sins, injustice).
Both are sham. The truth lies at the opposite end of the scale:
everything will be forgotten and nothing will be rectified. All
rectification (both vengeance and forgiveness) will be taken
over by oblivion. No one will rectify wrongs; all wrongs will be
forgotten.* —MILAN KUNDERA

We say "Holocaust" as if there were an established consensus on
the full range of historical meanings and associations that this
term is meant to designate. In fact, no such consensus exists.
The image of the Holocaust is a changing one, and just how it
is changing, who is changing it, and what the consequences of
such change may be are matters that need to be carefully and
continually pondered. Such reflection will be undertaken here
on the basis of the following assumptions:

1. It is not primarily from the work of historians that most
people gain whatever knowledge they may acquire of the Third
Reich and the Nazi crimes against the Jews but rather from that
of novelists, filmmakers, playwrights, poets, television program

writers and producers, museum exhibits, popular newspapers and magazines, internet web sites, the speeches and ritual performances of political figures and other public personalities, and the like.

2. Thus the "history" of the Holocaust that is made available to most people most of the time is largely a product of popular culture and does not always derive from or necessarily conform to the history of the Jews under Nazism that professional historians strive to establish. Indeed, in some ways the two might be seen as rival enterprises, and the contest between them regarded as a struggle between antithetical drives or ambitions.

3. The public at large remains readily drawn by the specter of the Holocaust and is, consequently, a receptive audience for stories and images of the Third Reich, yet one cannot assume that this popular fascination with extreme suffering and mass death is tantamount to a serious interest in Jewish fate during the Nazi period. Indeed, far from being an effective means of educating the public about the evils of Nazism and the catastrophe visited upon the Jews, a prolonged exposure to popular representations of the Holocaust may work in the opposite way. It can dull rather than sharpen moral sensibility and thereby inhibit a sober understanding of or sympathetic feeling for the victims of gross historical pain. Images of personal and collective suffering may awaken conscience, but they also have the power to perversely excite the imagination; and, depending on how they are presented and to whom, such images may evoke a broad range of responses, not all of them seemly or benign. A pornography of the Holocaust can accompany and undercut a didactics of the Holocaust.

4. In sum, the image of the Holocaust is continually being transfigured, and the several stages of its transfiguration, which one can trace throughout popular culture, may contribute to a fictional subversion of the historical sense rather than a firm consolidation of accurate, verifiable knowledge. One result of

such a development may be an incipient rejection of the Holocaust as it actually was rather than its incorporation by and
retention in historical memory.

This prospect and the subtle psychological, aesthetic, and cultural motives that underlie it are detectable in a broad range of
cultural phenomena, many of which will be examined in the
chapters of this book. As a start, let us consider a few noteworthy developments in political life and popular culture, primary
sources for the dissemination of information in an age dominated
by the mass media.

We can begin by acknowledging the obvious: most public
acts of remembering cannot be understood apart from the political culture of the moment. As one American historian puts it,
"Remembering is never just about the past. It's always about
the present."[1] As a vivid illustration of the truth of this insight,
it is helpful to recall a code name that is no longer in the news,
although for several weeks in the mid-1980s, it fairly dominated
it: Bitburg. Prior to the spring of 1985 it is doubtful that very many
people outside of Germany had ever heard of this small Rhen-
isch town (and inside Germany almost its only resonant association was with a locally produced beer, "Bit Bier"). Within a very
short time, however, "Bitburg" came to symbolize far more than
just its place name and pointed to an extraordinary tension in
historical awareness, moral evaluation, German-American political relations, and more. What came to the fore with "Bitburg,"
in short, implicated a number of major and obviously unresolved
issues rooted in the traumatic period of World War II and the still
unassimilated history of Nazi crimes against the Jews and others.
"Bitburg," it became clear, set in motion a debate about some of
the deepest values of Western culture. The imperatives of historical memory, national responsibility, forgiveness and justice, politics and morality—all of these were stirred up by "Bitburg," albeit
most often in inchoate and conflicting form.

How could so much of consequence emerge from what, on the face of it, started out to be little more than a ceremonial gesture between the heads of two allied governments? *Newsweek,* in a prominent story, summed up the matter as rooted in "one of the deepest moral quandaries of modern times—the tension between world Judaism's need to remember the crimes of the Holocaust and post-Nazi Germany's need to forget."[2] While this formulation is simplistic, it is not altogether off the mark and comes close to expressing the popular sense of what "Bitburg" was all about. For a more precise sense of what was actually involved, it is helpful to recall the words of one of the major actors in the Bitburg affair, Ronald Reagan.

Here is some of what the president of the United States had to say at his revealing news conference of March 21, 1985, in reply to a reporter's question about his reluctance to visit Dachau, the notorious Nazi camp located in a suburb of Munich:

Q. Mr. President, would you tell us [of] your decision not to visit a Nazi concentration camp site when you make your trip to Germany in May commemorating V-E Day?

A. Yes. I'll tell you. I feel very strongly that this time, in commemorating the end of that great war, that instead of reawakening the memories and so forth, and the passions of the time, that maybe we should observe this day as the day when, 40 years ago, peace began and friendship, because we now find ourselves allied and friends of the countries that we once fought against, and that we, it'd be almost a celebration of the end of an era and the coming into what has now been some 40 years of peace for us. And I felt that, since the German people have very few alive that remember even the war, and certainly none of them who were adults and participating in any way, and the, they do, they have a feeling and a guilt feeling that's been imposed upon them. And I just think it's unnecessary. I think they should be recognized for the democracy that they've created and the democratic principles they now espouse.[3]

This is a remarkable statement, not least of all for its striking linguistic fractures and imprecisions. One can lie, just as one can tell the truth, in a straightforward manner, but to express sentiments as ambivalent as President Reagan's requires that language be stuttered, not spoken straight out. Apart from the awkward mumblings, what is it about these words (and they presaged worse to come) that is so troublesome?

In part, one is offended by the note of historical ignorance they register and also perplexed by it: after all, it was common knowledge at the time that there were still large numbers of Germans alive who fought in the war and even larger numbers who remember it (knowledge never denied in Germany itself). Why, then, did the president of the United States not seem to know it? And if he did know it, what moved him to declare the opposite to be the case? Why, one wondered, was he so obviously intent on distancing Germany from its recent past?

The notion that "unnecessary" guilt feelings have been "imposed upon" the Germans is similarly wrong-headed and goes against the grain of common morality, which affirms that those who are guilty of wrongdoing should in fact feel guilty. Indeed, if they deny such feelings or acknowledge them only because someone else imposes them, then the guilty will never begin to acknowledge their misdeeds, let alone atone for them. For President Reagan to relieve the consciences of the guilty by suggesting that it is unfair to reawaken memory of the war years was another startling instance of presidential rhetoric gone astray.

Most troubling about President Reagan's words, though, was something else, namely the sense that what he was saying, as bizarre and objectionable as it seemed, might not be idiosyncratic at all but, on the contrary, might actually represent the sentiments of large numbers of people. The president of the United States was not unintelligent, and he certainly was not out of touch with popular feeling and common aspirations. Much of the success of his presidency, indeed, was probably owing to President Reagan's natural ability to express what was on the minds and in the hearts of his fellow citizens and to articulate some of their deeply felt and most basic views. If, in speaking as he did about Germany and the Germans, he conveyed not only his personal disregard of the past but that of significant numbers of his countrymen as well, the problem before us is even more troubling.

For a variety of reasons, many Americans have only scant knowledge of history. They also have difficulties relating to it, most of all if it is someone else's history, and especially if it is painful or otherwise upsetting. In looking to disconnect from recent German history, the American president probably did represent some of his countrymen's inclinations as well. One of President Reagan's aides in the White House, questioned about the prospects of a visit to a former concentration camp, recalled the president saying, "You know, I don't think we ought to focus on the past, I want to focus on the future, I want to put that history behind me." Another Administration official explained, "The President was not hot to go to a camp. You know, he is a cheerful politician. He does not like to grovel in a grisly scene like Dachau."[4]

These are familiar sentiments, then and now. Like the president, most people do not wish to be reminded of the brutalities of the past and are not eager to have them linger disturbingly in their minds. To the degree they know about Dachau at all, they would prefer to put that place, which *is* grisly, behind them. A forward-looking people, Americans in general endorse the notion that it is preferable to forgive, if not necessarily to forget, and get on with the business of living—even, if one can find a way, with a former enemy.

As he saw it, President Reagan's task at Bitburg, therefore, was to patch up old quarrels with the Germans and pardon them for old hurts, a task for which he devised a twofold solution: (1) to celebrate the achievements of the New Germany, and (2) to offer absolution to the Old Germany by blaming its sins on what he repeatedly called "one man's totalitarian dictatorship"—a dictatorship he portrayed as absolute and as responsible for victimizing not only the peoples of Europe but the German people as well. With respect to the first solution, most people recognize that German democracy in the postwar period has proven itself and that Germany today stands as a generally prosperous, strong, and reliable ally of the United States. For an American president to say as much is neither astonishing nor objectionable. But for him to do so as part of a planned visit to a German war cemetery situated just near the site of the Battle of the Bulge, and containing the graves of SS men, obviously was bound to raise troubling questions.

President Reagan's answers to these questions greatly deepened the embarrassment of his upcoming visit to Bitburg, yet they nonetheless showed his determination to proceed with his task of historical cleansing. Listen to the following words from the president's news conference of April 18, 1985, and recall that only a month before he declared that he did not want to visit a Nazi concentration camp for fear of reawakening old passions: "I think that there is nothing wrong with visiting that cemetery where those young men are victims of Nazism also, even though they were fighting in the German uniform, drafted into service to carry out the hateful wishes of the Nazis. They were victims just as surely as the victims in the concentration camps."[5] If ever a public utterance was designed to reawaken old passions, this one was, for in two simple sentences it succeeded in leveling the distinctions between those murdered in the camps and the comrades-in-arms of their murderers; at the same time, the president's words echoed a Nuremberg-style defense of the murderers, who appear in President Reagan's apologetic view as reluctant agents of somebody else's aggressive will.

Curiously enough, the "somebody else" was never mentioned by name, although on several occasions the president referred to "the awful evil started by one man," "one man's totalitarian dictatorship," and the like. There are aspects of Nazi Germany that we still do not understand fully, but by now it is clear that the Nazi state was not run by "one man," that the Nazi war machine was not and could not have been driven by "one man" alone, and that the terror carried out over a dozen years in the name of the Third Reich could not have come about had a great many people not actively and willingly followed the lead of this "one man." Nazism was a mass phenomenon, and in both large and small ways involved vast numbers of Germans over the course of the war. In attributing the evil of Nazism to Hitler alone, and, inexplicably, by never referring to him by name, President Reagan was reducing history to caricature, to a celluloid image of pervasive, if ineffable, malevolent force.

At Bergen-Belsen, a camp that he belatedly and awkwardly added to his German itinerary (and this only as a result of considerable public pressure), President Reagan referred to "the awful evil started by one man—an evil that victimized all the world with its destruction." He continued in the same figurative vein: "For year after year, until that man and his evil were destroyed, hell yawned forth its awful contents." Such sentences, employing old and by now empty abstractions, deflect from history in its particular features and have the effect of promoting the oblivion of its individual actors. Hitler appears in President Reagan's view as a terrifying but vague embodiment of evil, and Hitler's soldiers, "the young men" in their graves, as his innocent and unwilling victims. As for the real victims—mourned by President Reagan as those "Never to hope. Never to pray, never to love. Never to heal. Never to laugh. Never to cry"—they are sentimentalized out of mind. One victim and one alone is referred to by name— Anne Frank—but the passage from Anne Frank's diary that President Reagan quoted at Bergen-Belsen is the one always recalled by those who want to sanitize the past and put its horrors rapidly behind them: "In spite of everything I still believe that people are really good at heart." In the precarious safety of her Amsterdam attic hideaway there were moments when the young girl did experience such optimistic feeling, but surrounded by the dead and dying of Auschwitz and later herself a victim of the deprivations and diseases of Bergen-Belsen, it is doubtful that such a passage from the diary represented anything close to what Anne Frank must have felt at the end.

President Reagan's rhetoric, however, indicated that he was not much interested in the real Anne Frank or the real Bergen-Belsen. "We are here," he declared at the camp, "to commemorate that life triumphed over the tragedy and the death of the Holocaust—overcame the suffering, the sickness, the testing, and, yes, the gassings."[6] The fact that there were no gas chambers and hence no gassings at Bergen-Belsen was lost on President Reagan's speech-writers and obviously on President Reagan himself, but even if there had been, it would not have made much difference. The president had Germany's Chancellor Helmut Kohl and national reconciliation in mind, not Bergen-Belsen and the Holocaust; and, once his obligatory courtesy call at a Nazi concentration camp was concluded, he flew off to pay homage to the German war dead at the Bitburg cemetery.

To say that the whole misguided episode was the product of historical ignorance and bad planning is an understatement. It was a setback of major proportions in public education about the Holocaust, an education that relies overwhelmingly on image making and, thus, is vulnerable to manipulation by revisionists of every kind. Yet the American public, or at least half of it, saw the matter differently, and their reaction must have been a source of satisfaction to both President Reagan and Chancellor Kohl. For however incensed American Jews, ex-G.I.s, and others might have been over Bitburg, a New York Times/CBS News Poll taken after the visit to Germany revealed that there were as many people (41 percent) who approved of President Reagan's actions as there were (41 percent) who opposed them.[7] Beyond these statistics, a sampling of readers' letters to the editors of American newspapers reveals a similar degree of opinion for and against the Bitburg visit. The following letters are not a sufficient sample to represent the whole of popular perceptions, but one might take them as indicative of the range of feelings expressed at the time. Both letters appeared in campus newspapers in Midwestern college towns, and so they might be regarded as expressing a degree of educated opinion.

The first letter, written by a history professor who had himself fought in Europe during World War II, strongly objected to the president's visit to Bitburg and regarded it as a callous affront. The writer calls the president to task for not making proper distinctions between the German war dead and their victims and comments as follows: "Undoubtedly there were thousands of decent, honorable men in the German Army in the Second World War. But the army they fought in was not decent and honorable, and the regime they were serving was perhaps the most horrible in human history. As for the Waffen SS, they were not victims at all; they were ruthless victimizers." The writer praises Elie Wiesel's words at the White House beseeching the president to cancel his visit to Bitburg and then ends his letter on this note: "We are told that if the Bitburg affair is called off the Germans will be insulted. Too bad. I do not believe that decent Germans will be insulted. As for the others, if they do not yet realize how the rest of the world feels about the Waffen SS, it is time they found out."

The author of the second letter is a student and writes from another perspective altogether. His major concern is that preoccupation with the Holocaust prevents us from advancing confidently into the future and is also unfairly and negatively stereotyping Germans as a whole. He regards Wiesel's words to the president as an affront, chastises "the powerful Jewish lobby" for placing undue pressure on the Administration, and argues that it is time to stop harping on the Holocaust as an example of exceptional Jewish suffering. "Holocausts are a dime a dozen," he writes. "I can understand pleas for sympathy, but I refuse to be manipulated into pseudo-worship of the formerly persecuted." He continues, "Must we be sidetracked by a bunch of bones lying halfway around the world?" He urges the president to carry out his plans to visit Bitburg, a visit, he writes, "that is much more important than the whinings of people like Wiesel. It will signify that we are beginning to forgive the German people for their past sins, in much the same way that America has begun to seek forgiveness for Vietnam." The visit will also show, he continues, that we can refuse Jewish pleadings (understood as serving the interests of an Israeli government "which says 'gimme, gimme' when it wants and 'anti-Semitism, anti-Semitism' when it does not receive"). The letter ends by acknowledging that "the methodical murder of over six million Jews is indeed a tragedy" but that "those who killed them were undoubtedly of very warped reasoning" and hence also victims. Thus theirs is "a tragedy, too," one that the president can and should address by going to Bitburg.[8]

One observes in these two letters some of the mixed feelings about the Bitburg affair current at the time. Through this episode, one also gets a sense of the larger issue of a still evolving and highly variable American public memory of the Second World War and the Nazi persecution of the Jews.

There may have been a time when one might have assumed a degree of common understanding of the Holocaust and common feeling for its victims, but it is far from certain that any such consensus exists today. If pressed, most people probably would express revulsion over the crimes of the Nazis and sympathy for those who fell victim to them, but it is doubtful that very many would like to be subjected to such pressure for long. Who can blame them? A serious confrontation with the history of the Holocaust is a wrenching experience and places upon people greater demands than most can easily bear. As a consequence, many probably would prefer to let the past be past. It is too painful and incomprehensible, filled with nightmare images of cruelty and terror, deprivation and death, guilt and shame. To give in to the impulse to forgive and forget, therefore, is understandable, even if not especially commendable.

Against this background, the Bitburg affair might be taken as illustrative of a significant strain of American public sentiment. Among other things, it showed that, with respect to moral attention to the Holocaust, a point of surfeit probably had been reached. This point was painfully exemplified by President Reagan's words and actions, which revealed the true character of historical events beginning to give way to counter-histories, political calculation, and other kinds of fabrication. For however much the president may have insisted before the cameras that we must never forget, his words and actions unmistakably reflected a desire to have the past bear down less demandingly on contemporary consciousness. Some twenty-five years later, Bitburg is largely forgotten, but if it continues to trouble us at all, it is because it manifested so clearly the tenuous position of the Holocaust in popular awareness, a position that in earlier years few people would have thought to question.

If one looks critically at how the Holocaust has been represented to the public over time, though, one sees that an attenuation of its place in history is not, in fact, a sudden development but has been going on for years. Some erosion can be located within professional historical writings themselves, which have not been free of fictionalizing tendencies.[9] The greater part by far, however, is to be found in the popular media — in the countless novels and stories, poems and plays, and films and television programs about the Third Reich and the Jews. In reflecting upon these, one sees that the road to Bitburg was prepared long before Chancellor Kohl and President Reagan embarked on their stroll through the graves at the Bitburg military cemetery.

Consider, for instance, the figure of Hitler, by which I refer quite literally to the various shapes he has assumed in word and image and thus to his changing configuration in the popular mind. The dominant image of the man is one of menace, and usually, but not only, in the form, favored by President Reagan, of undifferentiated evil. Yet such larger-than-life figures not only repel, they also fascinate and attract. Not infrequently they have a human side, too. So it is with Hitler, who stands before us today as the twentieth century's most compelling figure of destructive power. Yet in some of the ways he has been represented, Hitler has also taken on overtones of humanity that balance his malevolent side with a sometimes comic, sometimes tragic appeal.

Review his image in film—from Leni Riefenstahl's heroic portrait (*Triumph of the Will*), through Charlie Chaplin's satiric one (*The Great Dictator*), to Hans Jürgen Syberberg's Wagnerian one (*Hitler: A Film from Germany*), to Oliver Hirschbiegel's sympathetic one (*Downfall*), to Dani Levy's highly dubious *My Führer: The Truly Truest Truth about Adolf Hitler*, which attempts to present Hitler's "funny" side, to, most recently, Quentin Tarantino's maniacal one (*Inglourious Basterds*)—and you will find a Hitler of the most variegated shapes, not all of them by any means repellent. Review his image in literature—from the self-serving political portrait of *Mein Kampf*, through Wyndham Lewis's apologetic portrait (*Hitler*), to George Steiner's neo-kabbalistic one (*The Portage to San Cristóbal of A. H.*), to Norman Mailer's dalliances with the metaphysical and demonological dimensions of his story (*The Castle in the Forest*)—and you will find much the same thing. On stage, Mel Brooks's musical adaptation of his film *The Producers* features a zany Hitler "with a song in his heart." You can even find Hitler featured romantically on stage, as in *Love Letters to Adolf Hitler*, a recitation with music of excerpts from letters written to the German Führer by dozens of his infatuated subjects.[10] Hitler on television, Hitler in oversized picture books, Hitler in popular magazines, Hitler in science fiction, song, joke, and cartoon—Hitler is a figure of omnipresent and infinitely plastic shape. As Gordon Craig has summed him up, "One and a half generations after his death in the bunker, Hitler was like the little man upon the stair in the old song. He wasn't there, but he wouldn't go away."[11]

Hitler has become an allegorical as well as an historical figure, then, a presence that summons the attention of this generation and undoubtedly will continue to be a compelling presence for years to come. While he remains a threatening figure on one level, on another he is undergoing a figurative process of domestication and normalization, which has the effect of disconnecting him from the criminal regime he established and the catastrophes he wrought. Consider, for instance, this little "biography" of the man from Norman Spinrad's novel *The Iron Dream*:

Adolf Hitler was born in Austria on April 20, 1889. As a young man he migrated to Germany and served in the German army during the Great War. After the war, he dabbled briefly in radical politics in Munich before finally emigrating to New York in 1919. While learning English, he eked out a precarious existence as a sidewalk artist and occasional translator in New York's bohemian haven, Greenwich Village. After several years of this freewheeling life, he began to pick up odd jobs as a magazine and comic illustrator. He did his first interior illustration for the science-fiction magazine Amazing in 1930. By 1932, he was a regular illustrator for the science-fiction magazines, and, by 1935, he had enough confidence in his English to make his debut as a science-fiction writer. He devoted the rest of his life to the science-fiction genre as a writer, illustrator, and fanzine editor. Although best known to present-day SF fans for his novels and stories, Hitler was a popular illustrator during the Golden Age of the thirties, edited several anthologies, wrote lively reviews, and published a popular fanzine, Storm, for nearly ten years.

He won a posthumous Hugo at the 1955 World Science-Fiction Convention for Lord of the Swastika, which was completed just before his death in 1953. For many years, he had been a popular figure at SF conventions, widely known in science-fiction fandom as a wit and nonstop raconteur. Ever since the book's publication, the colorful costumes he created in Lord of the Swastika have been favorite themes at convention masquerades. Hitler died in 1953, but the stories and novels he left behind remain as a legacy to all science-fiction enthusiasts.[12]

Bizarre? Outrageous? Amusing? Whatever one's response may be to this Hitler, he bears little resemblance to the Führer of the Third Reich. It may be, of course, that this is precisely the point that Spinrad wishes to make, but if so his parodic attempt has failed. Certainly it has not prevented others from reconceiving the figure of Hitler along equally original lines. Read Beryl Bainbridge's Young Adolf, and you will find him portrayed as something of a bumptious shlemiel. Read George Steiner's The Portage to San Cristóbal of A. H., and you will see him almost as a Torah-inspired visionary, purportedly responsible for the creation of the State of Israel. In story after story, we have had the raging Hitler, the contrite Hitler, the artistic Hitler, the tender Hitler. There are fictions that bring him back to life as a woman; others that recreate him as a Jew. Look at Joachim Fest's documentary about Hitler, and you will be hard put to find the man whose passion and program it was to murder the Jews. Look at Syberberg's phantasmagoric Hitler film (all seven hours of it), and you will see the Romantic artist bent on reaching an epic moment of apocalyptic fulfillment. In the work of various comedians he has been good for a gag. To certain rock fans, he was "the first rock star." To the pornographers, who like to recreate his private moments with Eva Braun (about which we know little), he is, as Nazism as a whole has become, an abundant source of imagery for sadomasochistic sex.

Just what he would have looked like in the once-infamous "Hitler Diaries" we do not know, for they were exposed as a fraud before serialization in the periodicals had a chance to progress very far, but you can be certain that Mr. Kujau, the talented forger of these "Diaries," would have cleaned him up. As it is, others have been intent on doing so on a more or less regular basis. The British historian David Irving and his various colleagues in the American and European "revisionist" movement have created a virtual industry out of Nazi makeovers. And they are hardly alone. Around the time of the Bitburg affair, Austria's best-selling mass-circulation daily, the *Neue Kronen Zeitung*, ran excerpts from a book by Christa Schroeder, one of Hitler's private secretaries, who portrayed her former boss as an amiable man, who liked flowers and dogs, pretty women and vegetarian food, and was generous with presents to his employees. The paper came under fire for presenting such a grossly apologetic view, which made Hitler appear, according to one critic, as "a blend of Robert Redford and a Boy Scout leader."[13] Such reproaches evidently do not have lasting value, however; Hirschbiegel's recent film, *The Downfall*, based on a memoir by another of Hitler's secretaries, portrays the German Führer in his last days as a man with a human touch, capable of sensitivity to others.

Some years ago, a handsome brochure was circulated widely that announced to prospective buyers "Adolf Hitler, the unknown artist." It advertised a large format picture book "in gold-embossed burgundy linen" containing "over 830 pictures, 94 in full color, most published for the first time." A descriptive account alluded to Hitler's "adolescent memories of pre-World War I Vienna, portraits of people who passed through his life, pastoral scenes long gone, glimpses of forgotten streets of old Europe, soaring churches, still-life floral arrangements, architectural plans for the future." Why anyone would want to pay good money to take possession of this "unknown Hitler," whose skills as a painter were slight, is a mystery, but the book's high price indicated that its publisher believed there is money to be made in marketing still one more version of Hitler, in this case, an aestheticized and benign one.

And there is money to be made, or otherwise we would not see so much Hitler on the market. Nazi memorabilia of all sorts gross over $50 million a year, according to one report.[14] Does Hitler on the market also mean Hitler on the brain? For many, undoubtedly it does. According to one of his biographers, "more will be written about Adolf Hitler than about anyone else in history with the exception of Jesus Christ."[15] Such a figure—who seems to be able to satisfy at one and the same time our fantasies for power, madness, money, sex, murder, politics, pageantry, ambition, and art—obviously has appeal. It is not an appeal that will help us better understand the Nazi persecution and slaughter of the Jews, but then it is not meant to. Rather, it is meant to fascinate us with the Holocaust, to some degree even to entertain us with it, and ultimately to distract us from it by turning it into something else—a source of vicarious danger and excitement, a new mythology of sometimes pleasurable, sometimes violent sensations.

The popularization and commercialization of Hitler, in short—and one could also say the same about other figures from the Third Reich—is not only unhistorical but at bottom antihistorical. Over time, these developments end up subverting the historical sense and blunting whatever moral implications it may carry. Just as the politicization of the Holocaust—as Bitburg makes clear—falsifies the past for its own ends, so, too, does the fictionalization of the Holocaust carry with it the potential to reshape the actors and events of the past to suit present-day fantasies. In both cases, the actual history of the Third Reich, once suffered by real men and women at the hands of other real men and women, is not of primary concern.

Richard von Weizsäcker, a former president of the Federal Republic of Germany, was one of the few public figures at the time of the Bitburg affair who saw fit to oppose these tendencies in a forthright manner. In his important speech to the German parliament of May 8, 1985, commemorating the fortieth anniversary of the end of the war in Europe, he spoke of the need "to look truth straight in the eye—without embellishment and without distortion." "The past had been terrible," he declared, and had to be remembered honestly. Yet in one respect even von Weizsäcker, whose intentions were noble, was not severe enough in his attack on revisionism. "All of us," he declared, "whether guilty or not, whether old or young, must accept the past. We are all affected by its consequences and liable for it. The young and old generations must and can help each other to understand why it is vital to keep alive the memories. It is not a case of coming to terms with the past. That is not possible. It cannot be subsequently modified or made not to have happened. However, anyone who closes his eyes to the past is blind to the present."[16]

The moral impulse behind these words is admirable, yet in one crucial respect they are not wholly correct: the activities surrounding Bitburg and numerous other tamperings with the Holocaust tell us that the past *can* be "subsequently modified," *can* be made "not to have happened." Far from being fixed, memory of the past is always susceptible to modification and even obliteration. The various Hitler examples presented in this chapter are but one instance of this process. There are many more. Taken together, they point to a refashioning and falsification of history, sometimes in small and subtle ways, sometimes wholesale.

The Nazi genocide of the Jews will not soon be forgotten, but how it is retained in memory and transmitted depends overwhelmingly on what we choose to recover from the past, on what we choose to ignore or suppress, and on what we choose to remodel or newly invent. The historical character of the crimes that we have come to call the Holocaust is open to alteration under the pressures of a broad range of cultural forces, including political expediency, commercial gain, and popular tastes and preferences. Even without these pressures, the horrific nature of these crimes, while a source of endless fascination, is subject to unconscious denial. While some live under the obligation to remember, for others remembrance is not a primary duty. And for still others, the temptation to exploit the sufferings of the Nazi era for personal and political agendas of the moment is too great to pass up. One result, as will be argued in the pages that follow, is the development of a culture of victimization that may have the Holocaust as its figurative centerpiece but, in reality, shows little genuine interest in those who suffered and died by the millions in Nazi-dominated Europe.

TWO

The Rhetoric of Victimization

*The agony of the Jews under Hitler is too important and too
outrageous to be forgotten; yet it can be remembered, it seems,
only in ways that distort its meaning and deny its importance.
. . . When Auschwitz became a social myth, a metaphor for
modern life, people lost sight of the only lesson it could possibly offer: that it offers, in itself, no lessons.*

— CHRISTOPHER LASCH

In *The Minimal Self*, a perceptive study of "psychic survival in
troubled times," Christopher Lasch noted that a preoccupation
with victimization and survival had become a prominent feature
of American culture since the early 1970s and that, as a consequence, everyday life was now infiltrated by "the rhetoric of crisis
and survival."[1] Lasch, an acute social historian and critic, located
the main source of this heightened concern with adversity in
the history of twentieth-century genocide. At the same time, he
was wary of the victim and survival mentality that was developing among Americans, thought it exaggerated, and warned about
its social exploitation and political misuse. Lasch acknowledged
legitimate causes for concern: in addition to the perils posed by
the continuation of the cold war, this was, after all, a century that
had already seen "the extermination of the Armenians, the kulaks,

the Jews, and the people of Cambodia" (p. 69). Nevertheless, he thought the responses to them were disproportionate to the actual reality of most people's lives and questioned the prevailing sense of helplessness that was coming to characterize the psychic tenor of the age. In line with this criticism, he was disturbed by the adoption of the concentration camp "as a compelling metaphor for society at large" (p. 72) and the ready identification of many Americans with the figure of the victim:

> Our perception not only of the past and the future but of the present has been colored by a new awareness of extremes. We think of ourselves both as survivors and as victims or potential victims. The growing belief that we are all victimized, in one way or another, by events beyond our control owes much of its power not just to the general feeling that we live in a dangerous world dominated by large organizations but to the memory of specific events in twentieth-century history that have victimized people on a mass scale. Like the idea of survival, the idea of victimization, inappropriately applied to everyday misfortunes, keeps this memory alive and at the same time deadens its emotional impact. Indiscriminate usage broadens the idea of victimization until it loses its meaning (p. 66).

As George Orwell and others have demonstrated, the inflation of political rhetoric is bound to lead to distortions and diminishments of meaning, and Lasch was right to call attention to the pernicious effects of this tendency. He recognized that the ready appropriation of "Auschwitz" as a convenient symbol for common anxieties had unfortunate psychic and social consequences, among them the normalization of atrocity and the artificial elevation of the "victim" as a privileged cultural type.

In this chapter, I want to pursue these developments beyond the point that Lasch reached in his study and explain some of the consequences of adopting a language of extremity as an expressive code for more or less everyday experience. The appropriation of the language of the Holocaust for such purposes is not a small matter, for over time it has the effect of trivializing the magnitude of real historical suffering and making of it little more than rhetorical gestures. And yet, thanks in no small part to the spread of the popular discourse of victimization and survivalism, these gestures are now part of the language-world we inhabit, so much so that an auditor of our current talk might conclude the times are tipping once more toward an all-too-familiar madness:

Item. The bird watchers in New York's Central Park are incensed when dozens of trees are cut down and make strong remonstrances to the Parks Commissioner over the tree clearing, which would deprive migrating birds of a traditional resting and feeding spot. The protest grows heated. To cap it off, the director of the New York City Audubon Society condemns the park's restoration plan as another "Mein Kampf."

Item. Aging is on the minds of America's elderly, and various "anti-aging" organizations want the government to do more to develop new medicines against the ravages of old age. One of these organizations, The Life Extension Foundation, "maintains an exhibit in Fort Lauderdale, Florida, which blames the Food and Drug Administration for dragging its feet on a host of desired substances. Its name? 'The F.D.A. Holocaust Museum.'"[2]

Item. In the nation's most popular televised courtroom drama ever, O. J. Simpson's principal lawyer, Johnnie L. Cochran, wraps up his closing argument by comparing Mark Fuhrman, the discredited Los Angeles police detective, to "another man not too long ago . . . who wanted to burn people, who had racist views. . . . This man, this scourge, became one of the worst people in the world, Adolf Hitler. . . . And so Fuhrman, Fuhrman wants to take all black people now and burn them or bomb them. That's genocidal racism."[3]

Item. Numerous book titles extend the reach of "genocidal racism," among them Larry Kramer's *Reports from the Holocaust: The Making of an AIDS Activist* and David Stannard's *American Holocaust: Columbus and the Conquest of the New World.* Not to be outmaneuvered by the left on proprietary rights to this language, John Powell gives us *Abortion: The Silent Holocaust,* and Jerry Falwell contributes an article to a popular Christian journal entitled "Let's Stop the Holocaust," in which he writes, "The Roe vs. Wade decision has brought about the genocide of more than 10 million helpless babies."

Item. A genocide of "10 million" clearly tops a genocide of six million. Trumping both, Toni Morrison dedicates her novel *Beloved* to the "Sixty Million and more." And the Black Muslim psychologist and Afrocentric activist Na'im Akbar, speaking at Wayne State University, states, it is "a simplistic notion of slavery which makes it easy for people to compare their holocaust to our holocaust. They don't understand that going to the ovens knowing who you are is damn well better than walking around for 100 years not knowing who you are. . . . Our holocaust in America is worse than the holocaust in Europe."[4]

This short list of rhetorical manipulations of the past could be increased almost without end through similar citations from television, the daily press, cinema, novels, popular songs, political speeches, internet blogs, and the like. Proving what? Not that a new Holocaust is on its way but that the old one has never altogether left us. At least the familiar signs and symbols have not left us. The Nazis are back, and so, in sometimes bizarre reconfigurations, are the Jews. Far from being a surprise, their return recalls nothing so much as Karl Marx's famous observation that "all great, world-historical [events] occur, as it were, twice. . . . The first time as tragedy, the second as farce."[5] In most instances the farcical element is unintended, yet its repeated occurrence has become commonplace and has a corrupting effect on public discourse. Listen often enough to Rush Limbaugh's verbal attacks on "feminazis," and before long the term "Nazi" gets redefined to mean whatever Limbaugh and others like him intend it to mean when they get angry. Or, in a similar rhetorical register, the language of the Third Reich becomes a part of political invective, as when a United States Congressman from Pennsylvania denounces the Environmental Protection Agency as an "environmental Gestapo." Or two New York Congressmen decry Newt Gingrich's "Contract with America" as a political instrument that will do to American blacks and other minorities what was done to the Jews in Hitler's Germany. Or in the latest American debate about health care reform, President Obama is routinely denounced by his opponents as a new version of Hitler. The Nazi metaphor also gets recycled for use in special lobbying efforts, as when the National Rifle Association attacks United States law-enforcement agents as "jack-booted government thugs" who wear "Nazi bucket helmets and black storm-trooper uniforms"; or, as illustrated above, when anti-abortion groups regularly decry the "abortion holocaust," comparing unborn fetuses to murdered Jews and the doctors who do the abortions to Dr. Mengele himself.[6]

To those who know better—presumably to anyone with even a modicum of historical memory—these analogies are not only in bad taste: they are subversive of good sense, sober judgment, and reason itself. Despite that, they have become omnipresent and call into question what had been one of the fundamental assumptions of postwar culture, namely, that the Nazi Holocaust was a defining event in modern history and one from which we may have learned something of lasting value. As Elie Wiesel put it, "We all agree that the centrality of the Holocaust to our lives is irrefutable. We all agree that the event was a watershed; there is a before and an after; nothing is the same any more. . . . Man's relationship to society, to his family, to his idea of himself. . . . all these have been affected by whatever took place inside the forbidden kingdom of malediction."[7] It is undoubtedly true that for those who survived the horrors of Auschwitz, the Holocaust marks a decisive turn in history, but for countless others the fact of Auschwitz evidently has not mattered in the transforming way that Wiesel claims it has. If it had the kinds of consequences that he describes, we would not encounter the debasement of Holocaust-related language that has become such a commonplace of contemporary rhetoric; nor, more ominously, would we be witness to the rise of a skinhead subculture in several European countries, or the political reemergence of racist and nationalist demagogues in some of these same countries, or the scourge of ethnic cleansing, or the obscene industry of Holocaust denial, or American teenagers killing their schoolmates and themselves on Hitler's birthday. Wiesel regards Auschwitz "as a kind of black hole in history," but in describing it in these terms, he speaks from the exceptional role of the victim. In fact, for many people the hole that the Holocaust survivor is likely to see in the heart of history is either scarcely visible or is being actively filled in by others, who draw on the language of Jewish victimization under the Nazis to assert their own strong claim to victim status. The stories they tell may benefit from the interest and sympathy generated by the sufferings of the Jews, but the "Holocaust" they invoke is primarily a metaphorical and not a historical reality. In a caustic but accurate formulation, the critic Edward Alexander has referred to this process as "stealing the Holocaust."[8] A few examples will reveal how it works.

In the summer of 1993, at a time when each day's news reports featured stories and pictures of the bombardments of Sarajevo, there appeared a little book that drew special attention to the Balkan crisis and, before long, even more attention to its youthful author. *Zlata's Diary*,[9] a reprise of this century's most celebrated wartime diary, was the work of Zlata Filipović, a sensitive and intelligent thirteen year old who was being hailed as "the Anne Frank of Sarajevo." Closely modeled on its world-famous precursor, *Zlata's Diary* reflected the aspirations and vulnerabilities of an adolescent girl trapped in a brutal, ever-threatening adult world. Like Anne Frank's book, the Sarajevo diary covered slightly more than two years. Like it, it also opened with jottings begun in the calm, carefree days of a pre-war existence ("Behind me—a long, hot summer and the happy days of summer holidays; ahead of me—a new school year," p. 1), then abruptly shifted focus to record the savagery of the outside world and the need to improvise a family defense against it ("It's horrible in Sarajevo today. People and children getting killed, shooting. We will probably spend the night in the cellar," p. 38). As in the *Diary of a Young Girl*, one finds in *Zlata's Diary* copious jottings of concern about "Mommy and Daddy," favorite pets, missing friends, a school that one could no longer attend, the absence of normal foods and everyday, out-of-doors activity; there are other diary entries about feeling hemmed in, bored, worried and deprived, yearning for a secure and more normal existence. All of these feelings commonly belong to adolescence, to be sure, but, more to the point here, they belong to *Zlata's Diary* because Zlata's words were generically derived from those of Anne Frank. In one of her early entries (March 30, 1992), Zlata openly acknowledges the source that was her inspiration and guide: "Hey, Diary! You know what I think? Since Anne Frank called her diary Kitty, maybe I could give you a name too. What about . . . MIMMY?" (p. 29). Taking "Mimmy," a close sound-mime of "Kitty," as her best friend and confidante, Zlata Filipović set about to write a wartime diary in a voice that is, according to her American publisher, "both innocent and wise, touchingly reminiscent of Anne Frank's." And, like Anne Frank's voice, Zlata's was meant to "awaken the conscience of the world."

Did the "world," a notorious slumberer, hear her and respond? Yes, in a sentimental sort of way, largely ignoring the political urgencies of Zlata's ravaged country and instead awarding the precocious young girl the kind of instant fame that has become characteristic of our media-driven, celebrity-centered world. *Zlata's Diary*, an early version of which was originally published in Sarajevo in 1993 by UNICEF, soon drew hordes of journalists and television cameramen to the Filipović apartment to interview the "wartime child," and before long she had become, in her own words, "a personality" (p. 167). Her situation, simultaneously harsh yet staged for special effects, was more than bizarre. For instance, the color plates in the American edition of her book include one that pictures her calmly seated in her room with her diary open before her, beneath which one finds a caption that reads, incongruously: "Zlata writes at her desk even as the sound of machine guns echoes from the hills" (p. 83). One searches the photograph to detect the effect on Zlata of those guns but finds little. As pictured here, Zlata is poised, studious-looking, unruffled; moreover, outside of her window the sun is shining, and inside her room everything projects good taste, middle-class order, and evident security. Thus, although the reader is fully aware that this is a wartime diary, the photograph of Zlata at her desk projects nothing remotely like a life lived on the dangerous edge of warfare.

In another photograph we see Zlata in bed, a book in her hand, but instead of reading it, she is smiling broadly at the cameras in a room that has been especially lighted for a posed photograph. Although the circumstances are clearly staged, we are nevertheless asked to imagine a young girl suffering from serious deprivation, because the caption under this picture reads: "Zlata, who loves books, reads by candlelight" (p. 118). A candle is indeed

positioned near her bed, but given the brightness of the cameramen's floodlights glancing off of Zlata's forehead, these words and
the scene they are meant to describe strain credulity. To imagine
anything similar taking place in Amsterdam in 1942–44 would
be impossible, for it would be like watching Anne Frank being
interviewed on CNN at the very moment when the Gestapo was
searching for the hidden door to her family hideaway. Yet *Zlata's
Diary*, promoted as the work of "the Anne Frank of Sarajevo," is
full of such discordant moments.

To cite one final example: in her entry of July 29, 1993, Zlata
writes about the city under siege — "SHOOTING, NO ELECTRICITY,
NO WATER, NO GAS, NO FOOD. Almost no life" (p. 168) — yet, during the very same week, she goes on to describe her "book promotion." The book is the very one that she is writing, whose "promotion," we learn, took place "in the cafe Jeñ, [which] was packed
with wonderful people." "Naturally," she continues, "there were
film cameras and photographers and a huge bouquet of flowers,
roses and daisies, . . . and at the end I read my message. This is
what I said:

> "Suddenly, unexpectedly, someone is using the ugly powers of
> war, which horrify me, to try to pull and drag me away from
> the shores of peace, from the happiness of wonderful friend-
> ships, playing and love. I feel like a swimmer who was made
> to enter the cold water against her will. I feel shocked, sad,
> unhappy and frightened and I wonder where they are forcing
> me to go, I wonder why they have taken away my peaceful
> and lovely shores of my childhood. I used to rejoice at each
> new day, because each was beautiful in its own way. I used to
> rejoice at the sun, at playing, at songs. In short, I enjoyed my
> childhood. I had no need of a better one. I have less and less
> strength to keep swimming in these cold waters. So take me
> back to the shores of my childhood, where I was warm, happy
> and content, like all the children whose childhood and the

right to enjoy it are now being destroyed. The only thing I
want to say to everyone is: PEACE!" (pp. 165–166)

For someone who twice recorded in her diary the worry that
she "not suffer the fate of Anne Frank" (pp. 171, 193), this is not
only maudlin, it is meretricious. Nevertheless, in a world evidently receptive to Anne Frank look-alikes, no matter how artificially constructed, sentimentality of this sort sells. In no time at
all, Zlata's Diary was picked up by a French publisher, Robert
Laffont, and quickly became a bestseller in France and a dozen
other countries. Flown with her family out of Sarajevo, Zlata was
soon living in Paris, giving interviews to the world's press about
the sufferings of her besieged city and her passionate desire for
peace. Newsweek ran a cover story on her, and on her American
tour she gave out more interviews and appeared on all of the
right talk shows. Before long, movie rights to her diary had been
sold to Universal Pictures, and, for all one knows, a search may
be launched someday to discover the next Milly Perkins who will
immortalize Zlata's story on screen for the millions.

What conclusions can one draw from Zlata's experience? Up
to a point, the old clichés still apply, but they need modification
to accommodate the new technological capacities of our day and
the recreational and commercial interests they are made to serve.
Thus, while it remains true that war is hell for those who suffer it
directly, for many others, who can now experience it vicariously
in the comfort of their living rooms, it has become a kind of spectator sport, an opportunity to indulge in the thrills and horrors of
extreme experience as it unfolds before one's eyes in real time.
Zlata, an intelligent girl, recognizes that she has become party to
the strangeness of this situation, and while she participates in it
willingly and to her advantage, she is ambivalent about the role
she is playing. In her diary entry of July 27, 1993, she writes: "Journalists, reporters, TV and radio crews from all over the world
(even Japan). . . . It's exciting" (p. 168). Yet one week later, in an

entry of August 2, 1993, it is not excitement she expresses but a touch of anxiety: "More journalists, reporters and cameramen. They write, take photographs, film, and it all goes to France, Italy, Canada, Japan, Spain, America. . . . Some people compare me with Anne Frank. That frightens me, Mimmy. I don't want to suffer her fate" (pp. 171–172).

With the protection that such extensive journalistic publicity gave her, there was little chance that Zlata would suffer Anne Frank's fate. That was her good fortune. And yet there is a peril to be recognized here: given the use and misuse to which Anne Frank's name and story have been repeatedly put, the looming danger, far from confronting the metaphorical "Anne Frank of Sarajevo," involves the history and memory of the Anne Frank of Amsterdam. As will be described at length in later chapters of this book, *The Diary of a Young Girl* has assumed a special place in postwar literature and culture, and it long ago established itself as the standard against which all other testaments of childhood courage and childhood loss are measured. Etty Hillesum, Hana Demetz, Charlotte Salomon, Jona Oberski, Selma Meerbaum-Eisinger, Hannah Senesh, Eva Schloss, and numerous others have all written books or had books published about their wartime experiences that were said to "take their place alongside Anne Frank's diary," or that were recognizably "in the tradition of Anne Frank," or that "continue where Anne Frank's diary ended," etc. Such puffery is a commonplace of contemporary book publishing and is not what is at issue here. The larger source of concern lies elsewhere — in the continuous evocation of Anne Frank as a metaphor for other people's stories, a practice that has had the effect of both narrowing and transfiguring her story to the point where it gets lifted off its historical base. Strong metaphors often work to dislodge or supplant the realities they invoke. That is especially the case with respect to unpleasant or disagreeable realities, which can be subtly disposed of through metaphorical extension and substitution. In the case at hand, the negative reality to be overcome is clear enough: Anne Frank's sufferings, unlike Zlata's, were unrelieved by the intervention of print journalists and television cameramen, and before she was yet sixteen, the author of the famous diary had been turned into a corpse at Bergen-Belsen. That is not a readily acceptable image of the young girl for most people, however, who greatly prefer to stress her "courage," her "indomitable spirit," her "hope for mankind," and other happier and more triumphant qualities. In her latter-day career as a cultural icon, these are precisely the qualities that have endeared Anne Frank to the world and won her a high degree of posthumous adulation and fame. This fame, however, has been purchased at the cost of historical veracity, for the Anne Frank who lives on as an inspiring figure in the popular imagination is a greatly caricatured version of the girl who was hunted down by the Nazis and dispatched to an early and gruesome death. Who, though, wants to contemplate the Anne Frank who lies among the tens of thousands of other anonymous Jewish dead in Bergen-Belsen when they can instead thrill to the pretty face of Milly Perkins playing the eternally bubbly young girl on screen?

For all of her lovable qualities, the ultimate fact about Anne Frank is that she was a youthful victim, one among millions, of murderous anti-Jewish violence. That, however, is also the least acceptable fact about her. And so for a long time now she has undergone a process of metaphorical transformation, which has had the effect of bringing her back to life symbolically as a "survivor." According to the terms of this fantasy, her "spirit" lives on and finds its reincarnation in others, who carry on her tradition of courage and affirmation in the face of life's worst threats. Typically, whenever Anne Frank's voice is invoked, as it is in the promotion of *Zlata's Diary*, it is intended that one hear in it those things that are meant to prevail against all odds—an imperishable innocence and a transcendent wisdom and hopefulness—and not the agony of its final death rattle. As one of her innumerable devotees declares, the Anne Frank we remember is "that great young woman with the Herculean faith in the good and the just of life."[10] To recall her in such terms—or, as it is often expressed, "to spread her spirit" in these terms—is to do a very American thing: to be positive, affirmative, uplifting, optimistic. And yet it is precisely through remembering her and countless others like her in such a consolatory manner that Anne Frank's voice and the collective voices of the other Jewish victims of Nazi genocide have become less and less audible with the passage of time.

In a famous essay written almost fifty years ago, "A Plea for the Dead," Elie Wiesel argued that rather than belittle the memory of the dead through small talk and other forms of irreverent evocation it is preferable to "leave them alone." Wiesel's plea was an impassioned one, triggered by the sense that the popularization of the Holocaust would rapidly be accompanied by its trivialization. He was right then, and he is even more right now, but we are well beyond the point where such admonitions are likely to be heeded. The dead have not been left alone, but neither have they always been properly mourned or faithfully remembered. As a result of the broad dissemination of Holocaust imagery through all of the media of popular culture, Hitler's victims have returned to assume a prominent place in contemporary consciousness. They have done so, however, in ways that often distort and banalize their true fate. Thus, while the idea of victimization has been elevated to prominence, attention has frequently been turned away from the actual victims of the Nazi genocide and towards the instrumentalization of their memory for personal, commercial, or political ends.

Some of the chapters that follow describe in detail how this phenomenon has evolved within American culture and what some of its consequences have been, but by way of further illustration, it will be helpful to cite two more examples here. The first is in the form of a poem, "An American Holocaust," by the contemporary American poet Louis Daniel Brodsky.[11] It opens with these lines:

The pain of having my children seized from me
Is more excruciating than being caught
In a rain of white-hot ash
Dropping from Bergen-Belsen's chimney stacks
Bellowing nonstop into a gaseous welkin. . . .

The "pain" that the poet describes in these lines is that of divorce, which results in a legal separation from his children. No doubt such separation is painful, but under the usual terms of divorce settlements in America, the pain is almost always mitigated through parental rights of visitation. To analogize such a family rupture with the fate of those who ended in the crematoria of Nazi concentration camps is to engage in a kind of rhetorical wildness that cannot help but undermine the credibility of any poem. To go beyond that point and add that the poet's pain is "more excruciating" still than that of the Holocaust victims surpasses the limits of rhetorical license and points to a state of mind that resembles lunacy. It simply makes no sense to revert to the use of Holocaust references to talk about the pains that accompany what has become, after all, a commonplace American experience. And yet the poet is relentless in his feverish quest to settle for nothing less than the most extreme of historical allusions to portray the sorrowful predicament of his marital divorce. Here, once again with a reference to being separated from his children, is how the poem ends:

But the greatest pain is witnessing them
From this distance not even Imagination can bridge
For the dense fencing my wife has erected
And spliced with Nazi hostility,
Envisioning them dying in her barbed-wire vengeance.

To say that "An American Holocaust" is merely a bad poem is to say too little. For what makes it bad—among other things,

its wildly disproportionate linkage of personal pain with the sufferings brought on by one of the twentieth century's most horrendous historical crimes—is symptomatic of a certain strain of
thought that has become all-too familiar in present-day American culture. Such thinking seeks to amplify individual predicament or group distress through analogizing it with the very worst
experiences of the past century. Hence the wife in Brodsky's
poem treats the bereft father not merely coldly or cruelly but
with nothing less than "Nazi hostility." And it is not enough that
the children have been taken from their father, they are envisioned as being trapped within the enclosure of their mother's
"barbed-wire vengeance." Everything but Hitler's mustache and
the brand of the swastika makes an appearance in "An American
Holocaust," a poem whose hyperbolic straining after emotional
affect is more than just objectionable. It is irresponsible, and yet,
sad to say, irresponsible in a way that is all too familiar. With the
imagination in the grip of something like moral hysteria, excess
has become contagious.

Consider Betty Friedan's reflections on the postwar condition
of American housewives, as set forth in her influential book, *The
Feminine Mystique* (1963):

> In a sense that is not as far-fetched as it sounds, the women
> who "adjust" as housewives, who grow up wanting to be "just
> a housewife," are in as much danger as the millions who
> walked to their own death in the concentration camps—and
> the millions more who refused to believe that the concentra-
> tion camps existed. In fact, there is an uncanny, uncomfort-
> able insight into why a woman can so easily lose her sense of
> self as a housewife in certain psychological observations made
> of the behavior of prisoners in Nazi concentration camps. In
> these settings, purposely contrived for the dehumanization of
> man, the prisoners literally became "walking corpses." Those
> who "adjusted" to the conditions of the camps surrendered

their human identity and went almost indifferently to their deaths. Strangely enough, the conditions which destroyed the human identity of so many prisoners were not the torture and the brutality, but conditions similar to those which destroy the identity of the American housewife. . . .

It was said . . . that not the SS but the prisoners themselves became their own worst enemy. Because they could not bear to see their situation as it really was—because they denied the very reality of their problem, and finally "adjusted" to the camp itself as if it were the only reality—they were caught in the prison of their own minds. . . . All this seems terribly remote from the easy life of the American suburban house-wife. But is [not] her house in reality a comfortable concen-tration camp?[12]

"In reality," her house is nothing of the sort, and a clear-think-ing person knows that the comparison is a foolish one. As in the case of Brodsky's "An American Holocaust," what we confront in Friedan's book goes beyond merely hyperbolic thinking to something close to the shut-down of thought itself. For no one who thinks at all lucidly can possibly see a connection "in real-ity" between the situation of middle-class American housewives of the postwar period, no matter how bored they might be, and the wartime condition of inmates in the Nazi camps. What can explain such confusion?

As Christopher Lasch and others have pointed out, a politics of suffering and victimization has been developing within Ameri-can society over the past several decades, a politics whose pro-ponents draw on the pervasive presence of Holocaust images in order to garner for themselves a certain moral superiority that victims have come to enjoy in our society. In the words of one commentator, "paradoxically, our era, which proclaims happi-ness as a universal goal, not only preoccupies itself with—even invites despair over—certain forms of suffering, but also on an ever escalating scale it recognizes, ideologizes, and politicizes some forms of suffering and victims, making them valid, fashionable, and even official." In such a manner, "suffering becomes a moral identity and a basis for political entitlement."[13] The philosopher Tzvetan Todorov takes these insights still further:

> What pleasure is to be found in being a victim? None; but if no one wants *to be* a victim, everyone wants to *have been* one. . . . Having been a victim gives you the right to complain, protest, and make demands. . . . Your privileges are permanent.
>
> What is true of individuals here is even more true of groups. If you succeed in establishing cogently that such-and-such a group has been a victim of injustice in the past, this opens to it in the present an inexhaustible line of credit. . . . Instead of struggling to obtain a privilege, you receive it automatically by belonging to a once-disfavored group; hence the frantic competition, not, as in international commerce, the status of "most favored nation," but that of the group most in disfavor. . . .
>
> What are six million dead Jews, and dead beyond our borders, asks Louis Farrakhan, the leader of the Nation of Islam: "The holocaust of the black people has been a hundred times worse than the holocaust of the Jews."[14]

Such manipulative strategies almost always involve recourse to rhetorical extremity, and within our inherited vocabulary of human suffering and pain, there is no rhetoric more extreme than that which derives from the Nazi Holocaust of the Jews. By projecting images of themselves as "victims" in these terms, however, writers like Filipović, Brodsky, and Friedan and demagogues like Louis Farrakhan not only fail to make their own cases plausible, but they do something to our use of language and our sense of history that is utterly reckless. For when everyone is proclaimed to be a "victim"—moreover, a "victim" on a par with or

even in excess of the condition of the victims of Nazi genocide—
then the very concept of "victim" is voided of any specific meaning that it once might have carried from the past. And so, a husband divorced from his wife and missing his children is
experiencing "an American Holocaust," middle-class American
housewives languishing in the suburbs are said to be undergoing
their own version of "genocide," and Zlata Filipović, writing her
wartime diary before the visiting journalists and television cameramen, becomes interchangeable with Anne Frank. The past is
neutralized by its impersonations and, in the end, reality itself is
reduced to little more than a figure of speech, so much so that
the very expression "in reality" becomes only a rhetorical filler.

Anne Frank and the other victims of Nazi genocide, in sum,
become victimized all over again, this time falling prey to a new
mystique of "victimization." Before long, people who may not consciously intend to manipulate the language of the now entrenched
victim culture are manipulated by it, and it becomes easy for them
to imagine themselves entrapped within a condition of suffering
and pain that is probably far in excess of their actual situations. It
is this unintentionally exaggerated association that helps to explain
the familiar phenomenon of young girls who instantly "identify"
with Anne Frank and come to see their lot in life as one with hers.
This as well has rendered the term "Holocaust" so plastic in its
application as to make it sometimes meaningless as an historical
referent. The scandal that should attach to the terrible suffering
and mass murder of the Jews is dissipated by a new social myth,
that of a universal "Auschwitz," which makes victims or potential
victims of us all. At the point when we all become "Anne Frank,"
Anne Frank herself is dislodged from history and begins to disap-
pear into metaphor. To see how she has evolved in this manner
will be the aim of chapter 4. First, though, it is necessary to look
more closely at certain developments within American culture
that influence the way people in this country see, and also are kept
from seeing, what the Holocaust actually was.

THREE

The Americanization of
the Holocaust

Looking back upon the devastation of European Jewry during World War II, what is it that most people see and how do they understand it?

In an effort to discover answers to questions of this kind, the American Jewish Committee carried out a series of studies in the 1990s to determine what people in several different countries—among them, the United States, France, Germany, and Great Britain—know about the Holocaust.[1] The findings were not encouraging, especially with respect to the levels of historical knowledge among Americans. When asked, "What does the term 'the Holocaust' refer to?" 38 percent of American adults and 53 percent of high school students either did not know or offered incorrect answers. Higher percentages of American adults (65 percent) and high school students (71 percent) seemed not to know that approximately six million Jews were killed by the Nazis and their allies. Presented with the names "Auschwitz, Dachau, and Treblinka," 38 percent of the same adults and 51 percent of the high school students failed to recognize these as signifying concentration camps. Furthermore, 59 percent of the adults and the same percentage of the students did not know that the symbol that Jews were forced to wear during the war was the yellow star. It is little wonder, then, that the scholars who carried out this survey concluded that a "serious knowledge gap exists for both adults and youth in the United States with regard to basic information about the Holocaust."[2]

The Europeans do better, with adults and students in Germany scoring the highest among the national population groups surveyed in these studies. But then we confront a seeming paradox, for while the Americans know the least about the Holocaust, they seem to *care* the most, with large percentages of those polled replying that they deem it "essential" or "important" that Americans "know about and understand the Holocaust."[3] Given the shockingly low levels of their own knowledge and understanding, how is it that these Americans—only 21 percent of whom are able to recognize that the "Warsaw ghetto" had some connection to the Nazi crimes against the Jews—regard the Holocaust as "relevant" today and strongly hold to the opinion that Americans should know about it?[4] It is pointless to lapse into an easy cynicism and suggest that they mean "other" Americans, for no doubt they include themselves in the picture. What kind of a picture is it, though, when people who know so little about an event as momentous as the Holocaust indicate that they care a good deal about it? This question prompts a series of related questions: what do Americans mean by the Holocaust anyway, and how do they come to acquire these meanings? What are their sources of information about the Holocaust, and what images do these sources project to them? How, in sum, do they come to know whatever it is they do know? Some answers to these questions have already been given in the previous chapters, but we need to probe them more deeply. Before proceeding to a consideration of how Americans have come to perceive and understand the Holocaust, however, it will be helpful to take up a few more general concerns.

Thanks to the valuable work of innumerable scholars and others, we possess a great deal of information today about the fate of the Jews of Europe during the Third Reich. Indeed, the crime that we have come to call the Holocaust is one of the most copiously documented crimes in history. Yet it continues to present massive problems to understanding. Why is that so?

In part, it is owing to the horrific nature of the Nazi assault against the Jews, an intended genocide whose scope and brutality surpass the limits of what most people are capable of imagining. It is hard for the mind to grasp the intentions behind this fury, just as it is hard to understand the passions that drove it, the system that sustained it, and the people who served its murderous ends. To admit as much is not to suggest that there was anything fundamentally "unreal" or otherworldly about the Holocaust. It was all too real an historical event, but one of such an unprecedented nature as to evade ready comprehension within the received categories of historical explanation. In addition to these problems of incomprehensibility, a second problem presents itself, which has to do with how the memory of the Nazi crimes has been represented within various national cultures. The injunction to remember is a constant of virtually every work of Holocaust testimony and reflection that has come down to us, yet the question of *what* is to be remembered is intimately tied to *who* it is doing the remembering and to the cultural priorities and pressures that determine or impede historical memory in the first place.

The term "historical memory" is in common usage, but, as previously noted, for most people a sense of the Nazi crimes against the Jews is formed less by the record of events established by professional historians than by individual stories and images that reach us from more popular writers, artists, film directors, television producers, political figures, and the like. We have already seen some examples of such popularization in the previous chapters of this book and observed some of their effects. Other instances will be cited in this chapter and the chapters that follow. All point to the same truth: we live in a mass culture, and much of what we learn about the past comes to us from those forms of communication that comprise the information and entertainment networks of this culture. By way of illustration, it is worth recalling that tens of millions of Americans watched the NBC docudrama *Holocaust* when this popular television miniseries was first shown in the spring of 1978. More recently, an even larger mass audience has seen Steven Spielberg's *Schindler's List.* It does not detract in the least from the scholarly value of a work such as Raul Hilberg's magisterial study, *The Destruction of the European Jews,* to recognize that far more people are likely to learn about Jewish victimization under the Nazis from these films or from reading Anne Frank's *The Diary of a Young Girl* or Art Spiegelman's *Maus* than from reading Hilberg.

What conclusions might one draw from these facts? The obvious ones: historical memory in a popular culture is determined chiefly by popular forms of representation. For this reason, if we truly wish to understand how Americans have come to view the Holocaust, it is necessary to give priority attention to those writers and artists whose works most people are exposed to. As a work of history, for instance, William Shirer's *The Rise and Fall of the Third Reich* does not carry the authority of the best books on Nazi Germany produced by academic historians. Nevertheless, it was extremely popular in its day and is still widely read. If one wants to identify those books that have helped to shape popular understanding of the Nazi era, then Shirer's work finds its place close to the top of the list and needs to be taken seriously.[5]

We also need to recognize that, more than sixty-five years after the defeat of Nazi Germany and the liberation of the death camps, there remain disagreements about how the Holocaust is to be understood and remembered. In its oldest and most normative conception, for instance, the Holocaust signifies the death of some six million Jews in Nazi-occupied Europe.[6] Simon Wiesenthal and those who follow his lead on this issue, however, have challenged this figure and advocate a much wider conception of the victims of the Nazi crimes. They point to eleven million dead.[7] This discrepancy in the numbers is no small matter, for it reflects a major conceptual difference about what the Holocaust was and who is to be included among its victims—only the Jews or all of those who perished under the Nazi tyranny, including Polish political prisoners, Soviet soldiers, Gypsies, homosexuals, the handicapped, the mentally ill, Jehovah's Witnesses, and others. In addition, there is ongoing argument today over whether the Holocaust is to be understood as but one example of a larger phenomenon—genocide—and, consequently, seen within the wider framework of state-sponsored mass violence, or whether its distinctive features make it a singular crime best comprehended in its own terms.[8] Similarly, the once widely shared view that the Holocaust was "unique" has eroded in scholarly circles, although it generally persists among people outside of the academy, at least in North America.[9]

One would think that more than six decades after the end of World War II these basic questions would by now be settled, but in fact they have not been. Nor has there been consensus on any of a number of other related issues. Indeed, a comparative study of the histories of World War II in different countries would quickly show that national myths and reigning ideologies have shaped the memory of the war years in diverse and often sharply contrasting ways.

For many years after the end of World War II, visitors to the remains of the Auschwitz camp system in Poland would find that the presentation of the main camp had been organized along lines largely meant to serve a Polish national interest. Auschwitz, in this rendering of it, was projected as a crucial memory site of the martyrdom of the Polish nation, and only in more recent years has it also been shown to be a place where over a million European Jews were destroyed.[10] Moreover, the numerous crucifixes that a visitor can sometimes see at Auschwitz-Birkenau and other former Nazi death camps mark these places symbolically as Christian burial sites. The fact that it was Jews who comprised the largest number of victims—90 percent or more of those murdered at Auschwitz-Birkenau were Jews—may not be apparent to people who visit these former killing centers and do not bring such knowledge with them.

And Poland is by no means a singular instance of this phenomenon. For decades the Russians resisted any proper acknowledgement of the Jewish dead at places like Babi Yar and instead have commemorated, without distinction, all of those who fell as "victims of fascism" during The Great Patriotic War. Germans have debated whether the crimes committed by their countrymen three generations ago constitute a singular chapter in history or are to be compared with other acts of barbarism and mass murder in the twentieth century such as Stalin's crimes. For those in Germany who pursue this latter course, the aim is to "normalize" the Nazi crimes by situating them within a broad-based history of brutality and mass murder, a move that may have the effect of dissolving the uniquely criminal features of German National Socialism within such conceptual frameworks as "totalitarianism," "fascism," and the like. Alongside this debate among historians, there has emerged a new and heightened emphasis on the role of Germans who resisted the tyranny of the Third Reich and also on those, especially in the eastern parts of the country, who perished under Allied bombing raids or were expelled in large numbers from their homes and lands. Over the years, in fact, many people in Germany have distanced themselves from any close identification with the perpetrators and have come to regard themselves increasingly as "victims." In this shift of psychological roles and moral responsibility, they have been preceded by Austrians, who long ago proclaimed themselves to be the first "victims" of the Third Reich. It is only of late and with notable reluctance that people in Austria have begun to see themselves as more willing partners of their countryman, Adolf Hitler. The French long postponed a national reckoning with their Vichy past and have been painfully slow to confront some of the ugly facts of active French collaboration with Nazi rule. Belatedly, and as a result of public scandal, the Swiss have come to understand that their country was not the neutral haven that it customarily has affirmed itself to be but, through some of its central institutions, may have been actively complicit with the Nazis. Among the Dutch there are to this day those who stress a proud campaign of citizens' opposition to the German occupiers of their country, this despite the fact that a sizable number of people in the Netherlands were organized in a native Nazi party and worked hand in hand with German rule. In Israel, the values of heroism and resistance have for decades been constituent features of national Holocaust memory and have been promoted as a positive counterweight to the otherwise overwhelmingly negative facts of Jewish victimization. In sum, national, cultural, ideological, religious, and political interests have shaped and continue to shape the ways in which the history of World War II and the crimes against the Jews have been presented to diverse publics.[11] Far from there being anything like a shared memory of the Holocaust, we find a multiplicity of historical memories and often a clash among them.

American culture, itself a dominant shaper of popular images, has not been exempt from these tendencies. Indeed, it is almost certainly the case that the future memory of the Holocaust will be determined to a large extent by America's role, along with that of Israel, Germany, and Poland, in projecting particular views of World War II and the Holocaust. In what follows I aim to examine some of the sources that contribute to the ongoing process of imagining and presenting the Holocaust along specifically American lines. As will soon become evident, the matter of who precisely is to be regarded as a Holocaust "victim," "perpetrator," "survivor," etc. is by no means clear or simple but is dependent on a complex range of determining cultural attitudes, political ideologies, religious values, and the like. To identify and explain these contemporary influences on our sense of the past is the major task of this chapter.

A good place to begin is with the term "Holocaust" itself. Although it is widely used today, the fact is that those Jews who suffered in the ghettos and camps of Nazi-occupied Europe did not think of themselves as victims of a "Holocaust." Nor did most of them employ such Hebrew terms as *churban* or *shoah*, which today sometimes alternate with "Holocaust" in popular usage. Rather, in referring to their fate in the immediate postwar years, they typically spoke about the "catastrophe," or the "recent Jewish catastrophe," or the "disaster." These more or less general terms remained dominant through the latter 1940s and into the early 1950s, when "Holocaust" or "the Holocaust" gained currency and took on the connotations it has largely retained until today.[12] Elie Wiesel had a prominent role in popularizing "the Holocaust" as the term of choice to designate the Nazi assault against the Jews, though he did not actually coin the phrase. In Wiesel's usage and, following him, that of countless others, "the Holocaust" has been intended as an exclusive term to point to the persecution and intended genocide of European Jewry. As already noted, however, there are others who have preferred to widen the application of the language of "Holocaust" so that it includes all those who suffered and perished at the hands of the Germans and their allies.[13]

The debate between those who reserve the term "Holocaust" specifically and exclusively for the Jewish victims of Nazism and those who opt for much wider inclusion of victim populations is an ongoing one. It is a debate of great consequence, for in terms of projecting an image of what the Holocaust was, a great deal depends on the numbers employed and the sense of the past that these numbers imply. Following Simon Wiesenthal, for instance, President Carter, speaking on Holocaust Remembrance Day in Washington in 1979, referred to eleven million victims of the Holocaust, among them six million Jews and five million non-Jews.[14] More recently, the language of "Holocaust" has been used by those who want to draw public attention to the crimes, abuses, and assorted sufferings that constitute social ills in today's America. In the passionate debates underway about abortion, for instance, one frequently encounters terms such as the "killing centers" where a "genocide" is being carried out against unborn baby "victims." Following this turn—and it is characteristically American in its intent to be broadly inclusive—"Holocaust" or "the Holocaust" is in the process of being transformed from a proper noun to a common noun, a semantic switch that signifies an important conceptual and ideological transformation as well. As a result, language that hitherto has been employed to refer primarily to Nazi crimes against the Jews is frequently applied to human sufferings of a diverse kind. In a globalizing age characterized by a high degree of standardization, "the Holocaust," as Daniel Levy and Natan Sznaider observe, "now serves as a universal 'container' for memories of myriad victims" and for many people has become a sign for the "universalizing of evil."[15]

There are those who oppose this tendency but also those who favor it. The Israeli scholar Yehuda Bauer has spoken out strongly against it, arguing that in the process of becoming Americanized, the Holocaust is in danger of becoming de-Judaized. As Bauer puts it, "In the public mind the term 'Holocaust' has become flattened" so that "any evil that befalls anyone anywhere becomes a Holocaust." Bauer recognizes that the semantic extension of the term "Holocaust" is accompanied by a cognitive shift, resulting in what he fears will be a "total misunderstanding" of the historical event that the term was originally meant to designate. What underlies this development? Its causes are various, but in Bauer's view, much of it relates to those people who were charged with the responsibility of creating the United States Holocaust Memorial Museum in Washington, D.C. They were faced with a difficult dilemma, moreover, one of a specifically American kind: "It was unclear how the uniqueness of the Holocaust and its universalist implications could be combined in a way that would be in accord with the American heritage and American political reality."[16]

Bauer did not spell out what constitutes the "American heritage," but anyone familiar with the ideological tendencies that inform American political culture would be able to fill in the picture for him. It is part of the traditional, mainstream American ethos to stress the prevalence of goodness, innocence, optimism, liberty, diversity, and equality. It is part of the same ethos to downplay or at least not dwell on the dark and brutal sides of life and instead to place a preponderant emphasis on the saving power of individual moral conduct and collective deeds of redemption. Americans by and large prefer to think affirmatively and progressively. The tragic vision, therefore, is antithetical to the American way of seeing the world, according to which people are meant to overcome adversity and not cling endlessly to their sorrows. Because Americans are also pragmatic in their approach to history, they are eager to learn what "lessons" can be drawn from the past in order, as many are quick to say, to prevent its worst excesses "from ever happening again." In short, one should take what one can from history and then move on, hopefully to a better day.

If it is values such as these that Bauer had in mind when he referred to the American heritage, it is little wonder that he found Americans culturally predisposed to "misunderstand" the Nazi persecution and mass murder of Europe's Jews. The right to life, liberty, and the pursuit of happiness, after all, had no place in Auschwitz, which denied its inmates all rights and subjected them instead to the punishments of forced incarceration, constant misery, and mass death. These cruelties and deprivations, systematized by state policy and willingly carried out by large numbers of citizens, are so antithetical to the American mind and moral imagination as to be virtually incomprehensible.

The Holocaust has had to enter American consciousness, therefore, in ways that Americans could readily understand on their own terms. These are terms that promote a tendency to individualize, heroize, moralize, idealize, and universalize. It is through such cognitive screens as these that human behavior is apt to be refracted through American cultural productions, and they have helped to shape the ways in which the Nazi Holocaust of European Jewry has been represented in this country on the popular level. In addition, "politically correct" attitudes and other ideological fashions of the moment also play a role in influencing how we read the past, including the years of destruction that characterize the Nazi era in Europe.

While significant attention has been focused on the Holocaust in recent years, during the war itself and for a number of years afterward the fate of Europe's Jews under Hitler was not a matter of central concern within American political and cultural life. Consider American films on the subject, for instance. According to Ilan Avisar, in *Screening the Holocaust*, Hollywood produced some five hundred narrative films on the war and war-related themes during the period 1940–1945. "In examining this harvest," Avisar writes, "we find striking avoidance of any explicit presentation of the Jewish catastrophe during the course of the war. *The Great Dictator* (1940) was a remarkable exception. . . . [Otherwise], Hollywood completely ignored the contemporaneous, systematic extermination of European Jewry."[17] Furthermore, Avisar notes, it was not until 1959, in filming the diary of Anne Frank, that Hollywood "addressed itself directly to the Nazis' genocidal treatment of the Jews."[18]

It is a matter of no small interest that it was the figure of Anne Frank that helped to break the relative silence within American culture about Jewish fate under Nazi tyranny. As the next chapter of this book will make abundantly clear, Anne Frank's diary was a popular success from the start, and to this day it can be taken as paradigmatic of the American reception of the Holocaust. For millions of Americans, the Holocaust is first made known and is vividly personalized in the image of Anne Frank.

What is it that defines her image for people in this country, and why have they come to cherish it so? There is a general understanding that Anne Frank was a Jew and for this reason was also a victim, but most of the stage and film translations of her diary do not make her appear "too Jewish," nor do they make her status as a victim too unbearably harsh. It is notable, for instance, that at no time during Goodrich and Hackett's prize-winning play does a Nazi soldier or Gestapo agent ever appear on the stage. The play has its anxious moments, to be sure, but these are never fixed visually on those who actually pursued Anne Frank and her family in their hiding places and made them into victims. Rather, anxiety builds towards a fate that is carefully kept hidden from the audience, which is spared any direct confrontation with Nazi violence. Consequently, one can leave the theater feeling somehow uplifted by Anne Frank's story rather than deeply disturbed.

As in this instance, Americans are typically given stories and images of the Nazi Holocaust that turn upward at the end rather than plunge downward into the terrifying silences of a gruesome death. The stage production of *The Diary of Anne Frank* ends with Anne's voice repeating what has become her signature line, informing us, as if from the heavens, "In spite of everything, I still believe that people are really good at heart." To which her father replies, humbly and affectionately, "She puts me to shame." Following these words the curtain comes down, ending Anne Frank's story not on a disconsolate note but an uplifting one.[19]

It is on a similar note that Gerald Green ended the hugely popular NBC miniseries, *Holocaust*; that William Styron chose to end his best-selling novel, *Sophie's Choice*; and that Steven Spielberg ends his extravagantly acclaimed film, *Schindler's List*. In these cases and numerous others like them, it is almost a given of American cultural engagement with the Holocaust that audiences not be subjected to unrelenting pain. Indeed, American "civil religion," as it has been called, places the stress emphatically on closures that are optimistic and affirmative. As one more example of this tendency, consider the following passage taken from a once widely circulated letter from the United States Holocaust Memorial Museum soliciting the support of new members:

Visitors will learn that while this is overwhelmingly a story about the extermination of the Jewish people, it is also about the Nazis' plans for the annihilation of the Gypsies and the handicapped, and about the persecution of priests and patriots, Polish intellectuals and Soviet prisoners of war, homosexuals and even innocent children.

Then, finally, when breaking hearts can bear it no longer, visitors will emerge into the light—into a celebration of resistance, rebirth, and renewal for the survivors—whether they remained in Europe, or as so many did, went to Israel or America to rebuild their lives. And having witnessed the nightmare of evil, the great American monuments to democracy that surround each departing visitor will take on new meaning, as will the ideals for which they stand.[20]

The topographical reference that gives rise to this note of American triumphalism is an important feature of the overall message that the United States Holocaust Memorial Museum means to convey. The museum is advantageously situated adjacent to the National Mall in Washington, D.C. The Washington Monument and the Jefferson Memorial are nearby and easily visible. These national monuments have the effect of reestablishing museum visitors in the familiar and consoling realities of American space, and in so doing they can also have the effect of telling visitors that the exhibits they just saw, for all of their horror, signify an essentially European event. To identify it as such is not to diminish the significance of the Holocaust for Americans, but it is to mark it as an alien experience, one that took place far from America's shores and even farther from the American spirit of fair play, decency, and justice for all. It is imperative, therefore, that some means to return people to this spirit be built into how the Jewish catastrophe in Europe is to be presented to the citizens of this country. In conformity with this need, the letter from which

I have quoted above concludes by urging all of us to remember "the six million Jews and millions of other innocent victims who died in the Holocaust" and, at the same time, to "also remember and renew our own faith in life . . . in civilization . . . in humanity . . . and in each other." How many people actually emerge in this spirit of renewal from the trip to hell that a visit to the United States Holocaust Memorial Museum takes them through is an open question. Americans are, for the most part, not a cynical people, nor do they like to see themselves or anyone else as permanent losers. Therefore many may *wish* to remember in the double sense described above, that is, by paying their respects to the victims of the European Holocaust and also by reassuring themselves that they live in a land that extends to all its citizens the rights to "life, liberty, and the pursuit of happiness."

It is noteworthy that as visitors enter the Holocaust Museum, they are greeted by these very words from America's hallowed Declaration of Independence, which are prominently engraved on a nearby wall. They might also be fortified against the terrifying pictures they are about to see by some famous words of America's first president, which likewise are prominently displayed near the museum's entrance: "The government of the United States . . . gives to bigotry no sanction, to persecution no assistance." It is, of course, bigotry and persecution in the most extreme sense that viewers will soon be staring at as they tour the Holocaust Museum's exhibits, but by bracketing the horror with some of the noblest principles of America's national credo, the museum's architects and program designers remind their visitors that the American vision of life is altogether different from that which brought on the catastrophe whose images are about to unfold before their eyes.

Given the story it tells in powerfully graphic fashion, the United States Holocaust Memorial Museum is not and cannot be a pleasurable museum to visit. Its aim, which it carries out admirably and effectively, is to educate the American public about a historical experience of a kind so excruciatingly painful that it would be a rare visitor who would emerge from this place unmoved. The emotional, moral, and pedagogical impact the museum makes upon the almost two million people who visit it each year is undoubtedly powerful. Just what it is that most of these people take away with them and retain as permanent knowledge, however, we do not know. The following account, which concludes an article by Estelle Gilson describing her own visit, may be representative of the responses of many who come to the United States Holocaust Memorial Museum:

> Do I think the United States Holocaust Memorial Museum will protect Jews in the future? Highly unlikely. Will it protect other minorities from genocide? Not likely. But it does what the United States does best. It informs. It bears witness to the Holocaust's existence, and provides a warning to whomever wishes to learn from it, that those who would dehumanize people in order to destroy them, dehumanize themselves as well.
>
> To have walked through this exhibition alongside fellow Americans—Caucasian Americans, African Americans, Hispanic Americans, Asian Americans, and yes, Jewish Americans—all in their bright summer tourist garb, left me feeling strangely comforted and surprisingly proud.[21]

Comfort and pride are no part of what one typically feels upon leaving the remains of the Nazi camps in Poland or Germany or upon concluding a visit to Yad Vashem in Israel. Why, therefore, are such feelings evoked at the United States Holocaust Memorial Museum? The answer probably lies less in what is shown in the one place and not in the others than in the site itself and the democratic ideals that America's capitol exemplifies. If one is to subject oneself to a serious confrontation with the history of the Nazi Holocaust at all, therefore, it may be somewhat easier to do so at the National Mall in Washington, D.C., than it is anywhere else in the world.

The United States Holocaust Memorial Museum annually attracts exceptionally large crowds (as of March 2010, it has drawn some thirty million visitors), and everything about it suggests that for years to come it is destined to be a powerful instrument for educating vast numbers of Americans and others about the Holocaust. As the museum grows and matures, however, will its conceptual base broaden, in familiar American fashion, to embrace a wider sense of its mission? As with other institutions situated in Washington, D.C., there will be an expectation on the part of some influential figures that the museum should become involved with American policy decisions regarding social and political problems at home and abroad. To their credit, to date the museum's directors and governing committees have successfully avoided submitting to such pressures, but they are sure to persist. So will the temptation to have the museum extend its scope beyond the period of Nazi rule in Europe. In its early years, the Holocaust Museum sponsored lectures on the genocide in Rwanda. Most people would regard that as appropriate and even admirable, but some objected. Somewhat later, the museum became the target of controversy because of a photographic exhibit it had mounted on the war in Bosnia.[22] More recently, under the mandate of its Committee on Conscience, the museum has devoted major resources and important attention to the ongoing killings in Darfur. Many will see such an inclusive focus as commendable and will argue that the sufferings in Rwanda, Bosnia, and Darfur cry out for public attention and are implicitly "Holocaust-related." To others, the inclusion of such topical lectures and exhibits in a Holocaust *Memorial* Museum tends to stretch the limits of the definition of Holocaust memory and confirm Yehuda Bauer's unease over the Americanization of the Holocaust.

Michael Berenbaum, who served as the museum's project director during the institution's planning and construction stages and, for a time, was also director of the museum's research institute, took issue with Bauer, arguing that the "Holocaust is only 'Americanized' insofar as it is explained to Americans and related to their history with ramifications for future policy. The study of the Holocaust can provide insights that have universal import for the destiny of all humanity. A national council funded at taxpayers' expense to design a *national* memorial does not have the liberty to create an exclusively Jewish one in the restricted sense of the term, and most specifically with regard to audience."[23]

Expanding on the connection between a museum's presentations and its audience, Berenbaum wrote that, as the United States Memorial Council took up its task of telling Americans about the Holocaust, it realized that "the story had to be told in such a way that it would resonate not only with the survivor in New York and his children in San Francisco, but with a black leader from Atlanta, a midwestern farmer, or a northeastern industrialist." Connecting such a diverse audience to history, Berenbaum noted, means connecting them to the past in a way that "inform[s] their current reality," including what he calls their current "social need."[24] The social needs of the different American types that he describes, however, are of a diverse sort, and it is hard to imagine narrating any story of the crimes of the Nazi era that will remain faithful to the specific features of European-based historical events of three generations ago and, at the same time, address a multiplicity of contemporary American social and political agendas. Berenbaum's formula for resolving such potential problems was to recognize that while the Holocaust was a unique event, it carries universal implications. That is no doubt the case. His successors at the United States Holocaust Memorial Museum have been sensitive to these complicated issues and, to date, have been effective in devising responsible ways to deal with them. Their successors will need to develop their own understandings of Berenbaum's formula and apply it in such a way as to make sure that the "uniqueness" of the Holocaust does not begin to yield some of its priority as historical fact to what is taken to be its wider metaphorical ramifications for today's American visitors. The challenge is a serious one. Kathryn Hill, at one time the museum's director of visitors services, was quoted in a *New York Times* article as being concerned with diversifying the museum's audiences: "We feel the museum has a special need to reach students in inner-city and rural schools." If one can actually meet such needs without compromising the historical integrity of the museum's presentations, it is certainly well worth doing, but one wonders about the losses that might be entailed in translating the story of the Holocaust into terms that would be comprehensible and meaningful to American youngsters from inner-city and rural schools. According to Naomi Paiss, a former director of communications, "The museum's ultimate goal [is] an 'en-masse understanding that we are not about what the Germans did to Jews but what people did to people.'"[25] Such a goal is at serious variance with the museum's mandate and, in fact, has fortunately not been pursued to date. But if those responsible for guiding the work of the United States Holocaust Memorial Museum in the future were ever to adopt a broadening of the mission this large, then the institution would cease to be a museum primarily devoted to educating the public about the Nazi Holocaust and become something else.

We need not wonder what this "something else" might look like, for it already exists, not at the United States Holocaust Memorial Museum in Washington, D.C., but at the Simon Wiesenthal Center's Museum of Tolerance in Los Angeles and elsewhere. The mission of the Los Angeles museum is twofold: to inform visitors about the history of racism and social prejudice in America and to represent what the museum calls "the ultimate example of man's inhumanity to man—the Holocaust."[26] Both are noble aims, but by situating the Holocaust within an historical framework that includes such quintessentially American experiences as the Los Angeles riots and the struggle for black civil rights, both of which are prominently illustrated, the Museum of Tolerance relativizes the catastrophe brought on by Nazism in a radical way. America's social problems, for all their gravity, are not genocidal in character and simply do not resemble the persecution and systematic slaughter of Europe's Jews during World War II. To mingle the victims of these very different historical experiences, therefore, is ultimately to widen the conceptual base of the Nazi Holocaust to the point where it begins to metamorphose into that high-sounding but all but meaningless abstraction: "man's inhumanity to man."

This tendency to relativize and universalize the Holocaust has been a prominent part of the American reception of Holocaust representations from the start. It is strong today and seems to be growing, especially within those segments of American culture that are intent on developing a politics of identity based on victim status and the grievances that come with such status. As illustrated in the previous chapter, the rhetoric of "oppression" has become a commonplace of contemporary American political, academic, and artistic discourse, and its exponents frequently take recourse to the signs and symbols of the Nazi Holocaust to describe what they see as their own "victimization" within American society.

To cite one egregious example among many within the cultural realm, consider one of the most celebrated works of the feminist artist Judy Chicago. Chicago (née Gerowitz) claims descent from twenty-three generations of rabbis; nevertheless, she freely admits that until the age of forty-five she knew virtually nothing about either Judaism or the Holocaust. In the early 1990s, though, she produced a large and ambitious art installation entitled the *Holocaust Project*, which combines her own work in several media with the work of her husband, the photographer Donald Woodman. The *Holocaust Project* had its opening at the Spertus Institute of Jewish Studies in Chicago in the fall of 1993 and since then has shown at museums in Boston, Los Angeles, and various other cities. Those who do not actually get to see the photo-paintings, tapestries, and stained-glass productions that make up this exhibition can have access to Chicago's work through an illustrated, oversized volume, also entitled *Holocaust Project*. The book presents colored plates of the art work along with numerous preliminary sketches, historical and contemporary photographs, excerpts from the artists' readings, and a detailed and highly revealing personal journal that Chicago kept as she set out to educate herself about the Holocaust.[27]

Her search, which she describes as one in quest of her latent Jewish self as well as of knowledge about the Nazi crimes, was intensive and demanding. It continued over a period of six or seven years and took Chicago and Woodman on trips to former camp sites and other places of wartime interest in France, Germany, Austria, Czechoslovakia, Poland, Russia, Latvia, and Lithuania. Journal entries, drawings, and photographs illustrate this ambitious itinerary and make clear that Chicago's search was not just for knowledge in the cognitive sense but, more passionately, for an emotional sense of the "Holocaust experience." To make this "experience" her own, as it were, Chicago did some things that go well beyond ordinary tourist behavior. During a visit to the former Natzweiler/Struthof concentration camp in France, for instance, she had herself photographed lying down on one of the long iron shovels that had been used to feed the bodies of victims into the flames of the crematorium oven. The large picture of her in corpse-like pose, stretched out and seemingly entering the mouth of the oven, is accompanied by this brief explanatory note: "When I lay on the shovel that carried bodies into the crematorium, I realized that, had I lived in Europe during the war, this would probably have happened to me. (Donald is too young.)"[28]

The *Holocaust Project* includes other illuminations of this order, which indicate that the more she learned about the Holocaust, the more she learned about herself as a person, a woman, and a Jew. For instance, following her simulated ride into the crematorium oven, she traveled with her husband to Nuremberg, where it was borne in on her that she was in Germany, "where it began." They went off to a restaurant, "an old beerhall-type place," and chatted away as they ate, "probably because we were afraid of the anguish we felt: the pain of *being* in Germany as Jews and letting ourselves know, feel, and experience this place, like no other place, where the Holocaust was born." It appears that in this German beerhall she experienced still another "revelation," this one confirmed by some readings she had been doing in the writings of Elie Wiesel: "The more I understand, the less I understand. I turn again and again to Wiesel for help, even though I don't always agree with what he says. But one remark of his was quite illuminating in terms of my inability to understand the perpetrators. I have written that I cannot inflict pain knowingly on others because I am a feminist and a conscious woman, and then I came upon Wiesel's statement that 'the Jews were told they were forbidden to diminish freedom.' *They were forbidden [by Scripture] to inflict pain.* Thus I find that I have carried a dual commandment, as a *feminist* and as a *Jew.* What an interesting revelation!"[29]

To someone who claims family descent from so lofty a figure as the Vilna Gaon, the great eighteenth-century intellectual and spiritual leader, this sudden rush of Jewish knowledge, for all of its belatedness, must have been both confirming and inspiring. Yet it is hardly a singular insight, for the text of the *Holocaust Project* includes other new insights of this order, some suggesting to the studious couple a close connection between "the oppression of women" and "the oppression of Jews," others indicating that the Holocaust may have been "a direct outgrowth of the patriarchal mind," still others linking the Holocaust to "the vulnerability of all human beings and, by extension, of all species and our fragile planet as well."[30] At one point, taking issue with Wiesel's claim that the Holocaust was a singular event in history, Ms. Chicago comes to the conclusion that, far from being unique, the Holocaust has to be understood as "*an aberration in the history of human cruelty*: The Nazis went too far, much too far, but there have been many, many cruel events in history."[31]

The culmination of the author/artist's growing wisdom about the Holocaust is probably reached when she concludes that it is futile to pin the blame for the Nazi crimes on any one group in particular. In her own words, "Everyone runs around trying to affix blame: The Germans did it; the French collaborated; the Poles were complicitous; the Americans and other Allies were indifferent. The list continues, trying to assign blame for something for which no one is to blame, but for which all human beings are responsible. *As a species, we are responsible for what we've done to each other, the Earth, and its creatures.* The Holocaust can be seen as the logical outgrowth of the rule of force, dominance, and power. It doesn't even matter which gender did it, though it falls on men."[32]

In translating these hard-won, self-empowering insights into her art work, Chicago is guided by a point of view that, as she says, sets her and her husband apart from most of the members of "the Holocaust community." Specifically, Chicago's "more comprehensive approach" situates the Holocaust as one "victim experience" among many and finds the root of all of these in "the injustice inherent in the global structure of patriarchy and the result of power as it has been defined and enforced by male-dominated societies."[33] Having sighted the enemy and given him his proper name, the artist then set out to make his violence graphic.

There is not room enough here to comment on all of the pieces that comprise the *Holocaust Project*, but suffice it to say that Judy Chicago's art work itself reflects the emphases and interpretations described above. One finds images of Nazi brutality side by side with images of slavery, atomic warfare, animal vivisection, and evil-looking gynecologists. Women are everywhere abused, attacked, tormented. And there are other victims as well whose sufferings draw Chicago's sympathies: *Pink Triangle* depicts both the torture and the solidarity of male homosexuals (as a special effect, their plight is set against a photographed background of pansies), and *Lesbian Triangle* does more or less the same for lesbians. A large tapestry entitled *The Fall*, conceptualized along the lines of a "battle of the sexes," depicts naked women being attacked by knife-wielding men while other women are being burned alive. In this same piece, a black slave plows furrows into the weeping earth-mother; a gaunt Jesus-like figure hangs helplessly in the background; other men wield bloody swords or feed people into the flaming ovens; and still others flay the hides of pigs and women hung side by side on a rack. In the middle of all this torment is a reworking of Leonardo's *Vetruvian Man*, which, an explanatory note tells us, is meant to show that the Holocaust had its true origin in "that moment in human history when men consolidated patriarchal power through force."[34] In Chicago's conception of history, all of our later troubles, including those brought on by the Nazis and their allies, have their root in the overthrow of matriarchy by cruelly aggressive, domineering men.

It is this tone and these understandings that inform the *Holocaust Project* from start to finish — or almost to the finish. The last piece, entitled *Rainbow Shabbat*, is a departure from all that precedes it and is intended to close the exhibit on a prayerful note. It is "an invocation for human awakening and global transformation," as the artist puts it.[35] A large stained-glass production, *Rainbow Shabbat* depicts twelve people around a Sabbath table. At one end of the table there stands a woman, covered in a traditional prayer shawl, blessing the candles. At the other end, a man, also in a prayer shawl, is making the traditional blessing over wine. Between these two and seated around the table are representatives of the world's people — an Arab in keffiyeh headdress, a Christian minister or priest with a large crucifix dangling on a chain beneath his clerical collar, Vietnamese, blacks, women, children, assorted whites. It is significant that the ten people around the Sabbath table all face away from the man and towards the woman, for it is through her and not him that the world will find whatever renewal and redemption may be possible. The faces of these Sabbath celebrants are expressionless but, inasmuch as they all have their arms about one another and seem to fall within the embrace of the praying woman's outstretched arms, we are given to understand that all is now well with the world or soon will be. Rainbow colors fill out the table scene from top to bottom, and on flanking side panels a large Jewish star, also surrounded by these bright colors, is inscribed with words that end the *Holocaust Project* on a prayerful note: "Heal those broken souls who have no peace and lead us all from darkness into light."[36]

It would be easy to see the *Holocaust Project* as one giant cliché from start to finish and dismiss it without any further ado. That would be a serious mistake, however, for Ms. Chicago's version of the Holocaust represents a number of trends that inform the American cultural and political mood today. We live in an age that is marked by narcissistic indulgences of a pronounced sort; everything is drawn back to the self and its desires, the self and its needs, the self and its pains. Combine this extreme emphasis on individualism with the pressures of an increasingly intrusive political correctness and you get productions like the *Holocaust Project*, according to which the genocidal crimes of Hitler's Germany are reduced to the deeds of a vicious "patriarchy" and Nazi victims are equated with monkeys in an animal laboratory and women during virtually every waking moment of their lives. Given the actual levels of atrocity that were enacted in Nazidominated Europe three generations ago, it is nothing short of a perversity for an American artist to validate herself as a victim in these terms today; but in a culture that seems to encourage and reward victimhood status, it is no longer seen as being especially perverse. And so we get proliferating images of the Holocaust serving as ready-at-hand emblems of accusation in the contemporary American debates about AIDS, abortion, child abuse, gay rights, the rights of immigrant aliens, etc. In fact, these are all matters of legitimate and serious social concern, but the analogy with the Nazi destruction of Europe's Jews adds nothing but sensationalism to the public discussion of what truly ails American society. And while the sensational is guaranteed to draw attention, it obfuscates and obscures more than it enlightens.

It also tends to make people lose their hold on reality. Listen to Judy Chicago one last time as she contemplates painting a rape scene for one of the panels of her *Holocaust Project:* "I am exhausting myself and depleting all my life's energy in fighting for the truth to be seen and heard. . . . I need to rest before I begin the rape image. Not only is it an intense, painful image, but it makes me very anxious. I keep thinking: am I going to get raped after I do this image? . . . But of course, I have no choice—so I'll just have to hope that art won't translate into life."[37] In this imaginary world, Holocausts threaten from every corner, and all are victims or potential victims. In more or less the same psychological register, even though with an eye on a different enemy, listen to the evangelical preacher Pat Robertson: "Just what Nazi Germany did to the Jews, so liberal America is now doing to evangelical Christians. . . . It's no different; it's the same thing. It is happening all over again. It is the Democratic Congress, the liberal-biased media, and the homosexuals who want to destroy all Christians. It's more terrible than anything suffered by any minority in our history." As the Reverend Robertson made this speech over his Christian Broadcasting Network, "footage of Nazi atrocities against the Jews appeared on screen."[38]

How, one wonders, does the Reverend Robertson's audience respond to rhetoric of this kind? Will most people recognize it as trumped up, a form of religio-political hysteria and, as such, seriously out of line with reality, or will they be prone to believe it? Does the Reverend Robertson himself believe it? We do not know, anymore than we know how much of a genuine belief Judy Chicago has staked in her own seriously skewed version of the Holocaust. What we do know is that if you expose thinking people long enough to images of atrocity, they will no longer remain fully thinking people, capable of recognizing differences and making distinctions between one order of human experience and another. Given the penchant among growing numbers of Americans to proclaim themselves "victims," one must wonder if the spread of Holocaust images throughout the various layers of our culture may not be having such a self-deluding effect.

What has been suggested above about the representation of Holocaust victims within American popular culture applies as well to the other principle types associated with the Holocaust. To reiterate, until recently it has been generally understood that the essential core of the Holocaust in its time was made up of victims, perpetrators, and bystanders. In more recent years, however, as thinking and writing about the Nazi crimes have taken a figurative turn, there has been a substantial augmentation of this core and also a shift of emphasis within it. I refer especially to the emergence of the "survivor" and "rescuer" as prominent figures, along with the "liberator," the "resister," the "second-generation survivor," the "avenger," and even the Holocaust "revisionist" or "denier." Interest in all of them has broadened the focus of the Holocaust "story" and influenced the point of view from which it is both narrated and received. In order to fully appreciate what Americans have come to know about the crimes of the Nazi era and how they have come to know it, therefore, one would have to look carefully at all of those whose actions and interactions collectively define the Holocaust for American audiences.[39] In what follows, I want to examine the prominence that two of these types, namely the "survivor" and the "rescuer," have enjoyed in recent years. To focus these observations, I turn to Steven Spielberg's hugely successful film, *Schindler's List*, and to the nature of the response to it among American filmgoers and critics.

For a number of years following the end of World War II, outside of the Jewish community relatively little public attention was paid in this country to those people who had managed to survive the Nazi assault against European Jewry and resettle in the United States.[40] Their status was that of the "D. P.," the "immigrant," the "war refugee," or the "greenhorn," and attitudes toward them were hardly adulatory. Generous-hearted people did what they could to help these newcomers adjust to their new circumstances in America and rebuild their lives here; others more or less ignored them. Throughout the late 1940s and well into the 1950s, a prevalent attitude was to put all of "that" behind one and get on with life.

Here is how the sociologist William Helmreich describes the situation:

> Most immigrants quickly learned not to talk about the war, often rationalizing their reluctance by saying that the stories were too horrible to be believed. Americans frequently responded to such stories with accounts of how they too had undergone privation during the war, mostly food rationing. Moritz Felberman [a survivor] was told by his aunt: "If you want to have friends here in America, don't keep talking about your experiences. Nobody's interested and if you tell them, they're going to hear it once and then the next time they'll be afraid to come see you. Don't ever speak about it."[41]

For some two decades or so following the end of the war, many of the "refugees" from Hitler's Europe probably were not inclined to "speak about it" much, even in the privacy of their family homes. Of course there were exceptions, but mainstream American culture and even segments of American Jewish culture did not promote public confessional outpourings of Holocaust atrocity stories. Just when this period of relative muteness ended is hard to say with any precision, but beginning in the mid-to-late 1960s and carrying up to the present day, a radical change of attitude has taken place, so much so that the "survivor" has become a much honored figure and, in some instances, enjoys something close to celebrity status. Elie Wiesel has played an important role in this regard, as have others. The result is that those who formerly had been regarded as "war refugees" have given up that unenviable status and taken on a new symbolic importance as "Holocaust survivors."

As "survivors" these aging men and women have been frequently sought as platform speakers in schools and universities, at *Yom HaShoah* (Holocaust Memorial Day) commemorative programs, and at other public occasions during the year, and sizable audiences often turn out to hear them tell their tales. Survivor memoirs have been published in large volume and now constitute a significant subgenre of Holocaust literature. In addition, institutions such as the Fortunoff Video Archives at Yale University and The Shoah Foundation for Visual History and Education, at the University of Southern California (originally established by Steven Spielberg) have been engaged in ambitious efforts to interview these aging witnesses and get their stories on tape while it is still possible to do so.[42] In short, the "survivor" now enjoys a greatly heightened public profile and has about him or her an aura that elicits honor, respect, fascination, and no small degree of awe. The writer Leon Uris summed up these attitudes by stating the case forthrightly: "These men and women are to be looked upon with wonderment."[43] And so, increasingly, they have been.

Schindler's List, dedicated as it is to narrating the story of eleven hundred Jews rescued from what doubtless would have been a gruesome death for most, is a film that celebrates "survivors." As such, it builds upon a momentum within segments of American culture, and especially American Jewish culture, which had been developing over a number of years. Many of those who managed to survive the ghettos, camps, and assorted hiding places of Nazi-occupied Europe have done well in this country, and in their latter years they have dedicated themselves energetically and successfully to seeing to it that their individual stories and the wrenchingly painful story of their era are preserved for future generations. Without the extraordinary commitment of these people, there probably would be no United States Holocaust Memorial Museum, no video archives for Holocaust testimony, fewer endowed chairs at American colleges and universities for the teaching of the Holocaust—and no *Schindler's List.* Their success in this respect is truly remarkable. The mission of these survivor activists, simply stated, is to carry on in perpetuity the memory work of a traumatized generation of European Jews who, in the short space of a generation, have transformed their former status as victims into unprecedented positions of influence and respect. Abandoning the reticence that marked their situation in the immediate postwar years, they have found their voice and are not reluctant to use it when the need arises. No one who recalls the Bitburg affair in the spring of 1985 will soon forget that it was a survivor who faced the president of the United States and, with all of the world's television cameras recording the moment, "spoke truth to power." Who but Elie Wiesel—a Holocaust survivor who has come to symbolize the moral authority of his generation— would have dared to publicly tell the president of this country that it was "not [his] place" to travel to Germany to join Chancellor Kohl for ceremonies at the military cemetery at Bitburg?[44]

The newly found strength, self-confidence, and self-assertion of survivors reached a high point during the 1994 Academy Awards ceremony when Branko Lustig, himself a survivor, and Steven Spielberg stepped before a vast and inordinately appreciative tele-vision audience and, in the name of the "survivors" as well as in the name of "the 6,000,000," accepted their Oscars as producer and director of *Schindler's List.* In so doing, they made emphati-cally clear that this generation of Holocaust survivors, which knows itself to be the *last* of its kind, will not depart without leav-ing behind its mark for this and future generations. In no small measure, that determination is symbolized through the creation of the United States Holocaust Memorial Museum and the many other institutions of its kind around the country.[45]

As *Schindler's List* demonstrates, if this is the age of the "survivor," it is also the age of the "rescuer." For along with a high degree of public attention focused on the "survivor," we have seen and continue to see the elevation through the popular media of "righteous Gentiles," "helpers," "liberators," "rescuers," and "saviors." These are the people who, in many instances, helped the "survivor" to survive, and so they, too, are increasingly looked upon with a degree of wonderment. Indeed, these people are now frequently regarded as the "moral heroes" of the Holocaust, the ones who managed to exemplify virtue during a time when basic human goodness was otherwise scarcely to be found. Those who speak of them unfailingly revert to such religious or quasi-religious metaphors as "the light that pierced the darkness," "the righteous," "the just," "the good Samaritans," etc. In a time when many feel the need to locate a moral counterweight to the overwhelming darkness and terror inherent in the Holocaust, the "helpers" and "rescuers" are the ones who supply images of "light," "hope," "affirmation," and "goodness." In this regard, it is notable that the United States Holocaust Memorial Museum in Washington, D.C., is situated on Raoul Wallenberg Place, a designation rich in symbolic implications and one that helps to "balance" the horrors awaiting visitors inside the building with a sense of righteousness duly honored on the outside.

Thanks to Steven Spielberg's film, the Swedish hero Wallenberg, one of Europe's most justly honored "rescuers," is now joined by the German Oskar Schindler as another one of the "righteous among the nations." Moreover, the attention newly focused on Schindler's wartime deeds of rescue has had the effect of renewing or creating interest in the stories of others who are praised for acting similarly—Aristedes de Sousa Mendes, Sempo Sugihara, Hermann Graebe, Miep Gies, Pastor André Trocmé and the people of Le Chambon, the Danes, etc. In one way or another, each of them is remembered for putting their lives at risk to help protect and save Jews during the war. And while their numbers are not huge, their actions, if confirmed, were clearly exemplary. The question that arises with respect to the "rescuers," therefore, is not one of their inclusion or exclusion from narrative accounts of the Nazi era but chiefly one of proportion: how central or peripheral are these "moral heroes" of the Holocaust to the larger history of the Holocaust?

Schindler's List answers this question in a way that moves "rescuers" like Schindler from the margins to the precise center of events. By doing that as successfully as he has, Spielberg has in effect repositioned the terms of the Holocaust "story" away from those advanced by Hilberg and others—the Holocaust encompassing essentially "perpetrators," "victims," and "bystanders"—and has placed the emphasis squarely on "rescuers" and "survivors." *Schindler's List*, after all, is a Holocaust film that focuses chiefly on the Jews who do *not* die at the hands of the Nazis but who, on the contrary, are actually saved by a Nazi who undergoes a moral conversion to goodness. If, as claimed by some, Spielberg's film is to be regarded from this point on as the "definitive" Holocaust film, and if, as claimed by others, it may actually do more to educate vast numbers of people about the history of the Holocaust than all the academic books on the subject combined, one has to recognize that it has achieved these ends as the result of a paradigm shift of major proportions. In their viewing of this film mass audiences are exposed to a version of the Holocaust that originates in long-standing American preferences for "heroes" and "happy endings," preferences that *Schindler's List* satisfies through its artful employment of tried-and-true Hollywood conventions of cinematic storytelling. To say as much is not to call into question Spielberg's achievement with *Schindler's List*, which is considerable, but it is to point up the fact that this is a film that presents a characteristically American way of reading and resolving an extreme history.

As for its impact, there was an extraordinary amount of press interest in *Schindler's List* even before the film had its premiere showing. Since then commentary on the film has grown exponentially and reveals both laudatory and highly critical attitudes. No less a political figure than President Clinton publicly "implored" people to see *Schindler's List*, and others in positions of political influence, including the governors of California and New Jersey, likewise gave the film their endorsement and promoted it as a primary source of historical information and moral education. Following its garnering of no less than seven prizes at the 1994 Academy Awards presentations, *Schindler's List* was even more lavishly acclaimed as a "great film," "a masterpiece," "an astounding achievement." Stephen Schiff, writing in *The New Yorker*, called the film "the finest fiction feature ever made about the century's greatest evil. . . . It will take its place in cultural history and remain there." Terrence Rafferty agreed with this evaluation and described Spielberg's film as "by far the finest, fullest dramatic film ever made about the Holocaust." Jeffrey Katzenberg, at the time head of Walt Disney film studios, remarked that *Schindler's List* "will wind up being so much more important than a movie. . . . It will affect how people on this planet think and act. . . . It will actually set the course of world affairs." If not at quite this level of hyperbole, many others weighed in with similar accolades.[46]

At the same time, the film has had its critics, some of them passionately opposed to what Spielberg has wrought. James Bowman, writing in *The American Spectator*, denounced *Schindler's List* as a film that "cheapens and trivializes the enormity of the Holocaust" and offers "no sense whatever of the political realities that allowed such things to happen." J. Hoberman, film critic of *The Village Voice*, found the film "sentimental," too much of a "feel-good" movie, and therefore bound to encourage attitudes of "complacency" in viewers. Donald Kuspit saw *Schindler's List* as "stereotypical," the work of an artist who simply does not "understand" the history of the Holocaust: "*Schindler's List* is a triumph of simplemindedness—always Spielberg's strength." Claude Lanzmann, the creator of *Shoah*, was harshly critical of Spielberg's film, denouncing it as one that is false to the essential facts of the Holocaust: "To tell the story of the Holocaust through a German who saved Jews can only lead to a distortion of the truth, because for the overwhelming majority of Jews things like this did not happen."[47]

While critical opinion on the film has clearly been divided, there is no question that Spielberg's cinematic statement is a major one and that from this point on *Schindler's List* is destined to play an influential role in determining how millions of people in this country and elsewhere will come to remember and understand the Nazi Holocaust. In light of this prospect, one is moved to ask: what version of the Holocaust does this film project? In particular, what images of Germans and Jews does Spielberg foreground in *Schindler's List?*

The fundamental dramatic confrontation in the film is not one between Jews and Germans but one between an evil German (Amon Goeth, the commander of the Plaszow labor camp) and a German who comes to exemplify righteous behavior (Oskar Schindler). As the movie progresses, the face-off between these two intensifies and takes on allegorical dimensions, and in the balance hangs the fate of the Jews. Otherwise, the Jews in *Schindler's List* are weakly imagined figures, for the most part either passive victims of random atrocity or venal collaborators with their persecutors. In just about every case they are presented as nondescript, anonymous figures or appear in stereotypical fashion, the men among them associated with money deals and other sorts of scheming and the women as temptresses and seductresses. Itzhak Stern, the only Jewish character developed at any length, is an inflexible, soulless type, whose expression throughout the film rarely changes from that of the professional bookkeeper that he is. In just about every other respect, the Jews in *Schindler's List* are irrelevant to the major drama of the film, which focuses on Oskar Schindler and Amon Goeth, the chief embodiments of "good" and "evil" in the film. In the contest between the two, it is Schindler, of course, who prevails and who, at film's end, is the recipient of the Jews' gratitude, respect, and love.

This ending takes Schindler and the Jews through two major rites of passage, both of which have about them an aura of the morally sublime, if not indeed of the sacred: through the presentation to him of a gold ring, the *Schindlerjuden* in effect "marry" themselves to this man out of heartfelt gratitude for his righteous deeds, which alone kept them from becoming victims of the Nazis. In the final cemetery scene the same Jews, now elderly "survivors," pay their respects to the memory of their savior through the ritualistic placing of tokens of honor and love on his grave. Both scenes convey tender feelings of affection, respect, and reconciliation, and most filmgoers doubtless will be moved to respond to these with similar feelings of their own. In addition, it is noteworthy that both scenes project Schindler as a figure defined by overtly Christian symbolism—in the first, he holds forth in a dramatic speech that may recall Jesus' Sermon on the Mount; and in the second, the camera pans lovingly over the crosses in Jerusalem's Latin Cemetery, coming to rest on the gravesite where Schindler himself is buried.[48] These two scenes bring to culmination and closure the career of a man who may have been a morally flawed character in many other respects but who is depicted as nothing short of a saintly hero with respect to the Jews.

As the Holocaust enters American public consciousness through *Schindler's List*, therefore, it can have the effect of dislodging earlier and more difficult feelings of shame and guilt that typically accompany reactions to images of the persecution and mass slaughter of Europe's Jews. As in the long and disturbingly powerful scene that depicts the clearing of the Cracow ghetto, Spielberg does not shy away from portraying brutality and bloodshed, but he places the responsibility for such atrocity in the person of Nazi types who are little more than psychopathic thugs. The political dimensions of Nazi behavior go altogether unexplored in *Schindler's List*, and in their stead one encounters raw sadism of an extremely personal rather than systemic kind. Identification with such a character as Amon Goeth, who is the incarnation of the murderous passions of limitless evil, is out of the question for most filmgoers, who are far more likely to align themselves sympathetically with the "good" German, Oskar Schindler, the "rescuer" of the Jews. At film's end, an unrepentant Goeth goes to his death on the gallows, Schindler goes to his eternal rest as a man of honor, and the *Schindlerjuden* survive to strike out for a new life as settlers in Palestine.

What version of the Holocaust, then, does *Schindler's List* present? A recognizably American one, by which I do not mean a historically "false" one but rather one that interprets history along lines that Americans seem to require or at least instinctively prefer. Michael André Bernstein is correct when he writes that by concentrating "on a small group of Jews who survived and on the good German who aided them rather than on all the millions who did not live and the millions of Germans and German sympathizers who did nothing to help," Spielberg satisfies "a characteristic American urge to find a redemptive meaning in every event."[49] That urge is not felt in such films as Alain Resnais's *Night and Fog* or Claude Lanzmann's *Shoah*, nor does one find it satisfied in the Auschwitz memoirs of such European writers as Primo Levi or Jean Améry. By contrast, it is on a note of redemptive promise that American productions on the Holocaust are likely to end. To reach such endings, however, it is necessary that a new paradigm of narrative construction be advanced, one focusing prominently on the more "affirmative" figures of the Holocaust story, notably "survivors" and "rescuers." *Schindler's List* is the most powerfully articulated example of this paradigm shift, but it hardly stands alone. Increasingly one finds a desire for a greater degree of "balance" in representing the Holocaust, a "balance" that might be achieved by modulating somewhat an emphasis on the Jewish victims and their German torturers and murderers and focusing a new kind of attention on "the righteous gentile," or "rescuer."

Within the American context, this search within the darkness and evil of the Holocaust for figures of luminosity and goodness seems to be part of a larger cultural quest for religious meaning, or what today is loosely called "spirituality." As Eva Fogelman states the case in her *Conscience and Courage: Rescuers of Jews during the Holocaust*, people "are hungry for role models," for inspiring examples "of moral courage during an immoral time." Her book is but one of many that identifies these role models with the "rescuers," whom she does not hesitate to define as the "spiritual heirs to the *Lamed Vav*—the thirty-six people of Jewish tradition whose sole task it is, in every generation . . . to do good for their fellow men."[50] André Schwarz-Bart revived popular interest in the figure of the *Lamed Vav* in his moving novel, *The Last of the Just* (1959), although as he presents it, this tradition reached its point of exhaustion during the time of the Holocaust. In an effort to revive it, Marek Halter produced a full-length film, *Tzedek*, which presents the stories of thirty-six righteous gentiles who rescued Jews. Numerous other books and films do the same.[51] In addition to these, at least half a dozen books on Raoul Wallenberg have appeared since the early 1980s, and several books on Oskar Schindler are on the shelves of most American bookstores.[52]

Eva Fogelman is hardly alone, therefore, in wanting "to give altruism back its good name."[53] Indeed, since 1980 we have been given at least forty films and as many books that relate stories of Christian rescue of Jews. Among those involved in shaping the configurations of Holocaust memory, a new accent on the "positive" is notable, so much so that *Moment* magazine saw fit to publish an article entitled "Is Elie Wiesel Happy?"[54] Other, less bizarre indicators likewise point to a new interest in the "positive" or "good" aspects of the Holocaust. In 1984 the United States Holocaust Memorial Council sponsored a major conference entitled "Faith in Humankind: Rescuers of Jews during the Holocaust." Other, smaller conferences have since been held elsewhere on the same theme. The Altruistic Personality Project has done programs and sponsored publications of a similar nature, and projects such as Friends of Le Chambon, Thanks to Scandinavia, and Tribute to the Danes direct attention to rescue efforts of a more specifically regional kind.[55] Seen within this context, Steven Spielberg's film, far from being exceptional in its focus on "rescue," is the culmination of a development in Holocaust narrative that has been building momentum for a number of years.

In Eva Fogelman's view, it is not difficult to explain what it is that accounts for this development: "The brutal testimony of the Eichmann trial set off an urgent quest for evidence of human kindness during the war. People around the world needed to feel that the heart of man was not unrelievedly black. Rescuers were discovered."[56]

Within the American discourse on the Holocaust, the person who has done the most to advance this discovery is Rabbi Harold N. Schulweis. In 1963, in the aftermath of the Eichmann trial, Rabbi Schulweis founded the Institute of Righteous Acts at the Judah Magnes Museum in Berkeley, California. Some twenty years later he went on to establish the Jewish Foundation of Christian Rescuers (Eva Fogelman served as its first director), which became an integral part of the Anti-Defamation League's International Center for Holocaust Studies. In addition to his work in establishing these institutions, Rabbi Schulweis has written a good deal about the desirability of directing public attention to the deeds of the "righteous." He is the author of the forewords to the books by Douglas Huneke, Samuel and Pearl Oliner, and Mordecai Paldiel, mentioned above, and wrote the afterword to Carol Rittner and Sondra Myers's *The Courage to Care: Rescuers of Jews during the Holocaust* (1986). In addition, he has published several articles on "rescuers," and he devotes a full chapter to them in his book, *For Those Who Can't Believe* (1994).

Through all of these writings Rabbi Schulweis has been concerned with how the Holocaust is being represented to diverse audiences in America: "How we interpret the Holocaust holds serious consequences for the character and morale of our children, not only for the Jewish child but for the non-Jewish child as well. . . . How effective, how constructive has been our way of relating this great atrocity? . . . It may be that we have unintentionally transmitted a morale-breaking pessimism in dwelling solely on the tragic past."[57] Rabbi Schulweis has consistently argued that in transmitting knowledge of the Holocaust, nothing should be done to mitigate the presentation of the severity of the Nazi crimes against the Jews but also that everything must be done to identify and call attention to those good people who put themselves at risk to protect Jews whose lives were imperiled. In his own words, "In remembering the cruelty and barbarity of the Holocaust, we must not forget the moral heroes of conscience. In an era of the anti-hero, the heroes of conscience must be exalted."[58] Rabbi Schulweis looks upon memory as a "healing art," one characterized by the imperative to establish "balance" in what is recalled and represented. In this view, memory is most meaningful when it is dedicated to the purposes of "moral education." Consequently, with respect to recounting the story of the Holocaust, Rabbi Schulweis argues that we face a question that is fundamentally ethical in its thrust: "How are we to remember without destroying hope?"[59]

In setting forth answers to this question, Rabbi Schulweis has developed both a pragmatic and a didactic approach to history and memory, one that seeks to interpret the Holocaust in ways that are fundamentally constructive. "Memory," he writes, "contains an ambiguous energy. It can liberate or enslave, heal or destroy. The use of memory carries with it a responsibility for the future." Thus, "it is to the moral act of remembering that we must be dedicated. How are we, as moral educators, to make memory the father of conscience and of constructive repentance?" His answer, not surprisingly, is to look to the "righteous among the nations" as a positive counterweight to what is otherwise an overwhelmingly negative and depressing record of villainy. "There is a moral symmetry in man," Rabbi Schulweis insists, and to help restore it, we must become newly attentive to the voices of heroism: "The world is hungry for moral heroes . . . , heroes whose altruism is lived out in action; models of exemplary behavior who realize our abstract ideals, human beings to be emulated." Hence the discovery and promotion of Oskar Schindler and the other "rescuers."[60]

These figures serve as a bridge in advancing the aims of Jewish-Christian dialogue in America, but beyond this pragmatic purpose they have reached a level of importance in Rabbi Schulweis's thinking that elevates their goodness to a theological principle. "Where was Adonai in Auschwitz?" Rabbi Schulweis asks. "Where was the power and mystique of Adonai within the hell of the Holocaust?" While numerous other religious thinkers have raised similar questions about God's absence or presence in the Nazi death camps, it would be rare to find among them very many who answer as Rabbi Schulweis does:

Where was Adonai in the Holocaust? Adonai was in Nieuvelande, a Dutch village in which seven hundred residents rescued five hundred Jews. . . . Adonai was in Le Chambon-sur-Lignon, whose citizens hid and protected five thousand Jews. . . . Adonai was in the rat-infested sewers of Lvov, where Polish sewer workers hid seventeen Jews. . . . Adonai was in Bulgaria . . . in Finland. . . . Adonai was with the Italian troops stationed in the southwestern half of Croatia. . . . in Yugoslavia, Greece, southern France, Albania. . . .[61]

The list goes on and on, an "affirmative" antiphony to that strain of severe religious doubt, if not outright theological despair, that has entered the post-Holocaust religious consciousness of so many other writers. One recalls the broken, stuttering prayer that concludes Schwarz-Bart's *The Last of the Just*: "And praised. *Auschwitz*. Be. *Maidanek*. The Lord. *Treblinka*. And praised. *Buchenwald*. Be. *Mauthausen*. The Lord. *Belzec*. . . ."[62]

As already noted, Schwarz-Bart seems to reach the melancholy conclusion that the Nazi assault against the Jews was so overpoweringly destructive as to bring to an end the ancient Jewish tradition of the Just. Rabbi Schulweis, by contrast, not only seeks to revive this tradition but, on the basis of its Christian exemplars, actually presumes to locate God *within* the Holocaust. In his insistence that Nazi villainy be "balanced" by Christian "heroes" who incarnate "hope" and "goodness," Rabbi Schulweis inscribes a new and characteristically American script for narrating the story of the Holocaust. It has yielded a large and still growing corpus of "rescue" literature and film, of which Spielberg's *Schindler's List* is, for the moment, the culminating expression.

The reception of Spielberg's film clearly indicates that a great many people respond enthusiastically to narrative employments of the Holocaust that help to restore what Rabbi Schulweis calls "the moral symmetry of man." In writing about the film, Rabbi Schulweis has argued that if *Schindler's List* "has become the defining symbol of the Holocaust, it is . . . not because of its artistry alone, but because it enables the viewer to enter the dark cavern without feeling that there is no exit. 'How far that little candle throws its beam.' Memory of the Holocaust is a sacred act that elicits a double mandate: to expose the depth of evil and to raise goodness from the dust of amnesia."[63] Eva Fogelman has put the same mandate in the form of a question: "Every child knows the name of Hitler, but how many know the name of Raoul Wallenberg?"[64]

The fact is that in the American population at large, and not only among children, pitifully little is known about either Hitler or Wallenberg.[65] But even if it were the case that knowledge of the former ran deep and knowledge of the latter was all but absent, the case for "balance" would not be convincing. There was not nor can there be any "symmetry" in the historical weights of Hitler and Wallenberg, or Hitler and Schindler, or Hitler and the good people of Le Chambon. The deeds of the righteous are assuredly worthy of remembrance, but by placing them on an almost equal level with the deeds of Hitler and by encompassing both within a "double mandate" of Holocaust memory, one ends up reshaping the history and memory of the Holocaust in ways that are bound to obscure how horrendous the Holocaust actually was. It is no part of Rabbi Schulweis's intention to bring about such a consequence—indeed, he has declared himself emphatically on this point time and again. Nevertheless, the inevitable end point of his moral "art of memory" is clear: by projecting "rescuers" as central figures in narrative accounts of the Holocaust—as if the morality of Wallenberg or Schindler truly were on a par with the evil of Hitler and could somehow offset it—one changes the core of Holocaust remembrance in ways that will almost certainly vitiate any sober understanding of the deeds of the murderers and the sufferings of their victims.

As a consequence of such a change, religious faith may revive for some and the tenor of Jewish-Christian dialogue in America may improve for others, but there is reason to suspect that the exaltation of the "righteous" may, over time, serve to foster a greater complacency about one of the most harrowing historical events of this past century. Those who advocate "balance," therefore, also need to keep proportion in mind—that is to say, the lineaments of historical reality itself. The Israeli writer Aharon Appelfeld has written on this matter in a way that restores some much-needed perspective: "During the Holocaust there were brave Germans, Ukrainians, and Poles who risked their lives to save Jews. But the Holocaust is not epitomized by the greatness of these marvelous individuals' hearts. . . . I say this because survivors sometimes feel deep gratitude to their rescuers and forget that the saviors were few, and those who betrayed Jews to the Nazis were many and evil."[66]

Appelfeld's sobering words call attention to a parallel development in the literature of rescue—namely, the rescue that did *not* happen—that has been developing over the years, especially in the

United States.[67] Beginning at least as far back as Arthur Morse's *While Six Million Died: A Chronicle of American Apathy* (1967) and continuing in a major way with David Wyman's influential book, *The Abandonment of the Jews* (1984), a counter-narrative to stories lauding "saviors" and "the righteous" has emerged.[68] It documents and decries indifference and antisemitism at the government level, in the news media,[69] and within segments of the public at large and is harshly critical of the failure to do more to save Europe's endangered Jews. Raphael Medoff, Director of the David Wyman Institute for Holocaust Studies and co-author, with Wyman, of A *Race against Time: Peter Bergson, America, and the Holocaust* (2002), has been particularly intent on focusing on the deficiencies of the Roosevelt administration's wartime policies. With others, he has kept alive important debates about the status of refugees and the American military's failure to bomb the Nazi death camps or the railroad tracks leading to them.[70] If one reads deeply enough in this literature, a far darker picture of American responses to the Holocaust emerges, which challenges the more positive arguments that Rabbi Schulweis sought to advance.

While the views of Morse, Wyman, Medoff, and others have scholarly merit, however, it is unlikely that they will be able to contend with the overwhelmingly affirmative views presented in the still-growing body of "rescue" literature. Like others, Americans can acknowledge only so much historical pain and, while not denying someone else's suffering, prefer to retrieve a remnant of moral idealism from a history of mass murder. As already demonstrated, this tendency has been growing stronger in recent years, although within American responses to the Holocaust one can trace it back to earlier decades, when the evil character of the Nazi genocide appeared simply too much for some to bear. One hears the keynote to a religious counter-response to atrocity in Father John A. O'Brien's foreword to Philip Friedman's *Their Brothers' Keepers*, the first book in English on Christian "rescuers." Father O'Brien begins soberly enough: "The story of Hitler's efforts to solve the 'Jewish problem' in Germany and in all the countries which fell under the yoke of the Nazis, by the simple expedient of exterminating them, . . . is a ghastly and shocking tale of brutality, torture, and murder, which in deliberate, systematic savagery on a grand scale is probably unsurpassed in all the annals of human history. From such a rehearsal readers instinctively recoil, for it does not make pleasant reading." Father O'Brien is correct on both counts: the story of the Nazi crimes against the Jews is one of unparalleled horror and, if presented in terms that do not mitigate its ghastliness, most people may indeed recoil from it. Recognizing as much, American representations of the Holocaust, from the time of *The Diary of Anne Frank* in the late 1950s to the appearance of the *Holocaust Project* and *Schindler's List*, seek ways to "balance" a history of unbearable suffering with affirmative images of hope. Thus, memory of Anne Frank's hideous fate in Auschwitz and Bergen-Belsen is softened by her transcendent "message of faith in humankind"; the "victims" portrayed in Judy Chicago's *Holocaust Project* are not only the European Jews who were slaughtered by the millions three generations ago but a much vaster and more generalized collective of suffering humanity, animal life, and the earth itself; and the Jews of Cracow and other European cities and towns who were rounded up and deported to their deaths in the Nazi killing centers of Poland are rendered as merely background figures in *Schindler's List*, whereas the foreground is occupied by a small number of Jews who owe their lives to a "good" Nazi who turned out, against all expectations, to be their savior. In these and so many other instances one confronts an American memory of the Holocaust evolving in ways that present "victims" but *also* "survivors," "perpetrators" but *also* "rescuers," "bystanders" but *also* "liberators," etc. Such a "balanced" portrait, which is intended to restore "the moral symmetry of man," enables American educators to teach what is commonly called "the lessons of the Holocaust" to diverse and sundry audiences. In place of the scandal that, now and forever, should accompany any earnest encounter with the unprecedented evil of the Nazi crimes against the Jews, we see the emergence of moral leavening agents of various sorts—the "righteous among the nations," the "rescuers," the "bearers of light in a time of darkness," etc. Through these figures Rabbi Schulweis finds a way to a renewed faith in Adonai, and Father O'Brien finds a means to celebrate Christian virtue: "It is needed to balance the degradation and baseness of the Jew-baiters with the gallantry and heroism of the Jew-aiders. . . . [*Their Brother's Keepers*] shows that nineteen centuries of Christian teaching were not without results. So deeply had the fundamental law of the Christian religion, the duty to love one's neighbor, been woven into the warp and woof of the Christian conscience that thousands in all lands defied the sternest edicts and threats of the Gestapo and sheltered Jews. . . . They proved that they *were* their brothers' keepers and that not in vain had Jesus of Nazareth related the parable of the Good Samaritan."[71]

To end on this note is to offer hope and consolation but also to obscure a history of human betrayal, degradation, and destruction almost without parallel. Nevertheless, most people, and especially most Americans, prefer Father O'Brien's stress on the affirmative to a more disconsolate view of history. As further evidence, we turn now to an examination of Anne Frank's critical and ever-changing role in this story.

FOUR

Anne Frank:
The Posthumous Years

To me she is one of the survivors.   —AN INSCRIPTION LEFT BY
AN ANONYMOUS VISITOR TO THE ANNE FRANK HOUSE

It has been estimated that, among the almost six million Jews who fell victim to the Nazis during World War II, at least one million and perhaps as many as one and a half million were children. Yad Vashem in Jerusalem and other research institutions elsewhere have many of their names on record. To the world at large, however, these children all bear one name—that of Anne Frank. It is not that we lack information about the others, for more than a few of them were youthful authors and wrote diaries or other personal testimonies that have come down to us. For the most part, though, these other books remain relatively unknown while the diary of Anne Frank is almost certainly the most widely read book of World War II. It is as if the broad public has chosen to pay tribute to the memory of the others by remembering the one child who today stands for all the child victims of the Nazi era. To the million or more who perished we have given the collective name: *Anne Frank.*

What accounts for this remarkable metonymy? How has it evolved, and what might it tell us about the evolution of a more broadly encompassing popular understanding of the Holocaust?

These questions will form the heart of my inquiry in this chapter, one that aims to clarify how, on the level of popular perceptions, a sense of the past seems to be decisively shaped through the projection of single images of ubiquitous and compelling power. Through a study of the development of the image of Anne Frank, I hope to be able to reveal some of the ways in which a public memory of the Nazi era has itself been developing since the end of World War II.

About the persistence and power of the figure of Anne Frank there can be little doubt today. Simply put, she may be the most famous child of the twentieth century. Her book has been translated into dozens of languages and has been read by many millions of people throughout the world. Millions more are acquainted with her story through the dramatic and film versions of her diary. Streets, schools, and youth centers bear her name, just as public statues, stamps, and commemorative coins bear her image. Youth villages, forests, and foundations have been named after her; ballets, requiems, and cantatas written for her; poems and songs composed in tribute to her; and public figures of every kind, from politicians to religious leaders, regularly invoke her name and quote lines from her book. In all of these ways her name, face, and fate are kept constantly before us.

To illustrate this phenomenon that, far from lessening with the passage of the years, seems to be increasing in scope and intensity, consider the following. In June 1989, a series of events was held in New York City to commemorate what would have been the sixtieth anniversary of Anne Frank's birth. Mayor Koch officially proclaimed the week beginning June 12 as "Anne Frank Week." A major exhibition of photographs and texts from the Nazi era, entitled "Anne Frank in the World: 1929–1945," opened at the City Gallery on Columbus Circle and later was shown at the Cathedral of St. John the Divine and other places in New York. It drew tens of thousands of people. A gala celebrity concert honoring Anne Frank in words and music was performed under the title "Remembering Anne Frank" on the evening of June 12. Later that same night a prominent New York television channel offered the American premiere of Willy Lindwer's Emmy award–winning documentary, *The Last Seven Months of Anne Frank.* A second film about Jews who had been hidden by Christians during the war was also shown. Books released that day included the Doubleday critical edition of *The Diary of Anne Frank*[1] and a new school curriculum, *The End of Innocence: Anne Frank and the Holocaust.*[2] An art exhibit that opened at a prominent gallery in Manhattan featured "The Anne Frank Series." On June 13 Bill Moyers hosted on prime time television a special program about "The Legend and the Legacy of Anne Frank." The day after there was an international symposium on Anne Frank; the following day a teacher-training workshop was convened to introduce secondary school educators to "Anne Frank and the Holocaust"; and so it went through the week.

Similar events took place outside of New York City; in Pennsylvania, New Jersey, Texas, and elsewhere, films on Anne Frank's life were screened, lectures on and readings from her book were held, musical programs were performed, and theater productions of *The Diary of Anne Frank* were dedicated to her memory. United States Senator Paul Simon, of Illinois, introduced a resolution to the Senate designating June 12, 1989, as "Anne Frank Day." In his resolution he noted that more than twenty cities nationwide would be marking the day in commemoration of Anne Frank. In Philadelphia, a new educational foundation called the Anne Frank Institute presented its annual Anne Frank Youth Award and announced plans to develop the country's first Anne Frank Museum (it was never built).

In Frankfurt, the city of her birth, a plaque marks the building where she was born, and a major exhibition on Anne Frank was mounted in 1989 at the city's historical museum. Elsewhere in West Germany large numbers of people visited the touring exhibition "Anne Frank in the World," attended lectures and participated in symposia about her, viewed films of the period in which she lived, recalled the way she and so many others died. The exhibition, organized by the Anne Frank Foundation in Amsterdam, has also toured cities throughout the United States, Europe, and Asia. To date, it has been seen by millions of people in over one hundred cities throughout the world.[3]

The above is by no means an exhaustive list. It is given merely to illustrate the manifold ways in which the figure of Anne Frank has won such a prominent place among us and stands today, almost unrivalled, as a contemporary cultural icon. The question, therefore, is not one about the constancy of her presence, which by now is a given, but about its symbolic character. Why is it that, among the many millions who perished during the Nazi era, it is Anne Frank who almost singularly stands out as such a commanding figure? What is it that she has come to represent to vast numbers of people around the world who feel so powerfully drawn to her image? Who, in short, is the Anne Frank we remember?

In seeking answers to these questions, we would do well to reflect first on the earliest signs that Anne Frank would eventually emerge from among the anonymous dead at Bergen-Belsen and assume a posthumous existence of such unusual force and magnitude within popular culture. In fact, the initial reception of her diary was not so auspicious. According to reports by the historian Louis de Jong and others, several Dutch publishing houses turned down the manuscript of *Het Achterhuis* before it was finally accepted by Contact, an Amsterdam publisher.[4] The first edition, which appeared in June 1947, was relatively small, consisting of only fifteen hundred copies, no doubt reflecting the sense that people were tired of the war and probably did not want to be reminded all over again of the sufferings that had marked the years of occupation. The first critical notice, written by Jan Romein, Professor of Dutch History at the University of Amsterdam, sounded a strong note of pessimism about the prospects of such a story as Anne Frank's finding many readers. After praising her diary for its intelligence, vivacity, and humaneness, and also noting that the young author had perished in one of the worst of the German concentration camps shortly before liberation, Romein offered the following reflections:

> The way she died is unimportant. More important is that this young life was willfully cut off by a system of irrational cruelty. We had sworn to each other never to forget or forgive this system as long as it was still raging, but now that it is gone, we too easily forgive, or at least forget, which ultimately means the same thing.[5]

What is so remarkable about this statement is its date: April 1946. The war had ended less than a year before, and yet, as is obvious from Romein's downcast words, the question of memory was already a worried one; indeed, in terms of its outcome, it may already have been a lost one. Romein's response to Anne Frank's diary (he read it in manuscript and wrote his little essay a full year before Contact brought out the first edition of the book) was conditioned by his sense that the war had swept away whatever sources of culture might effectively have opposed Nazism and that, in the postwar period, there were few signs that an active democratic counterforce could be quickly established in its stead. And so, he concluded pessimistically, "we have lost the battle against the beast in man. We have lost because we have not been able to substitute something positive for it. And that is why we will lose again."

Had this view prevailed, it is clear that Anne Frank's story would have remained a minor affair, one among the hundreds of wartime diaries kept in the archives of the Netherlands Institute for War Documentation but otherwise hardly known. As it happens, Romein's reading of Anne Frank was not to be widely shared, for within a decade of his review, the diary was to capture huge audiences the world over. Later readers evidently were to fix upon aspects of Anne Frank's story that Romein either overlooked or upon which he placed only secondary stress. Clearly, however, he was not "wrong" in his view of Anne Frank, nor was he reading her book "badly." Rather, the discoveries that he made in the diary pointed him back to the devastations from which the countries of Europe were only just emerging. The book showed him "the real hideousness of fascism, more than all the trials of Nuremberg" and summed up "the worst crime of that abominable spirit . . . the destruction of life and talent only because of a senseless desire to destroy." Moreover, he sensed that the force of the spirit unleashed by Nazism was far from spent and that Anne Frank would hardly be its last victim. "No matter in what form inhumanity may lay traps for us, we will fall into them as long as we are unable to replace that inhumanity with a positive force." The name that Romein gave this positive force was "democracy," and he concluded his meditation on the conflict between fascism and a vital opposition to it with these melancholy words: "And with all our good intentions, we are still as far away from this kind of democracy as we were before the war."

Romein's essay presented a dark view of recent history and an apprehension of its legacy for Europe in the immediate postwar period. Within this framework, he read Anne Frank's diary in the only way he could, as an admonitory text. The book's youthful author, after all, had been murdered by the Nazis, and her death appeared to him as a warning of further devastations to come unless the spirit of nihilism unleashed by Nazism could be permanently overcome. Romein recognized Anne Frank's precocious talent, to be sure, but he found nothing in her diary that transcended his sharp sense of her horrible end and the monstrous system that destroyed her.

Romein's essay, "A Child's Voice," appeared on the front page of the Dutch newspaper *Het Parool* on April 3, 1946, and is credited with stimulating interest in Anne Frank's then still unpublished manuscript. When the book appeared the following June it carried an introduction by Romein's wife and, on the dust jacket, extracts from his essay. The early reviews, according to the Dutch scholar Gerrold van der Stroom, were uniformly favorable and spoke of the book as "a moral testament," "a human document of great clarity and honesty," and as a text that "transcends the misery" it records.[6] These terms, which were far more optimistic than those used by Romein, were to be repeated and amplified elsewhere as the diary found its way into foreign-language translations. A French edition was brought out in Paris by Calmann-Levy in 1950; that same year, the Heidelberg publisher, Lambert Schneider, issued the first German-language version; in 1952 Valentine, Mitchell released the British publication, and at the same time Doubleday offered it to American readers; translations into numerous other languages were to follow within a few years. In 1955 the popular theater version, by Frances Goodrich and Albert Hackett, first played in the United States and soon was introduced to highly receptive audiences around the world.[7] Four years later, in 1959, George Stevens's Hollywood film version was produced and likewise proved to be an international success. The "child's voice" that had been silenced in Bergen-Belsen had now become audible to vast numbers of people around the world.

What was it that they heard in this voice, and why did it appeal to them so? Unlike Romein, who took away from Anne Frank's story the heavy sense "that we have lost the battle against the beast in man," most later readers found a far more buoyant message in the book. They saw Anne Frank as a young, innocent, vivacious girl, full of life and blessed with an optimistic spirit that enabled her never to lose hope in humanity, even as its worst representatives were intent on hunting her down and murdering her. They understood her story as deeply sorrowful but perhaps not as ultimately tragic, for they also found in it strains of tenderness and intimacy, courage and compassion, wit and humor, sincere religious feeling, and an aspiring romantic idealism, all of which undercut the sense of historical catastrophe that Romein stressed. Indeed, whereas he read it primarily as a revealing historical document, most others preferred to see the diary as a moving personal testimony, a war-time story, to be sure, but also a work of bright adolescent spirit, one that portrayed a life shadowed by daily tension and lingering threat but also inspired by nascent love and humane intelligence. In her introduction to the American edition, for instance, Eleanor Roosevelt acknowledged that Anne Frank's book made her "shockingly aware of war's greatest evil—the degradation of the human spirit," but "at the same time, Anne's diary makes poignantly clear the ultimate shining nobility of that spirit."[8] The affirmation inherent in this evaluation, its reaching for psychological harmony reflected in the syntactic balance of the sentence, typifies much of the early response to Anne Frank's book among American readers. A reviewer for *Newsweek* used the heading "Distressing Story" but highlighted Anne Frank's "courage and faith," praised her resolve to maintain her ideals in the most difficult of circumstances, and concluded by predicting that "with her vivid and appealing diary she will be remembered as a talented and sensitive adolescent whose spirit could not be imprisoned or thwarted."[9] A review in the *Saturday Review* ran under the heading "A Glory and a Doom" and, as this phrasing suggests, likewise offered a balanced reading of the book, pointing up its sorrowful aspects but ending on a note of affirmative belief that "from this one girl's diary a gleam of redemption may arise."[10]

Meyer Levin, who was to take an intense, even obsessive interest in Anne Frank, wrote a highly appreciative review for the Sunday *New York Times Book Review,* a front page article that undoubtedly contributed to the book's early success in the United States. It also may have helped to set the terms by which the book would be understood by many of its first readers. Levin noted that "Anne Frank's voice becomes the voice of six million vanished Jewish souls," but otherwise he subordinated the historical aspect of the diary and stressed its more intimate side. He hailed it as "a warm and stirring confession," a "virtually perfect drama of puberty," which should be read "over and over for insight and enjoyment."

While it was a story shaped by the conditions of the recent war, he emphasized that readers need not shy away from it, for "this is no lugubrious ghetto tale, no compilation of horrors." Rather, it was a book representative "of human character and growth anywhere," a book "that simply bubbles with amusement, love, and discovery," and that expresses "a poignant delight in the infinite human spirit." For someone who later was to carry on an impassioned campaign against those whom he accused of willfully distorting Anne Frank's diary by universalizing it, Levin did not do very much in his *New York Times* review to stress its particularistic aspects. Instead, he wrote that the diary was "so wondrously alive, so near, that one feels overwhelmingly the universalities of human nature." The types portrayed were human types, so much so that the Franks and the Van Daans were people who "might be living next door." As for the author herself, "one feels the presence of this child-becoming-woman as warmly as though she was snuggled on a near-by sofa." "Surely," Levin concluded, "this wise and wonderful young girl . . . will be widely loved."[11]

In order to give the book this emphasis—one that urged readers to cherish its youthful author rather than to mourn her—one had to read the diary in such a way as to have Anne Frank's story appear an uplifting and not a harrowing experience. The only way to do that, though, was to dehistoricize her story, view it as emblematic of Jewish fate during the Nazi period, to be sure, but also as transcending that fate. The girl was gone, but something precious about her spirit—its ebullience, its youthful optimism, its magnanimity—would outlast her murderers. Levin, like so many others who wrote about the diary, fixed on those passages that highlighted Anne Frank's cheerfulness and serenity and tended to play down its gloomier aspects. Obviously, neither Levin nor anyone else could ignore the young girl's ultimate end, but by emphasizing the tender and more ennobling aspects of youthful sentiment in the book and deemphasizing its darker dimensions, it became possible to project an image

of Anne Frank that softened somewhat the revulsion and horror that otherwise might have directed readers' responses to the
diary. One wanted, in short, to be able to regard the book as an
inspiring text and not a disconsolate one and to come away from
it with feelings of affection for the author rather than fear for her
fate or loathing for those who brought it about.

This tendency to idealize her story characterized much of the
early response to Anne Frank's writing, especially among readers
in America. Thus Anne Birstein and Alfred Kazin, in their intro-
ductory essay to *The Works of Anne Frank*, quoted the young girl's
bedtime prayer—"I thank you God, for all that is good and dear
and beautiful"—and suggested that "perhaps this was Anne's last
prayer in hiding. Perhaps when she went to bed on the night of
August 3, 1944 [the following day the family was to be discovered
and taken away], her last thought was of her own blessedness:
her youth, her strength, her love for all the people and the growing things around her, her closeness to God, who had provided
them." Perhaps. But, as Birstein and Kazin add, "there is no way
of knowing." A lack of knowledge, however, did not impede the
two authors from endowing Anne Frank's last night in relative
freedom with an aura of prayerful hope and consolation. Indeed,
Birstein and Kazin place a prominent stress on the inspirational
aspects of the diary and write that it has survived "because the faith-
fulness with which it records an unusual experience reminds us
. . . of the sweetness and goodness that are possible in a world
where a few souls still have good will. The *Diary* moves us because
its author had the strength to see, to remember, to hope."[12]

As illustrated here, a strong desire to regard Anne Frank's story
as a testament of hope characterizes much of the early reception
of the diary. This wish found both a powerful fulfillment and
a new impetus in *The Diary of Anne Frank*, the 1955 stage play
by Frances Goodrich and Albert Hackett, which was to prove
extraordinarily successful in moving mass audiences to pity and
love the image of the bright young girl without, at the same time,

having them overly frightened or repelled by too stark a sense of her end. More than any other "reading" of the diary, the Goodrich and Hackett adaptation was responsible for projecting an image of Anne Frank that would be widely acceptable to large numbers of people in the postwar period. In essence, the two authors recreated Anne Frank as a triumphant figure, one characterized by such irrepressible hope and tenacious optimism as to overcome any final sense of a cruel end. As Walter Kerr, reviewing the play for the *Herald Tribune*, put it, "Soaring through the center of the play with the careless gayety of a bird that simply cannot be caged is Anne Frank herself. . . . Anne is not going to her death; she is going to leave a dent on life, and let death take what's left."[13] Echoing this view, the reviewer for the *New York Post* wrote that the play "brought about the reincarnation of Anne Frank—as though she'd never been dead."[14] Given the forcefulness and attractiveness of the young girl's personality, audiences would leave the theater knowing, of course, that Anne Frank had died, but nevertheless feeling that she had not been defeated.

How did Goodrich and Hackett manage to create this effect? As is well known, the playwrights took some large liberties with the text of the diary and, by playing down or simply suppressing outright the more foreboding entries and highlighting more affirmative ones, they shaped an image of Anne Frank that varied more than a little from the girl's self-image in the diary. In particular, they tended to understate the specifically Jewish aspect of her story and instead universalized her experience as the experience of suffering humanity in general. In this, as will soon become clear, they had the encouragement and close cooperation of both Otto Frank and Garson Kanin, the play's first director. They also placed a preponderant emphasis on her most cheerful side, ending their play with the consoling affirmation that "in spite of everything I still believe that people are really good at heart," a line that does not appear in the diary in anything like the climactic role it is made to assume in the play. As Lawrence

Langer has written, this line, "floating over the audience like a benediction assuring grace after momentary gloom, is the least appropriate epitaph conceivable for the millions of victims and thousands of survivors of Nazi genocide."[15] Langer, of course, is right in his criticism, or at least would be right if the play had been conceived to honor the memory of the millions of victims of Nazi terror. In fact, though, the play was shaped along very different lines. As Garson Kanin put it in a revealing *New York Times* interview, "This play makes use of elements having mainly to do with human courage, faith, hope, brotherhood, love, and self-sacrifice. We discovered as we went deeper and deeper that it was a play about what Shaw called 'the life force.'"[16] No brooding sense of mass death registers here. Rather, what shows through this string of lofty abstractions is nothing but an idealized sense of history, or, more accurately, no sense of it at all.

History, as Anne Frank and millions of other European Jews suffered it, was a perilous affair, but neither the playwrights nor the director had it in mind to present a grim or gloomy play. It is clear from other remarks that Kanin made to the press at the time of the play's New York opening that exposing theater audiences to anything remotely reminiscent of genocide was simply not part of his intention:

> I have never looked on it as a sad play. I certainly have no wish to inflict depression on an audience; I don't consider that a legitimate theatrical end. I never thought the original material depressing. I've never seen it as sociological, historical, or political—but as a human document. . . . Looking back, Anne Frank's death doesn't seem to me a wasteful death, because she left us a legacy that has meaning and value to us as you look at the whole story.[17]

Kanin summed up what he understood to be the "meaning and value" of Anne Frank's story in an essay he published in *News-*

week in 1979, almost twenty-five years after the first stage production of *The Diary of Anne Frank*. Comparing her to Peter Pan
and the Mona Lisa, among others, "Anne," he wrote, "remains
forever adolescent. . . . [She] reminds us that the length of a life
does not necessarily reflect its quality. . . . Anne lives on. She
remains for us ever a shining star, a radiant presence who, during
her time of terror and humiliation and imprisonment, was able
to find it within herself to write in her immortal diary, 'In spite of
everything I still believe that people are good at heart.'"[18] Thus
sentimentality, reduced here to an almost naive level, is made to
triumph over history.

Given the liberties that the playwrights took with the text in
reworking it for the popular theater and given as well this maudlin
rendering of it on the part of the director, it is little wonder that
audiences responded as they did. The reviewer for *Variety* had
this to say about the opening in New York: "Theoretically, after
seeing this new play . . . one should come out depressed, hating
the Nazis, hating what they did to millions of innocent people,
and most particularly what they did to a little Jewish Dutch girl
whose name was Anne Frank. . . . Yet 'Diary' comes off as a glow-
ing, moving, frequently humorous play that has just about everything one could wish for. It is not grim."[19] The reviewer for the
Daily News wrote that "as it appears on the stage of the Cort, 'The
Diary of Anne Frank' is not in any important sense a Jewish play.
. . . It is a story of the gallant human spirit. . . . Anne Frank is a
Little Orphan Annie brought into vibrant life." About the family
in hiding, this reviewer continued in his same hyperbolic fashion: "Without the gallantry of the human spirit, this apartment
could be a hell a few stories above the earth. . . . But this place is
not a hell above ground; it is a testing place in which men and
women and children earn the blessed right to be alive."[20] Others
responded in a similar vein, one pronouncing that Anne Frank
"was destined to become a symbol of man's hope for the survival
of the human spirit," another prophesying, in lofty but equally

meaningless fashion, that "wherever and whenever man's inhumanity to man erupts, these characters and their conflicts will be humanly and dramatically valid," etc.[21] In brief, the Anne Frank who emerged through this play was fashioned to evoke the most conventional of responses about "man's inhumanity to man," the "triumph of goodness over evil," the eternal verities of "the human spirit," and other such banalities. The harshness of history was left behind, and in its place softer, more acceptable images of a young girl's gayety and moral gallantry came to the fore.

Lawrence Langer sums up the inevitable impact on theatergoers of a play of such character: "An audience coming to this play in 1955, only a decade after the event, would find little to threaten their psychological or emotional security. . . . The authors of the dramatic version of Anne Frank's *Diary* lacked the artistic will—or courage—to leave their audiences overwhelmed by the feeling that Anne's bright spirit was extinguished, that Anne, together with millions of others, was killed simply because she was Jewish, and for no other reason."[22]

One did not encounter much criticism of this kind in the late 1950s. On the contrary, most of the reviews of *The Diary of Anne Frank* were laudatory, and the play enjoyed an instant success. It swept all of the major theater prizes—in 1956, the Pulitzer Prize, the Critics Circle Prize, and the Antoinette Perry Award—and soon was playing before theater audiences everywhere. To this day it remains a popular play and is frequently performed in major cities and small towns throughout the world. It was followed in 1959 by a full-length motion picture, also scripted by Goodrich and Hackett, which proved to be equally popular, and, in 1967, by the first of several television adaptations. Videos, children's books, and other tie-ins have followed, as have any of a number of reissues of the original diary. As a consequence, it is no exaggeration to say that more people are probably familiar with the Nazi era through the figure of Anne Frank than through any other figure of that period with the possible exception of Adolf Hitler himself.

Hers is often the first story of that time that large numbers of people come to know; for many, hers may also be the last story of its kind that they encounter and the one whose images they are most likely to retain. It would be reasonable to surmise, indeed, that if people have read one book and only one book about the victims of Nazism, it is likely to be *The Diary of a Young Girl.* If they have seen one play and only one play, it is probably Goodrich and Hackett's *The Diary of Anne Frank.* The several film and television versions have played to millions, and millions more have been to Amsterdam to visit the house on the Prinsengracht where the diary was composed. In sum, the impact of Anne Frank on shaping the historical consciousness of vast numbers of people is almost inestimable. More than any other single work of the postwar period, her diary, in its several permutations, must be counted among the first and most abiding popular representations of Jewish fate in the era of Nazi persecutions.

Who, though, is the Anne Frank of *The Diary of Anne Frank?* What version of the author of the original diary comes through the Goodrich and Hackett play? From some of the theater reviews that have already been cited, it is evident that the Anne of the stage resembles the Anne of the printed page in some respects but differs from her significantly in others. The major differences, as has been pointed out by more than one critic in the past, is that the Anne of the stage has been fashioned as a more universal type than the Anne of the original diary. She also appears to be imbued with a more permanently optimistic, indeed all but indestructibly affirmative, spirit. To be sure, one can find entries in the diary that illustrate Anne Frank's cheerfulness but, if one is open to them, one can also find passages that reflect a far graver sense of the times and more than a little anxiety about current events. Peering out of her hideaway windows, for instance, Anne Frank saw and recorded the brutality of the German occupation (entry of November 19, 1942):

Evening after evening the green and gray army lorries trundle
past. The Germans ring at every front door to inquire if there
are any Jews living in the house. If there are, then the whole
family has to go at once. If they don't find any, they go on to
the next house. No one has a chance of evading them unless
one goes into hiding. . . . It seems like the slave hunts of
olden times. But it's certainly no joke; it's much too tragic for
that. In the evenings when it's dark, I often see rows of good
innocent people accompanied by crying children, walking
on and on . . . bullied and knocked about until they almost
drop. No one is spared—old people, babies, expectant moth-
ers, the sick—each and all join in the march of death.[23]

The scene is vividly drawn and shows the degree to which Anne
Frank was aware of what was taking place just below on the streets
of Amsterdam; however, no such passage as this one appears in
the stage play. Nor did Goodrich and Hackett see fit to carry over
the following entry (October 9, 1942), which extends still further
the young diarist's consciousness of Jewish fate during this time:

Our many Jewish friends are being taken away by the
dozen. These people are being treated by the Gestapo without a shred of decency, being loaded into cattle trucks and
sent to Westerbork, the big Jewish camp in Drente. Westerbork sounds terrible: only one washing cubicle for a hundred people and not nearly enough lavatories. There are no
separate accommodations. Men, women, and children all
sleep together. One hears of frightful immorality because of
this; and a lot of the women, and even girls, who stay there
any length of time are expecting babies. . . . If it is as bad
as this in Holland whatever will it be like in the distant and
barbarous regions [the Jews] are sent to? We assume that
most of them are murdered. The English radio speaks of
their being gassed.[24]

As it happens, Anne Frank and her family were themselves to be sent to Westerbork and from there to those regions in the east that are described here in such chillingly direct terms, but this is knowledge that, once again, was not incorporated into the play in any substantial way at all. By stripping the text of such passages as these, Goodrich and Hackett may have "spared" theater audiences from knowing some of the worst that Anne Frank herself knew or feared, but in the process they reduced the figure of the young girl considerably. They also detached her from her own vivid sense of herself as a Jew. For instance, in thinking about the hardships of her family's situation, the Anne of the diary was drawn to reflect upon the nature of Jewish historical experience and wrote thoughtfully about the relationship between her suffering people and their God (April 11, 1944):

We have been pointedly reminded that we are in hiding, that we are Jews in chains, chained to one spot, without any rights, but with a thousand duties. We Jews mustn't show our feelings, must be brave and strong, must accept all inconveniences and not grumble. . . .

Who has inflicted this upon us? Who has made us Jews different from all other people? Who has allowed us to suffer so terribly up till now? It is God that has made us as we are, but it will be God, too, who will raise us up again. If we bear all this suffering and if there are still Jews left, when it is over, then Jews, instead of being doomed, will be held up as an example. Who knows, it might even be our religion from which the world and all peoples learn good, and for that reason and that reason only do we have to suffer now. We can never become just Netherlanders, or just English, or representatives of any country for that matter, we will always remain Jews, but we want to, too.[25]

This passage is striking for the maturity of its religious insight and also for what it reveals about Anne Frank's understanding of herself as an actor within the stream of Jewish history. It was, however, deleted from the play entirely and, in its place, there appears the following weak substitution: "We're not the only people that've had to suffer. There've always been people that've had to . . . sometimes one race . . . sometimes another. . . ."[26] As Lawrence Graver explains, it was Garson Kanin, the play's director, who was responsible for this unfortunate change. While reading an advanced draft of the Goodrich and Hackett manuscript, Kanin encountered lines that more or less faithfully followed the diary's Jewish sentiments about suffering and objected to them as "an embarrassing piece of special pleading." Throughout history, he told the writers:

> people have suffered because of being English, French, German, Italian, Ethiopian, Mohammedan, Negro, and so on. I don't know how this can be indicated, but it seems to me of utmost importance.
>
> The fact that in this play the symbols of persecution and oppression are Jews is incidental and, Anne, in stating the argument so, reduces her magnificent stature. It is Peter here who should be the young one, outraged at being persecuted because he is a Jew, and Anne, wiser, pointing out that through the ages, people in minorities have been oppressed. In other words, at this moment, the play has an opportunity to spread its theme into the infinite.[27]

Goodrich and Hackett took Kanin's point to heart and radically changed their script to accommodate their director's wishes: "We're not the only people that have had to suffer," etc. As dramatic prose, these lines are pallid in comparison to those cited above, but more grievously, they are altogether without source or analogy in the diary itself and have the effect of generalizing the figure of Anne Frank to the point of deracinating her. They are, however, typical of the major thrust of the play, which has given to the world an Anne Frank who is emotionally much thinner, intellectually less thoughtful, and spiritually and psychologically far less serious than the Anne of the diary. In the play's final scene, indeed, Goodrich and Hackett sentimentalize their heroine to the point of silliness by having Otto Frank remark, "It seems strange to say this, that anyone could be happy in a concentration camp. But Anne was happy in the camp in Holland where they first took us. After two years of being shut up in these rooms, she could be out . . . out in the sunshine and the fresh air that she loved."[28] In the bathetic quality of the sentiment they express, these lines are of a piece with the Birstein and Kazin fantasy, cited earlier, about Anne Frank's bedtime prayer and may even have provoked them. Both posit an Anne Frank of the beatitudes, a saintly figure who ultimately could not be brought down by her persecutors. "No longer a child," as Goodrich and Hackett describe her at play's end, "but a woman with courage to meet whatever lies ahead." She is last seen on stage "with a soft, reassuring smile"—this, supposedly, in the presence of the armed Gestapo, which has burst in upon her family in hiding—and her final words in the play, twice repeated, are, "In spite of everything, I still believe that people are really good at heart." Adding point to this affirmation, which is intended to lift one above whatever fear or sorrow one might otherwise feel at this moment in the play, Otto Frank says just before the curtain falls, "She puts me to shame."[29] And so *The Diary of Anne Frank* ends not on a note of final doom but of moral triumph, one's faith in humankind supposedly restored by the inspiring example of the girl who, "in spite of everything," could leave us with a credo affirming belief in the goodness of man.

This credo was Otto Frank's even more than it was his daughter's, although it has been associated with the latter for so long now that today it is almost universally embraced as the defining quality of Anne Frank's "spirit." In fact, though, this buoyant "spirit," while present in certain entries of the diary, was largely the postwar creation of Otto Frank, whose role in shaping a positive, inspiring image of his daughter was in many ways decisive. Indeed, in no small measure, the Anne Frank we remember is the Anne Frank that her father wished us to remember and labored tirelessly to project.

Together with his wife and two daughters, Otto Frank was transported to Auschwitz and was the only member of his family to survive the Nazi camps. Upon his return to Amsterdam, he was given the pages of his daughter's diary by his loyal co-worker and protector, Miep Gies, and, with the help of some others, he set about to prepare the text for publication. It appeared in 1950 as *Het Achterhuis*. In the years that followed, Otto Frank devoted himself to perpetuating his daughter's memory in a variety of ways—through his close, often laborious, and sometimes painful dealings with translators, publishers, playwrights, producers, directors, agents, and attorneys involved with the book, stage, and film versions of Anne Frank's diary; through the establishment and supervision of the Anne Frank Foundation in Amsterdam, whose purpose was both to preserve the house at 263 Prinsengracht as a memorial museum and also to carry out broad-based educational programs against manifestations of discrimination and racism in the postwar period; through decades of correspondence with hundreds of people around the world who wrote to him after reading the diary or seeing the play; and in other related ways. Otto Frank's chief occupation in the postwar period was his single-minded devotion to transmitting the story of his daughter's life and "legacy," a legacy, as he understood it and wished it to be understood, that placed a preponderant emphasis on hope, peace, and the advancement of tolerance and understanding among peoples of different kinds. Liberal-minded, rationalist, and broadly cosmopolitan by education and conviction, Otto Frank was guided in his mission by admirably humane concerns and the strong belief that his daughter's story, if seen in its most universal aspect, could serve as a source of inspiration for countless others. For it to have these effects, however, the image of Anne Frank had to be shaped in ways that would be acceptable to large and diverse audiences. In some of his early correspondence with Meyer Levin, who was setting about to write a dramatic version of the diary, Otto Frank made clear just how he wanted his daughter to be seen:

> As to the Jewish [issue] you are right that I do not feel the same way you do. I always said, that Anne's book is not a warbook. War is the background. It is not a Jewish book either, though Jewish sphere, sentiment and surrounding is the background. I never wanted a Jew writing an introduction for it. It is (at least here) read and understood more by gentiles than in Jewish circles. . . . So do not make a Jewish play out of it![30]

As is well known, Levin's script, which tended to foreground the very features that Otto Frank understood as being of only background relevance, was rejected, and the non-Jewish playwrights Goodrich and Hackett were engaged to write the dramatic version of the diary. Their Anne Frank, crafted through close consultation with Otto Frank, faithfully follows the latter's wishes and specifically carries out Garson Kanin's prescription for a more positive, appealing, and universally inspiring Anne Frank.

The formula worked, and following upon the initial success of the play, which was enormous, there was renewed public interest in the diary itself. Contact had not reprinted *Het Achterhuis* since 1950, but in 1955 it reissued the diary in three separate printings. There were three more printings in 1956, nine in 1957, five in 1958, and numerous other printings up to today. In fact, when it first appeared the diary had not had a notable success in Holland, but as a result of its much greater appeal in America and the wide attention given the Goodrich and Hackett dramatic version, the book returned to the country of its origin, as Gerrold van der Stroom describes it, "via an international detour."[31]

There was a similar response elsewhere. In West Germany, *Das Tagebuch der Anne Frank* also had only a modest beginning. The original Lambert Schneider edition numbered only 4,500 in 1950. In 1955, however, Fischer Bücherei took it over and reissued the book as a paperback volume, with a cover that featured the words that by now had become canonized: "Ich glaube an das Gute im Menschen." Within the first five years Fischer printed the diary no less than eighteen times and sold more than 700,000 copies to German readers.

In 1958 Fischer also brought out Ernst Schnabel's *Anne Frank: Spur Eine Kindes,* a book that traced the story of Anne Frank beyond the point of her last diary entry to her death in Bergen-Belsen. In describing the aftermath of the Frank family's experience in Amsterdam, Schnabel performed a valuable service. His book, however, is problematic on two counts: one, since it is altogether undocumented, it is impossible to verify the personal accounts of Anne Frank that the author ascribes to the various eye-witnesses he interviewed; and, two, the book tends to idealize Anne Frank and thus contributes to the mystique that was rapidly growing up around her. In his opening pages, for instance, the author asks, "What was the source in this child of the power her name exerts throughout the world? Was this power, perhaps, not something within her, but something outside of and above her?"[32] He never answers these questions in so many words, but their metaphysical thrust is apparent and would seem, once again, to point in the direction of some special beatitude. This emphasis is heightened by the account of Anne Frank's period of incarceration in Auschwitz that Schnabel attributes to witnesses—"Anne still had her face, up to the last. Actually she seemed to me in Auschwitz even more beautiful than in Westerbork"[33]—and even more so by the account he gives of her end in Bergen-Belsen: "She died, peacefully, feeling that nothing bad was happening to her."[34] Schnabel attributes this sense of Anne Frank's death to one of the many unnamed witnesses he interviewed, but without any way to confirm the validity of the testimony, one is simply at a loss to know the truth of the matter. Birstein and Kazin, however, take up this description of a peaceful death and quote it approvingly in their own account of Anne Frank, as do any of a number of others. It may be that Anne Frank did die in such a manner, but given the conditions that prevailed at Bergen-Belsen during her time in the camp, it is more likely that the ravages of typhus, malnutrition, exposure, and other related horrors culminated in a far more gruesome death. The fact is, we do not know and cannot know with any certainty how Anne Frank died. What is clear, however, is that the idea of her coming to a miserable end was simply incompatible with the image of Anne Frank that was developing in the period following the Goodrich and Hackett play. Most people preferred to entertain a vision of the girl that connected her to a sustaining strength rather than debilitating weakness, to abiding goodness rather than evil triumphant. Far from being remembered as one dead child among a million or more murdered Jewish children, she was instead to be taken up and cherished as a general symbol of martyred innocence, who stood for but also transcended the lot of suffering humanity.

As we have already seen, this image of her received a kind of spiritual-political apotheosis at the time of the Bitburg affair when President Reagan, looking to "balance" his ill-conceived visit to the German military cemetery at Bitburg, traveled to Bergen-Belsen to pay homage to the victims of the Holocaust. Here is a fuller account of what the American president had to say on that occasion:

Here they lie. Never to hope. Never to pray. Never to love. Never to kneel. Never to laugh. Never to cry.

And too many of them knew that this was their fate. But that was not the end. Through it all was their faith and a spirit that moved their faith.

Nothing illustrates this better than the story of a young girl who died here at Bergen-Belsen. For more than two years, Anne Frank and her family had hidden from the Nazis in a confined annex in Holland, where she kept a remarkably profound diary. Betrayed by an informant, Anne and her family were sent by freight car to Auschwitz and finally here to Bergen-Belsen.

Just three weeks before her capture, young Anne wrote these words: "It's really a wonder that I haven't dropped all my ideals, because they seem so absurd and impossible to carry out. Yet I keep them, because in spite of everything I still believe that people are really good at heart. I simply can't build up my hopes on a foundation consisting of confusion, misery and death. I see the world gradually being turned into wilderness, I hear the ever approaching thunder, which will destroy us too, I can feel the sufferings of millions, and yet if I look up into the heavens, I think it will all come right, that this cruelty, too, will end, and that peace and tranquility will return again."[35]

By the time of President Reagan's speech in May 1985, these words had already been cited so many times as to have taken on the character of a cliché. To recite them in Bergen-Belsen, where Anne Frank and all those other anonymous dead met their end, was to make of them little more than a kitsch of hope. In themselves, to be sure, Anne Frank's words express a noble sentiment, but given our sense of what awaited her beyond the secret annex, it is scarcely possible to quote them today and pretend that the idealism they express remains altogether intact. When the American president then added his belief that the memories evoked at Bergen-Belsen "take us where God intended his children to go—toward learning, toward healing, and, above all, toward redemption,"[36] it was clear that the Anne Frank he had hoped to conjure at the gravesite had dissolved into a public rhetoric of empty piety, her image reduced to little more than vague plati-tudes about the power of faith to transcend human suffering. As for her historical substance, after so much had been diffused into the gathering legend of a secular saint, little was left.

With only few exceptions, this is the image of Anne Frank that prevails to this day within a large and receptive public. By and large, it is an image produced in America along the conventional lines employed by the major entertainment media. Given the power of American popular culture in the postwar period and the influence it has exerted in countries around the world, the American version of Anne Frank quickly took hold elsewhere. The "exceptions" alluded to above, however, are of the utmost importance to understanding the place of Anne Frank within the evolving memory of the Holocaust. The fact is, her reception has not been uniformly the same at all times and in all places any more than public perceptions of the Nazi period as a whole have been the same. For obvious reasons, the crucial agents of mem-ory with regard to this history are the Germans and the Jews, among whom one finds complex and often subtly differentiated responses to the story under review here.

As has already been mentioned, *Das Tagebuch der Anne Frank* was originally published in 1950 by Lambert Schneider Ver-lag. According to contemporary reports, some booksellers were reluctant at first to show the book in their shop windows out of concern it might provoke a hostile reaction; apparently no such thing occurred. The book sold moderately well and then, in the Fischer Taschenbuch edition, which first appeared in 1955, sold extremely well and went on to become one of the most popular books of postwar German literature. The circulation numbers bear out the extent of its reception: as of spring, 2010, the Fischer paperback edition was in its 135th printing and had seen well over three million copies in print.[37]

The play was also to reach an unusually large audience. It opened on October 1, 1956, at major theaters in seven different cities (West Berlin, Hamburg, Düsseldorf, Aachen, Karlsruhe, Konstanz, and Dresden) and, according to the reviews, had a profoundly moving effect on audiences everywhere. Within a short time it played in dozens of cities across Germany and, in the late 1950s alone, reached hundreds of thousands of people. While the play continued to be performed in the next two decades, its popularity waned somewhat. Then, in the fall of 1979, following the huge success of the NBC program "Holocaust" on German television, there was a renewal of interest in *The Diary of Anne Frank*. The play was performed numerous times in Düsseldorf, Oldenburg, Bielefeld, Wilhelmshafen, and other cities; in some of these places it was accompanied by an exhibit of photographs of Anne Frank and her family.

Numerous other events characterize the German reception of the diary and show the extent to which the figure of Anne Frank has become established as an important presence within postwar German consciousness. In the 1950s, Anne Frank clubs and discussion groups formed among German youths in various cities. In 1957 some two thousand of these young people, mainly from the Hamburg area, made a pilgrimage to Bergen-Belsen to pay homage to the memory of Anne Frank. The following year more than eight thousand people participated in a similar visit to the camp. In June of 1959 an Anne Frank Village, conceived of as a haven for refugees, was inaugurated in the city of Wuppertal. That same month special commemorative services honoring Anne Frank were held at the university and at the Paulskirche in Frankfurt and attracted large crowds. Through the 1950s and '60s, schools were named for Anne Frank in dozens of cities and towns across Germany, and German school children began to take up her diary as part of their reading. They regularly crossed the border into Holland in busloads for visits to the Anne Frank house in Amsterdam. Also in the 1960s German newspapers gave wide coverage to the trial of Karl Silberbauer, the Austrian Gestapo agent who had arrested the Frank family, and to the trials of former SS Major General Wilhelm Harster and two of his aides, Wilhelm Zoepf and Gertrud Slotke, who were charged with complicity in the murder of eighty-three thousand Dutch Jews; Anne Frank's name and fate were prominently mentioned in all of these news stories. In 1979, to mark the fiftieth anniversary of her birth, the Deutsche Bundespost brought out a commemorative Anne Frank postage stamp. That same year, Lambert Schneider Verlag published a commemorative picture book chronicling the life and times of Anne Frank. In more recent years Miep Gies's memoir, translated into German, has kept the memory of Anne Frank alive for German readers, as Ernst Schnabel's book did in earlier years. Television programs and the touring exhibit, "Anne Frank in der Welt," which has been shown in numerous German cities, have done the same up to the present moment. This list could be extended but, for present purposes, it need not be: it is clear that from 1950, the date of the original German publication of the diary, until today Anne Frank has been projected to German audiences on an ongoing basis and through virtually all of the media of popular culture. The question, therefore, is not "Do the Germans know her?," for assuredly they do. Rather, one wants to know how Germans have responded to her, what it is she means to them, and how they identify themselves with her story.

To grasp the nature of this response at its core necessitates placing the German reception of Anne Frank within the context of that struggle over historical memory that Germans call "Vergangenheitsbewältigung." This coming to terms with the past, a challenge that strikes to the heart of German national identity in the postwar period, has been going on with greater or lesser degrees of willingness and success for more than sixty-five years now. Its history is a tortuous one, for it intermingles personal and collective memory with politics and morality in ways that are extremely demanding. Left to themselves, the majority of Germans doubtless would prefer to remain disengaged from this history, even as they know, on some level, that it continues to exert powerful claims upon them.

Willing or not, there has been an on-again, off-again engagement with the traumatic history of the Third Reich since the period immediately following the end of the war. In the beginning, this encounter was an enforced one and was met with a general resistance. Most Germans did not respond well to the Nuremberg trials any more than they did to the documentary films of wartime atrocities that the allies encouraged them to see. These things were intended to get people to acknowledge the worst of the crimes committed by their countrymen, but in the immediate postwar period most were in no mood to wrestle with the sins of their nation, especially when they felt they were being compelled to do so by their conquerors. In contrast to this general resistance, Anne Frank's diary, in both the book and the dramatic versions, seems to have brought numbers of otherwise reluctant Germans to look back at the war and to recognize, many of them for the first time, the real nature of the Nazi persecutions. Whereas most could not allow themselves to register any shock of personal recognition in the faces of the Nazi officials brought before the Nuremberg tribunals or acknowledge any association at all with the terrifying images of the corpse-mounds shown to them in the films, many were genuinely moved by the story of Anne Frank. The theater reviews of the time tell of audiences sitting in stunned silence at the play and leaving the performance unable to speak or to look one another in the eye. Many of the early book reviews also make clear that the diary of Anne Frank broke through to German readers as almost nothing previously connected to the war had been able to do. In all of these respects, the emergence of Anne Frank as a factor in postwar German consciousness signaled something new—indeed, she was among the first prods to public memory and began a debate that continues, unresolved, to this day.

In its essence, this is a debate about the nature of World War II and, in particular, about postwar Germany's understanding of and sense of responsibility for Nazi Germany's murderous treatment of the Jews. As evidenced by numerous public debates, including the notorious "historians' debate" that began in 1989 and continued for several years thereafter and, a decade later, by the intensely ambivalent German reception of Daniel Jonah Goldhagen's *Hitler's Willing Executioners*, Germans are divided in their efforts to make the war years comprehensible to themselves, let alone in their efforts to explain them to others. As for their nation's persecution and mass murder of European Jewry, the crimes are broadly acknowledged by virtually all responsible sectors of German society, but a consensus of explanation for them is lacking. These are huge and unsettling issues, and whenever they are raised they awaken complex emotional responses, ranging from indignation and rejection to shame and guilt.

The story of Anne Frank could not fail to provoke this full range of responses, and indeed it did. Following productions of the play, there were often turbulent discussions within families about the Nazi period. President Heuss himself gave a well publicized speech in Munich, in October 1957, in which he referred to these debates and wanted to see them continue lest the past be forgotten. While Anne Frank's story was painful for Germans to confront, it was also deemed to be necessary. Its greatest effect was to get people to see the "other" side of the wartime experience and to enforce a realization of the sufferings their nation had caused to millions of innocent people.

No doubt it was for these reasons that many responded powerfully, almost desperately, to the message of hope that they detected in the diary and to which they gave such a heightened emphasis. The Anne Frank they would favor, indeed almost the only Anne Frank they could bring themselves to acknowledge, was the one who spoke affirmatively about life and not accusingly about her torturers. According to one contemporary commentator, the appeal of the diary to German readers was "the appeal of the forgiving faith which pervades the book and appears to make the murdered absolve the murderer."[38] According to another, the extraordinary popularity of the play should not necessarily be taken as an unqualified good, for "it lets the Germans off too lightly. It does not even begin to suggest how frightful German actions were."[39] One sees, therefore, that the response to Anne Frank had to be a highly ambivalent one among German audiences. If they were forced into too close an identification with the girl's persecutors, most would have felt assaulted by the oppressive feelings of guilt and shame evoked by a vicarious sense of complicity. As it happens, the play is constructed in such a manner as to keep these feelings from becoming overwhelming. The drama builds towards violence but never represents it as such. No one is killed, nor is a single member of the Gestapo or SS ever brought on stage. The audience observes only the people in hiding, and while it surely knows from whom they are seeking shelter, a face-to-face encounter with Germans in the role of persecutors never takes place. It is no doubt for this reason that some in the audience would be moved to identify more closely with the victims, if not specifically as Jews, then as people in a state of extreme difficulty. In the words of one of the contemporary German drama critics, "We see in Anne Frank's fate our own fate—the tragedy of human existence per se."[40]

This tendency to generalize Anne Frank's experience so that it becomes an existential and not a specifically historical one was especially strong among the young. Norbert Muhlen, who attempted to gauge public reaction to the diary of Anne Frank shortly after the play first showed in West German theaters, wrote as follows:

> Many young Germans identify with Anne Frank, see in her the prototype of all youth—helpless, imprisoned, at the mercy of elders, defiant of the outside world and terrified within. And the persecution and murder of Jews seems to them to be merely a peculiar external

circumstance—secondary in importance to the personal tragedy of the heroine. . . . The political basis for the tragedy shrinks in their eyes into the remote historical background.[41]

It would be impossible to suppress altogether the Jewish factor in the story of Anne Frank, any more than it would be to deny the German factor, but as indicated above and, in a curious way, as illustrated by the character of the German translation of the diary, a degree of suppression seems to be a constituent feature of the German reception of Anne Frank.

Some of the early reviews noted that the German translator, Anneliese Schütz, was not very successful in carrying over into her own language the youthful style of the teenage author of *Het Achterhuis*. What was not remarked was the more serious matter of her alterations and the outright suppression of material from the original diary. A few examples will suffice. In her entry of October 29, 1942, Anne Frank mentions that she has been reading in her mother's German prayer book. The Frank family was originally from Germany, so it is not at all surprising that Mrs. Frank would pray in her native language or that Anne could read in it. In the Schütz translation, however, the reference to Anne reading the prayers "in German" is omitted. It is omitted as well in numerous other instances. In her entry of June 13, 1943, Anne refers to a birthday poem that her father has written for her and mentions that it was composed in German. German readers of the diary, however, would never know that, for once again Schütz chose to eliminate the reference to the parent's language. She did so as well in her translation of the entry of November 17, 1942, in which Anne cites a humorous "Prospectus and Guide to the 'Secret Annexe,'" a parody of a hotel guide that describes various "Do's and Don't's." Among these is the following reference to language usage: "Speak softly at all times, by order! All civilized languages are permitted, therefore no German!" In the Schütz translation this becomes: "Alle Kultursprachen . . . aber leise!!!"

("All civilized languages . . . but softly!!!"). The original reference to German is simply stripped from the text as if it never had
appeared. There are other instances of this kind as well, all of
which would seem to indicate a determined effort on the translator's part to detach the Franks from any connection to their own
mother tongue. Inasmuch as language is a cultural possession
that binds its speakers to one another more naturally and intimately than most other things, the severance of the Franks from
German would necessarily effect a degree of severance between
them and German readers of the diary. Whatever natural links
would have existed between the two would have been cut by the
translator's tampering with the text.

Cuts were also made elsewhere, although it is doubtful that
German readers of *Das Tagebuch der Anne Frank* have been
aware of them. For instance, in her diary entry of November 19,
1942, Anne describes the nightly search for hidden Jews, already
cited above, and remarks that "the Germans ring at every front
door to inquire if there are any Jews living in the house." The
German translation carries over the reference to the manhunt
but submerges in vaguer terms the national identity of the hunters. In her entry of May 18, 1943, Anne records the fact that "all
students who wish either to get their degrees this year, or continue their studies, are compelled to sign that they are in sympathy with the Germans and approve of the New Order." The
Schütz translation once again omits the specific reference to
"the Germans" and in its place substitutes, more vaguely, "die
besetzende Macht" ("the occupying power"). In her entry of January 28, 1944, Anne writes that "although others may show heroism in their war or against the Germans, our helpers display heroism in their cheerfulness and affection." Schütz again eliminated
the reference to "the Germans" and substitutes, more abstractly,
"die Unterdrückung" ("the oppression").

When one looks carefully at these changes a pattern begins to
emerge. Whereas the effect of the previously mentioned series

of alterations was to weaken the German-Jewish identity of the Franks by disconnecting them from German, and thereby also perhaps to weaken any natural sympathy with the Franks that German readers of the *Tagebuch* would have, the effect of this second series of changes works the other way: it disconnects German readers from any shared identity with the persecutors of the Franks by eliminating specific references to the German nationality of the criminals. Thus, German readers are discouraged from entertaining a full awareness of the fact that the Jews, like themselves, are also native Germans, and they are further discouraged from focusing on the fact that the persecutors of these Jews were their own countrymen. In a general sense, of course, readers of the diary would be aware of the German identity of both the Franks and those who were responsible for terrorizing them; however, the act of reading well never proceeds "in a general sense" but always depends upon the apperception of minute particulars. As has been shown, however, some of the most telling features of Anne Frank's story were not told to German readers, who without knowing it had for years been reading a bowdlerized version of the diary.[42]

The loss in this instance is not just the familiar one that always obtains when one reads literature in translation but something far more troubling: through reading a distorted text, and not being aware of it, German readers of the *Tagebuch* have become familiar with a version of Anne Frank that is incomplete and in some serious ways inauthentic. One final illustration will bear out this point. In her diary entry of October 9, 1942, Anne records what she has come to learn about the camp at Westerbork to which the Dutch Jews were being sent. She describes the physical conditions at the camp as being woefully inadequate and then writes, "One hears of frightful immorality because of this; and a lot of the women, and even girls, who stay there any length of time are expecting babies." As a girl who had apprehensions about being arrested and sent to this very same camp (apprehensions, we know,

that were borne out by her later experience), Anne had cause to
worry about the victimization of young women at Westerbork. The
German translation of the diary, however, skips this reference in
its entirety and thus keeps German readers from any knowledge of
the young girl's fears. Furthermore, the German translation makes
no mention at all of Anne's reference, in the same diary entry, to
Jews being murdered in the east. The diarist writes: "If it is as bad
as this in Holland whatever will it be like in the distant and barbarous regions they are sent to? We assume that most of them are
murdered." The second of these two sentences—"We assume that
most of them are murdered"—was simply dropped from the German translation, as if it were a matter of no importance that the
young girl lived day by day with such terrifying assumptions. Once
again, therefore, German readers would be deprived of gaining a
full sense of the psychology of Jewish victimhood as Anne Frank
experienced it. Finally, as the result of still another excision from
this same entry, they would be spared the shock of knowing the
full extent of Anne's bitterness about the Germans. She wrote, at
the conclusion of her day's notes for October 9, 1942, "Nice people, the Germans! To think that I was once one of them too! No,
Hitler took away our nationality long ago. In fact, Germans and
Jews are the greatest enemies in the world." The German translation handles most of this in more or less straight fashion, but then
renders the final sentence as follows: "Und eine grössere Feind-
schaft als zwischen *diesen* Deutschen und den Juden gibt es nicht
auf der Welt!" ("And there is not a greater enmity in the world
than the one between *these* Germans and the Jews!"; italics in the
original.) In its original Dutch version, Anne's pronouncement is
unqualified: as she sees it, Germans and Jews are enemies, the
worst enemies in the world—period. The German translation seriously qualifies her view, however, and tells German readers that
Anne regarded only "*these* Germans"—the "bad" Germans—as
her enemies. The others, presumably themselves included, did
not fall within her judgment and therefore need not wrestle with

its implications, for Anne evidently did not mean to include *them* in her harsh comment. Of course, though, she did, and in the long run it is no kindness to German readers to spare them from the full truth of her views and to encourage them instead to take comfort in her more benign sentiments about the goodness of man. She had plenty of reason to believe otherwise.

There is no doubt that for many Germans in the postwar period, the discovery of Anne Frank marked the beginning of a long-delayed but necessary process of self-examination, but the hard work of personal introspection and historical scrutiny has gone on fitfully and produced reactions of a highly ambivalent sort. Out of both sorrow and shame, Germans have named streets, schools, and youth centers after Anne Frank, but to this day most probably do not comprehend why, three generations ago, a significant number of their countrymen deemed it necessary to hunt down a fifteen-year-old Jewish girl and send her off to suffer and die in places like Auschwitz and Bergen-Belsen. Until that issue is joined, the German encounter with Anne Frank is destined to remain incomplete.

The Jewish reception of Anne Frank, if one can use such a unitary phrase to describe a complex, multifaceted phenomenon, comes in part as a critique of the German response just outlined above. Hannah Arendt, the distinguished German-Jewish political philosopher, was by no means alone in expressing distaste for the way Germans and others took to Anne Frank. "I think the admiration for Anne Frank, especially in Germany, was phony and that the whole business was highly unpleasant— cheap sentimentality at the expense of a great catastrophe," she wrote.[43] In expressing this view she followed Bruno Bettelheim, the Austrian-Jewish refugee and famous child psychologist, who quarreled at length with the popular reception of Anne Frank and denounced it as a means of evading the issue of the death camps. "There is good reason," he wrote, "why the enormously successful play ends with Anne stating her belief in the good in all men. . . . If all men are basically good . . . then indeed we can all go on with life as usual and forget about Auschwitz. . . . [Anne Frank's story] found wide acclaim because . . . it denies implicitly that Auschwitz ever existed. If all men are good, there was never an Auschwitz."[44]

Arendt and Bettelheim, in other respects embattled critics of the Jewish role during World War II, here represent a powerful strain of Jewish resentment toward the popular treatment of the Holocaust. They object in particular to that familiar response to Anne Frank's ordeal that reduces the enormity of Jewish suffering under German National Socialism to sentiment of the most puerile sort. Norbert Muhlen illustrates this tendency even as he seems, unwittingly, to contribute to its banal character:

> The extent to which Anne Frank has become a symbol struck me again when a young Berlin dancer—a girl raised in a strong Nazi home but without any political interests—said on mention of Anne Frank's name: "Isn't it wonderful that a girl who went through so much suffering could still say, 'I believe in the goodness of man.'"
>
> The dancer had never read the book or seen the play, yet she repeated the quotation accurately. For Anne Frank's influence has been infinitely wider than the immediate audience for the play and book. Anne Frank has become a witness and a teacher to her survivors. Thus her homecoming to the country which expelled and then killed her has become a strange but heartening kind of triumph.[45]

We have on record no reply by either Arendt or Bettelheim to this report, but it is not difficult to imagine what either one of them would have had to say to Mr. Muhlen. They would have been highly critical of his conclusions precisely because they encourage the reduction of Anne Frank to a symbol of moral and intellectual convenience. In the example Muhlen cites, Anne Frank has been seized upon by someone who has neither read her book nor seen her story on stage but nevertheless savors a sense of her as a redeeming presence. In a word, Anne Frank has become a ready-at-hand formula for easy forgiveness. Far from this development representing her triumphant homecoming to the country that first expelled and then killed her, it represents quite the reverse: the triumph of Anne Frank's former countrymen over her. In her name, they have, after all, forgiven themselves. If there is any "teaching" to be deduced from this strange turn-about, it can only be the one that Hannah Arendt pointed to—the ascendancy of cheap sentimentality over any responsible sense of history.

Others wrote out of similar concern and expressed analogous worries and resentments. Martin Dworkin, in a highly critical essay in *Jewish Frontier*, argued that both the dramatic and film adaptations of the diary "perpetrated a fundamental falsity" by presenting to the world an Anne Frank who looked like "a signally American figure of thoughtless youth." He found that the work of Goodrich and Hackett diluted the richness of Anne Frank's writing to "a familiar soft-drink flavor" and stated that the audiences seeing the film and the play "know little of the facts of the extermination of six million Jews by the Nazis and will not be led to [such] knowledge in the theater."[46] *Commentary*, which was among the first English-language journals to bring the diary to the attention of readers, likewise denounced the work of Goodrich and Hackett, its reviewer calling the play "seriously dishonest" and a "failure." "If we in America cannot present her with the respect and integrity and seriousness she deserves," the *Commentary* reviewer stated, "then I think we should not try to present her at all."[47]

When one contrasts these criticisms and others like them that appeared in the Jewish press in the late 1950s and early 1960s with the general reception accorded the dramatic and film versions of the diary, one sees that Jewish opinion was on the whole much harsher. Jews recognized, to be sure, that the figure of Anne Frank on the stage and screen would reach very large audiences who otherwise knew little of the fate of the Jews in the recent European catastrophe, but many could not sanction the serious historical compromises that accompanied the popularization of the diary. The Anne Frank projected through these media looked to them too much like an American adolescent and too little like a Jewish youth of European background. Hence, the criticism that one finds expressed time and again by Jewish writers of the period frequently turned on questions of representation. Was Anne Frank being portrayed faithfully or was her image and that of the larger Jewish catastrophe she symbolized being cheapened and distorted? These questions, which remain with us still today, marked the Jewish reception of Anne Frank right from the start.

In contrast to what one sees elsewhere, one also finds Jews placing the diary of Anne Frank within the broader context of a crime they began to call "the holocaust" and within the corpus of a body of writings that some referred to as "*hurban* literature." These terms were used as early as 1952 in places like the *National Jewish Monthly, Congress Weekly,* and *Jewish Social Studies.* They contrast sharply with the often more abstract terminology that one finds in the mainstream newspapers and periodicals of the time, where the discourse more readily employs phrases like "man's inhumanity to man" and "the evil of our time." Jewish opinion was shaped by the conviction that Anne Frank's death was part of the larger destruction of European Jewry and should be grasped as such. Her story, far from being unique, was, in the words of Ludwig Lewisohn, part of "the literature of the Jewish martyrdom of this age." Many others, Lewisohn wrote, "left prose and verse, left cry and chronicle, as poignant as the diary of Anne Frank."[48] To understand her properly, therefore, one should read her as a representative voice and not a singular one.

Interestingly, Meyer Levin also advocated that she be read in these terms, although he did not do so in his *New York Times* review. However, at the same time that he wrote about Anne Frank for the *Times,* he published two independent review articles in Jewish periodicals, and in these he placed a greater stress on the specifically Jewish features of Anne Frank's story. He began his piece for *Congress Weekly* with the sentence, "At last, the voice of the six million may be heard in America," and he went on to say that "this diary is without doubt the most important human document to have come out of the great catastrophe. . . . The holocaust at long last comes home, and our defenses are shattered. We weep."[49] That is not the tone Levin took in the *New York Times*. Writing as well for the *National Jewish Post*, Levin praised the diary as "the book that makes us live with all the Jews who disappeared in Europe. It is the book with which we can identify, . . . the purest record we possess of the lives of those who were exterminated." In exhorting his readers to come to know Anne Frank's story, and to get others to know it, Levin employed a mode of address that he never would have used in writing for the mainstream press: "If it means buying no other book this year, I urge every reader to get hold of this Diary. If your budget permits you ten books a year, I urge you to buy ten copies of the Diary, and to distribute them amongst your non-Jewish friends." Levin also made a plea for Jewish institutions to devote a sizable portion of their public relations budgets "to disseminate this book and its contents in every possible form." It should be "a play and a film, it should be on television and radio." Levin was clearly embarked upon a mission here. He wanted Anne Frank's story known because he detected in it "the very pulse, the frightened but courageous pulse of the six million Jews" who perished in the Holocaust.[50] To get her story out to as broad a public as possible and to preserve it in what he took to be its essential character, Levin, as is well known, wrote the first dramatic version of the diary of Anne Frank and then, when it was aborted, engaged in a furious, protracted public quarrel with Otto Frank, Kermit Bloomgarden, and others connected to the Goodrich and Hackett play. The controversy went on for a long time. Levin wrote a whole book about it, which he entitled, fittingly enough, *The*

Obsession, and then turned his obsessions into a novel, which he called, tellingly, *The Fanatic*. Along the way he marshaled public support for his cause from dozens of rabbis, writers, and other prominent figures and thus managed to turn a one-man crusade into an affair that seemed to speak symptomatically of a larger Jewish anxiety.

It was an anxiety that grew out of a double sense of victim-hood—first, the victimization of the Jews during the war itself, and then their revictimization in the postwar period, when it sometimes seemed that others did not understand the singularity and enormity of Jewish suffering. As Ludwig Lewisohn put it, "A million Anne Franks died in horror and misery."[51] In the aftermath of that catastrophe, the least one could do was remember the dead with a proper respect.

It was against this background that Bruno Bettelheim set Jewish nerves on edge through his severe critique of the public reception of Anne Frank. In writings that he published in several different places in the early 1960s, he leveled a strong attack against the wartime behavior of the Frank family and the postwar adulation of Anne Frank. As Bettelheim saw it, the girl's fate "was certainly not a necessary fate, much less a heroic one; it was a senseless fate."[52] Her family was foolish to stick together when they would have had a better chance apart. They were also foolish to try to carry on their daily existence as if the danger just outside their door could not reach them. They should have armed themselves to fight their enemies. At a minimum, they should have recognized the death threat they were under and not given in to the illusion that they could go on living their lives as they had been accustomed to in the period before the German occupation. At the very time when the death camps were being readied to receive them, Otto Frank was giving school lessons in conventional subject matter to his two daughters. Thus, Anne, in Bettelheim's view, "may well have died because her parents could not get themselves to believe in Auschwitz." Through indulging in traditional "ghetto thinking," the Franks rendered themselves defenseless and helped to bring on their terrible end.[53]

Bettelheim's charge that the Jews, in effect, had prepared the way for their own victimization was received in a hostile manner by most others, and a public debate over the wartime behavior of the Jews quickly developed. The controversy escalated a short time later when Hannah Arendt, in writing about the Eichmann trial, argued that the Jews of Eastern Europe were condemned by the Jewish councils in the ghettos and thus perished in far greater numbers than they would have had they had no leaders at all.[54] By this time Anne Frank had already attained symbolic status as the quintessential Jewish victim, and her name and her fate were part of the argument that ensued. The polemic was so impassioned because the stakes were so high: the argument turned on nothing less than how Jewish historical memory was to understand and transmit the story of "the million Anne Franks who died in misery and horror."

In framing the question in these terms, it is evident that Jewish preoccupation with the war years centered on issues that scarcely arose in the discussion elsewhere. As Bettelheim put it, "The present generation of Jews cannot stop being haunted by the question: How was it possible that six million Jews died? How was it possible that we did not rush to halt the slaughter? . . . For our own protection, now and in the future, we must try to find answers."[55] The answers are still to be discovered, but the anxiety that gives rise to the questions remains and is, indeed, a constituent feature of Jewish consciousness in the postwar decades. There is no doubt that it has helped to influence the Jewish reception of Anne Frank and to give it a shape that one does not find elsewhere. Like others, Jewish readers of the diary know the famous passages in which the young girl speaks of her belief in the goodness of man, but most Jews do not see these passages as constituting the central teaching of the text. Haunted by an overwhelming sense of Jewish victimization, they tend to

respond skeptically to idealizations of Anne Frank as a heroic figure and instead see her as one among the six million. When they
speak of her legacy, therefore, they do so in very different terms
than others use. The following, written as a prefatory note to a
1967 article by Otto Frank, can serve as illustration:

> Anne Frank, 15, a dark-eyed girl-child, died in the concentra-
> tion camp of Bergen-Belsen in 1945. . . . She became a symbol
> of the Jewish past. . . . Hitler killed her and six million oth-
> ers. But the events recorded in her diary became part of the
> national memory that built the State of Israel—and the spirit
> behind its six-day war last June. No longer would Jews try only
> to survive. There would be no more martyrs. Dead heroes, if
> need be, but no more Anne Franks. That is her living legacy.[56]

It is doubtful that others would define Anne Frank's legacy in
these terms, but among Jews this language expresses a sentiment
that is by now familiar and tends to displace the more optimistic
sentiments found elsewhere. Interestingly, and revealingly, when
the Goodrich and Hackett drama was first performed in Israel by
the Habimah Theater group in 1966, the director, Israel Becker,
changed the last line of the play. In the original version Otto
Frank hears his daughter's voice repeating the celebrated words,
"In spite of everything, I still believe that people are really good
at heart," and he replies, "She puts me to shame." Particularly in
Germany, these words registered a powerful effect. In Israel, however, where theatergoers would have been reacting against the
background of a very different historical experience, such a line,
spoken by the dead girl's grieving father, would have made little
sense. In the Habimah Theater version, therefore, Otto Frank
hears his daughter's voice, shakes his head, and says, uncertainly,
"I don't know, I don't know."[57] The curtain then falls leaving the
audience unconsoled, sharing the father's grief and doubt. In this
response, unrelieved as it is by any uplifting sense of the girl in

her more buoyant moments, one may find a significant measure of the difference between a Jewish understanding of Anne Frank and her reception elsewhere.

In another bold rejoinder to the Goodrich and Hackett dramatization of the diary, Wendy Kesselman also set out to loosen the hold of the universalizing trend in her adaptation of *The Diary of Anne Frank.* Kesselman was not free to rework the earlier version of the theater piece as extensively as she might have wished but was bound by contract to retain the main lines of Goodrich and Hackett's presentation. Nevertheless, in some important ways she managed to neutralize some of the feel-good sentimentality of the 1955 stage play. Through dialogue that makes explicit references to Judaism, Jewish suffering, and a sense of Jewish national belonging, and also by having prayers recited in Hebrew, Kesselman reshaped the earlier version to emphasize the Jewish identities of Anne and the others in hiding with her. By foregrounding the yellow stars these Jews were forced to wear right from the beginning of act 1 and by bringing Nazis on stage at the end of act 2, she makes more graphic some of the horror of the Holocaust, which was muted in the Goodrich and Hackett play. Here, too, one is presented with the famous credo, "In spite of everything, I still believe that people are really good at heart," but the voice-over of this line at the end of act 2 is immediately followed by a Nazi officer shouting "Raus!" His harsh command, delivered as a scream, not only drowns out Anne Frank's optimistic words but shows that, in the face of Nazi terror, they lose their resonance. The final words of the play are spoken by Otto Frank, but this time there is no mention of Anne being happy in a concentration camp. Instead, Mr. Frank's closing speech reveals the overwhelmingly sad fact that, of the eight former occupants of the secret annex, all but he lost their lives in the Nazi camps. As the curtain falls, his daughter's diary is in his hands, but nothing suggests that the diarist herself has somehow transcended her death. Her story remains, but it is far from being a consoling one.

From this point on, Kesselman's rewriting of Anne Frank's story will vie with the Goodrich and Hackett version for the attention of theater audiences. If the cultural preferences of the past continue, popular perceptions of Anne Frank will still be molded in the main by the more cheerful portrait of the girl who first stepped on theater stages in the mid-1950s. But at the very least, Kesselman's play serves notice that we need not remain forever wedded to such sentimentalized notions of who Anne Frank was and how she came to suffer such an early and cruel death.[58]

What can be said, by way of conclusion, about the Anne Frank we remember? She is, without doubt, an omnipresent figure of postwar consciousness, but like the war itself she means different things to different people. Like the Germans, the Israelis have also named streets, schools, and youth centers after Anne Frank. Unlike the Germans, however, who have paid such tribute to the memory of the young girl as an act of atonement for the past and a warning for the future, the Israelis have acted out of a sense of national mourning and solidarity with the dead. Thus, in both Germany and Israel, one finds a common history marked by a common symbol but shaped by very different motives and yielding diverse interpretations of the past. Elsewhere, one finds the figuration of Anne Frank similarly diverse. Among certain Catholic writers Anne Frank is described in language of a kind usually reserved for saints. In Japan, where she is widely known, it was common at one time for teenage girls to euphemistically refer to their monthly days of menstruation by using the name of Anne Frank. Yevgeny Yevtuschenko helped to immortalize Anne Frank in his famous poem on Babi Yar, but he did so through a figure of love and fantasy as well as victimization. If one were to carry out a study of the reception of the diary in the various other countries and cultures where Anne Frank is known, one would almost certainly find still other responses to the girl and the history her image reflects.

The past, as we know, is never permanently fixed but rather shifts in contour and meaning with the changing shapes of symbolization and interpretation. As we have seen, strong symbolic figures such as Anne Frank evoke a broad range of responses and call up associations of a varied kind. A comparison of the numerous prefaces to the foreign language editions of the diary, for instance, also reveals several different versions of Anne Frank. Albrecht Goes, the author of the foreword to the Fischer edition of *Das Tagebuch der Anne Frank*, speaks abstractly about a "spirit of love" that pervades the diary. Daniel Rops, who wrote the preface to the French edition, gives us an Anne Frank as, on the one hand, sensuous and, on the other, as artist and mystic. In Storm Jameson's foreword to the British edition we confront still another Anne Frank, one who wrote brilliantly and then went to her death at Bergen-Belsen with "a profound smile . . . of happiness and faith."[59]

I cite these versions of Anne Frank in order to emphasize the plastic nature of the figure we have been examining. In looking at the Holocaust through the figure of Anne Frank we see that "the Holocaust" is itself a variable term and is explained and understood in ways that resist easy consensus. There is nothing particularly surprising about this development, although the pace at which it seems to be proceeding and the degree of divergence that it may yield are matters that warrant serious pondering by anyone interested in observing how the past is variously reconstructed and transmitted to diverse publics. We already have been given numerous versions of Anne Frank, and in the future we almost certainly will be given others. "We shall read her diary/until the Messiah comes," as a poem about her says.[60] No doubt we shall, although how we shall read her and what we shall make of her and the history that her story reflects are questions that right now remain open.

FIVE

The Anne Frank We Remember/ The Anne Frank We Forget

I would like to read in a published book what people think about Anne Frank. —AN INSCRIPTION LEFT BY
AN ANONYMOUS VISITOR TO THE ANNE FRANK HOUSE

People think that she is very special. Once, when my daughter was in the Netherlands with her twin daughters, one of the first things they wanted me to show them was the Anne Frank House. I didn't feel up to it; actually, I didn't want to go at all. For more than forty years I had pushed that aside because I really wanted to live normally, and I didn't want to talk about it anymore.

Nonetheless, I went to the Anne Frank House, and I had a very special feeling there. I had seen her, after all, from the time she came to Westerbork. People took pictures there [in the Anne Frank House] of every corner, every plank, everything. . . . My daughter panicked, because she knew that I had known Anne. She looked around and she said, "Mama, shouldn't you tell these people that you knew her? Shouldn't you do something? Tell them, tell them."

I couldn't do it; I absolutely couldn't. I wouldn't have known how to tell it. Because it was so bizarre, that entire Anne Frank House. All those people, all those cameras. I saw Anne again, and I thought that this really wouldn't have been anything for

her. In the Anne Frank House, you can see what I wrote in the
registration book: "Anne Frank didn't want this."
— FROM AN INTERVIEW WITH A VISITOR TO THE ANNE FRANK HOUSE

Whether she would have wanted it or not, people come to the
Anne Frank House by the hundreds of thousands every year.
What motivates them to make this pilgrimage no doubt varies
from person to person, but that they are drawn to the house on
the Prinsengracht in very large numbers is clear. They ascend the
narrow stairs, enter the "secret annex" through the hidden door
behind the fake bookcase, tour the rooms where Anne Frank and
the seven others hid from their oppressors, stare in silence at the
furnishings that remain, look at the child's pin-ups still on the wall
of Anne Frank's room, peer out the windows to see what she saw.
Most visitors probably do not realize that these rooms have been
redone more than once since August 4, 1944, that fateful day when
the Gestapo burst in upon the hidden Jews, arrested them, and
soon after had them dispatched to the camps where all but Otto
Frank were to perish. It hardly matters, for over the years 263 Prinsengracht in Amsterdam has become a memory site of primary
importance. Reconstructed or not, it now houses something akin
to sacred space, and for at least a brief moment most who visit the
"secret annex" are stirred by the sense that they are in touch with
a rare and profoundly important moment in history.

Elsewhere in the building, they reenter their own time and
walk through more familiar, less sacralized space. They can see
a display of Anne Frank's diary in replica copy and also copies of
her book in many different foreign-language translations, watch a
short film on antisemitism, study the historical documents in the
showcases and on some of the walls, get an update on contemporary manifestations of racism and the dangers of extreme political
nationalism, and purchase souvenir postcards, books, and tapes
about Anne Frank and the house.

Upon leaving, many register comments in the guest books, as Rachel van Amerongen-Frankfoorder did in the words quoted above. In her case, the transformation of the young girl she knew into a popular legend was clearly objectionable. Here is what some others have had to say:

—"A child expressing such optimism gives everyone hope."
—"Why did this have to happen?"
—"Teach the children about the hatred of their parents."
—"You smiled at me and you spoke of nothing and I knew that this is what I had long been waiting for."
—"Anne is crazy."
—"Anne Frank did not really understand people. Did she?"
—"Why the Jews?
  Why this death?"
—"To have been Jewish was to have been Anne Frank.
  To be Jewish is not to become Anne Frank."
—"Why are we always being reminded of it?"
—"We should forget."
—"We should remember."
—"I'm glad that I'm not a Jew."

As is evident from these inscriptions, culled from the guest books in the Anne Frank House, Anne Frank conjures up a range of responses from those who think about her. What commonality there is seems to lie in the recognition that she was a victim, although to many a victim whose "spirit" has managed to transcend her death. Many of the German visitors to the Anne Frank House record words of shame and regret. Many of the Jewish visitors express feelings of sorrow and defiance and the resolve that "it" should never happen again. Some visitors jot down romantic messages—some of them, posthumous love letters to the murdered girl. Others express anger, bewilderment, guilt, remorse, hostility, annoyance, aggression. Whatever else one can say about her, Anne Frank is not a neutral symbol.

Can one, though, get beyond the legend she has become to the person she was? At this late date, decades after she first began to be mythologized, such an act of rehistoricization is difficult. Anne Frank's story is no longer her own but the world's, and the "world" has chosen to make of her what it will—the quintessential child victim but also the eternally bright and cheerful adolescent, the martyred innocent but also the apostle of hope. Anne Frank is all of these things and more. To this day, more than sixty-five years after her death, children write letters to her, as if she were a secular saint and not a more-or-less typical Jewish youth, one among many, of her exceptionally tragic generation.

When one thinks about her in these terms—and especially when one places her among the six million dead Jews—one encounters numbers and a fate that the mind cannot readily absorb. At the conclusion of her book, *One, By One, By One: Facing the Holocaust*, Judith Miller spoke to this dilemma: "Abstraction is memory's most ardent enemy. It kills because it encourages distance, and often indifference. We must remind ourselves that the Holocaust was not six million. It was one, plus one, plus one. . . . Only in understanding that civilized people must defend the one, by one, by one . . . can the Holocaust, the incomprehensible, be given meaning."[1] Just what kind of "meaning" the systematic persecution and slaughter of millions of innocent people like Anne Frank can have is a question that Miller does not answer, but nevertheless the point she makes about the need to personalize the Holocaust is well taken. Otherwise, as she correctly puts it, memory of the Nazi crimes can fade into a meaningless abstraction of mass, anonymous death.

In fact, memory has already taken such a turn. The widely viewed photographs and films of the corpse mounds that so many have seen inevitably project anonymity—a heart-stopping image of inert, intertwined limbs that defines and compounds the specter of a grossly dehumanized horror. One is simultaneously drawn to and repelled by such images. In encountering them, it is easy to lose sight of the fact that these pictures of faceless, frozen agony in fact are composed of individual men, women, and children, who, before being put to the slaughter, were often diminished to the point of non-recognition by their Nazi murderers. There is nothing one can do today about these countless dead except remember them and mourn them. But how precisely does the work of memory and mourning proceed in a culture that chooses not to place a very high value on either?

The question of memory's attenuation, which in one form or another haunts all Holocaust survivors, was posed in particularly sharp ways in Primo Levi's last book, *The Drowned and the Saved*. Among other things, Levi was troubled by what he recognized as a "gap that exists and grows wider every year between things as they were 'down there' and things as they are represented by the current imagination fed by approximative books, films, and myths. It slides fatally toward simplification and stereotype. . . ."[2] One way to keep this slide from accelerating is to focus on individual stories, to see precisely how the Holocaust claimed its victims "one, by one, by one." Levi noted as much when he wrote that "a single Anne Frank excites more emotion than the myriads who suffered as she did but whose image has remained in the shadows. Perhaps it is necessary that it can be so. If we had to and were able to suffer the sufferings of everyone, we could not live."[3] Levi's own writings are as forceful and lucid an evocation of the sufferings of the victims as any we have been given. Yet it is not he who stands today as the most widely known writer of the Holocaust but the figure he names: Anne Frank. As we have seen, however, the Anne Frank who has been projected to many millions of people over the years is a figure already broadly diffused into legend. Even if that were not the case, she cannot fairly be said to represent the victims of the Nazi slaughter. Her tale, set as it is in Amsterdam, unfolded far away from the places in eastern Europe where most Jews were murdered. During the time when she was hidden in her secret annex, Anne Frank was shielded from the worst aspects of the Nazi terror and knew about them only distantly. It is true that ultimately she came to share the fate of millions of other Jews in the Nazi camp system, but inasmuch as her diary stops before this final, grim chapter of her story, most readers are unaware of the actual circumstances of her end. Probably most would prefer to remain unaware, for were they to be confronted with a full account of Anne Frank's suffering, it is doubtful that their response would remain as ardent as it has been over the years.

Thanks to Willy Lindwer's *The Last Seven Months of Anne Frank*, which prints the texts of interviews with Dutch women who had been incarcerated with the Franks in Westerbork, Auschwitz, and Bergen-Belsen, we have a sense of Anne Frank's condition at the end of her life. Here, for instance, from an interview with Rachel van Amerongen-Frankfoorder, is a description of Anne Frank during her last days in Bergen-Belsen:

> I saw Anne and her sister Margot again in the barracks [of Bergen-Belsen]. . . . The Frank girls were almost unrecognizable since their hair had been cut off. They were much balder than we were.
> . . . And they were cold, just like all the rest of us.
> It was winter and you didn't have any clothes. So all of the ingredients for illness were present. They were in bad shape. Day by day they got weaker. . . . You could see that they were very sick.
> The Frank girls were so emaciated. They looked terrible. They had little squabbles, caused by their illness, because it was clear that they had typhus. . . . They had those hollowed-out faces, skin over bone. They were terribly cold. They had the least desirable places in the barracks, below, near the door, which was constantly opened and closed. You heard them constantly screaming, 'Close the door, close the door,' and the voices became weaker every day.

You could really see both of them dying, as well as others. But what was so sad, of course, was that these children were still so young. I always found it so horrible that as children they had never really lived. They were indeed the youngest among us. . . .

They showed the recognizable symptoms of typhus—that gradual wasting away, a sort of apathy, with occasional revivals, until they became so sick that there wasn't any hope. And their end came. I don't know which one was carried out earlier, Anne or Margot. . . .

The dead were always carried outside, laid down in front of the barracks, and when you were let out in the morning to go to the latrine, you had to walk past them. That was just as dreadful as going to the latrine itself, because gradually everyone got typhus. In front of the barracks was a kind of wheelbarrow in which you could take care of your needs. Sometimes you also had to take those wheelbarrows to the latrine. Possibly it was on one of those trips to the latrine that I walked past the bodies of the Frank sisters. . . . The heaps [of bodies] would be cleared away [from the front of the barracks]. A huge hole would be dug and they were thrown into it. That I'm sure of. That must have been their fate, because that's what happened with other people. I don't have a single reason for assuming that it was any different for them than for the other women with us who died at the same time.[4]

Needless to say, this image of the emaciated, disease-ridden girl lying dead amidst the human waste of the camp latrine, then dumped into a huge hole that served as a mass grave, forms no part of the cherished "legacy" of Anne Frank. And yet precisely this was Anne Frank's fate, as it was the fate of innumerable other Jewish victims of Nazi Germany. Following prevailing cultural norms, however, the image of Anne Frank that has evolved over the years has been largely sanitized of any realistic sense of her life and death. As already shown, her life has been idealized to the point where it can be summed up by a single, often quoted sentence from the diary—"In spite of everything I still believe that people are really good at heart"—and her death is either glossed over or given a hopeful, even beatific character.

Indeed, it may well be the case that Anne Frank's popularity is owing to the fact that her story remains only imperfectly known and, by and large, has been sentimentalized and romanticized. In some crucial respects it has also been de-Judaized. What remains, although certainly moving, is relatively mild, given what one finds elsewhere in Holocaust literature. Anne Frank's tale draws a vast audience to the private life of an admirable young girl but at the same time shields it from a closer knowledge of the brutal fate she shared with millions of other European Jews. By learning the little one comes to learn about the Nazi crimes through the story of Anne Frank, one can "know about" the Holocaust in some distant, preliminary way, yet keep from confronting the Nazi horrors at their worst. Primo Levi's anxious concern that the history that he and so many others suffered would end in a slide toward simplification and stereotype tends to be borne out as one reviews the nature of the responses to Anne Frank. A number of the essays collected in David Rosenberg's *Testimony: Contemporary Writers Make the Holocaust Personal* (1989) refer to Anne Frank, for instance, but do so in ways that demonstrate just how weakened a figure she has become.

Rosenberg asked his contributors, most of them American writers born during or after the war years, to describe "the shadow of the Holocaust" on their lives. Furthermore, he wanted them to state how and when they first learned of the Holocaust and how it has shaped or been absent from their careers as writers. These questions are interesting enough, but many of the responses are disappointingly shallow.

Francine Prose, one of Rosenberg's contributors, cites *The Diary of a Young Girl* as an early formative influence on her and remarks that, as a young girl, she read the book again and again. What did it tell her? "For me," she writes, "the book was the story of a girl who had a love affair and a girl who died, and in retrospect I am not sure I knew the difference. . . . I think that I would have been willing to suffer the death if I could have had the romance." Prose writes about the links she felt between herself as a young girl and Anne Frank ("Anne Frank, our sister, our double,") and remembers feeling the Holocaust as a focal point for the voluptuous commingling of sex and death. "And so," she notes, "the Holocaust for me became invested with an air of the romantic. It was terrible and glamorous, dark-toned and nostalgic. . . ." Whatever else these words may say, they register almost no sense of the extreme character of the events that unfolded in Europe three generations ago. Rather, to quote this author one last time, the Holocaust was diminished to the status of "a pin with which to prick yourself." Astonishingly, it became little more than an instrument for the stimulation of painful but somehow highly desirable sensations, "at once terrible and exciting." Like a good horror film to be watched on a lazy Saturday afternoon, it provided "a kind of half-scary, half-pleasurable chill, . . . a heady mix of melancholy and exaltation."[5] Understood in these terms, a catastrophic history is emptied of any serious meaning it might possibly have and is reduced to the banal.

A reduction to even lower depths is evident in the essay contributed to *Testimony* by Daphne Merkin. She notes that she likewise felt a close personal connection to Anne Frank and valued the diary as an inspiring record of intensely private experience. Like many others, she looked at Anne Frank solipsistically and found in her what she wanted to find: not a young Jewish victim of Nazi terror but an image of herself at her writing desk. "The reality of her own mind was as valid as the life-threatening reality external to her mind," Merkin writes. "You could be living right in the eye of the Nazi storm and still take your own little angst seriously. Better yet, you could emerge from

the Holocaust a literary heroine! The thought was exhilarating."
Exhilaration, achieved through the determined provocation of
her own darkest impulses, is important to this writer, so much
so that she indulges a wild Holocaust fantasy in which she finds
herself "in the embrace of the young Adolf Hitler" ("He played
with my hair, the hair of a Jewess, the wrong color hair, not an
Aryan blonde."). Elsewhere, in an extension of these perverse
imaginings, Merkin writes that Jewish men of her generation
are bound to Nazi-inspired erotic fantasies of their own, and
that "in a toss-up between having Anne Frank or Eva Braun
(Hitler's mistress) as a date, it was clear to me whom these men
would choose."[6] How she knows who would come out ahead in
this crazy toss-up is not clear, but all the same Merkin is convinced that her Jewish men are led on by what she calls "shiksa
hunger," an insatiable longing for blonde, Christian women (a
charge not unlike that often made against black men, who are
sometimes stereotyped as being unable to resist the purported
allure of these same fair-haired women). Although Anne Frank
may be the initial trigger for these obscene musings, she is soon
left behind in Merkin's reflections, which in the end really have
little to do with the Holocaust and much to do with the author's
own self-indulgent fantasies of persecution and vengeance.
That, however, seems to be one of the prices one pays when
one sets out to "make the Holocaust personal."

Following these examples, one realizes that the conceptual
problem with which we began remains, for to look at the victims
of the Holocaust "one, by one, by one" is not necessarily to see
them clearly. In the case of the popularization of Anne Frank, in
fact, a far greater part of this history may be kept from view. To be
sure, there are others who regard the crimes of the Third Reich
in more sober and responsible ways, but tendencies to "personalize" or politicize the Holocaust are prominent today and represent a cultural trend that is troubling. It is a trend that has the
effect of either denying the realities of Auschwitz or transmuting

them into something else—erotic indulgences of various sorts or political action programs that dramatize their appeals through emotionally linked references to the Nazi campaign of genocide. The citations from *Testimony* given above illustrate the former. As an illustration of the latter, one need only look at the rhetoric routinely employed in the debates about abortion and AIDS to realize that "genocide" and "Holocaust" are terms that are being applied to social realities that, for all of their gravity, do not resemble the Nazi crimes against the Jews.

Those crimes had genocide as their aim and the organized force of a powerful political state to implement them in a determined, systematic way. With respect to both intentionality and means, therefore, the Nazi Holocaust was radically destructive. An event without identifiable historical precedent, it does not lend itself readily to comparison or analogy. To say as much is obviously not to say there are no people today who are suffering, for every day's news shows us that the opposite is true. Nor is it to suggest that we have succeeded in eliminating from our society the various forms of prejudice, intolerance, and injustice that are at the root of so much personal and collective pain, for clearly we have not. However, it is to say that we are likely to obscure rather than to clarify the nature and causes of present-day suffering when we see such suffering as a new form of "genocide." When every instance of human distress is transfigured as another "Holocaust," the Holocaust itself tends to become less real, little more than a figure of speech—its moral claims upon us diminished rather than enlarged by metaphorical extension.

Anne Frank has been appropriated as a symbol in these ways almost from the start. In addition, there have been repeated attempts to deny her story any value whatsoever. For decades, neo-Nazi and other far right-wing groups have attacked the authenticity of the diary through the publication of polemical tracts meant to "expose" Anne Frank's writings as a forgery. The intention is to nullify the historicity of the Holocaust by calling into question the legitimacy of one of its central texts. Thus, if Anne Frank's diary can be shown to be a "hoax"—a literary fabrication rather than an authentic historical document—then the reality of Jewish suffering under the Nazis can likewise be "proven" to be bogus. What is truly bogus in all of these cases, of course, is the "scholarship" that is used to advance this kind of radical revisionism. But for all of its sinister methods and pernicious effects, the literature of Holocaust denial is widespread today and has given us such meretricious books and pamphlets as *Anne Frank's Diary—A Forgery, Anne Frank's Diary—A Hoax, Anne Frank's Diary—The Big Fraud,* and related tawdry works. The fact that such literature is driven by a palpable bad faith does not mean it lacks for readers, unfortunately. The opposite seems to be true, as the reception for revisionist claims that the Holocaust never happened appears greater today than it has been in the past.[7]

On the other end of the political spectrum one finds troubling tendencies of another sort. Those on the left typically do not seek to attack or suppress the historical memory of the Holocaust, but some are disposed to instrumentalize it for their own political ends. In the 1960s, for instance, it was common practice for the figure of Anne Frank to be pressed into service in the struggle against "fascism." There was a time during the Vietnam War when the Anne Frank House in Amsterdam itself became a prominent focal point for the "anti-fascist" campaign, which, among other things, sought to expose visitors on the Prinsengracht to vivid denunciations of America as a successor state to Nazi Germany. These visitors undoubtedly came to pay homage to the memory of Anne Frank, but they frequently were confronted by displays of another kind, some of them featuring attack slogans like "Amerika, Amerika, über Alles." S. H. Radius, a co-director of the Anne Frank Foundation in the late 1960s, presented the rationale for such activities in these terms:

We are gratified that so many people come here. The trouble is, most of them come for the wrong reason! They regard the house as a shrine to a martyred Jewish girl. That is the least of its meanings. . . . All of these people are thinking in terms of the past. But the object of the Anne Frank Foundation is to use the past only to illuminate the present and the future. What we try to do is to make visible the effects of any kind of persecution on any group.[8]

Few well-meaning people would want to argue with the aims of combating the evils of persecution whenever and wherever they appear, but the programmatic exploitation of history for contemporary political purposes creates problems of its own. When, for instance, the figure of Anne Frank was made to serve as a rallying point of opposition to American policy in Vietnam, as was the case in the late 1960s, it is clear that the past is no longer valued in its own terms and instead becomes a tool in the ideological struggles of the moment. To "use" history in this way is almost always to misuse it, with all of the attendant consequences.

To observe such misuse today at its most blatant, consider the following efforts to poach on Anne Frank's story for partisan political goals. In January 2008, a stenciled image of a smiling Anne Frank wearing a red and white keffiyeh appeared on the walls of buildings in Amsterdam. Soon after, an enterprising Dutch business firm called Boomerang transferred this image to designer T-shirts and postcards. The cards were distributed free throughout the Netherlands, no doubt to boost sales for Boomerang's politically chic new line of shirts. But it was a risky marketing move to promote a product featuring the face of Amsterdam's most famous martyr made over to look like Yasser Arafat's daughter. The Israeli Ambassador to the Netherlands expressed outrage. So did Dutch Jewish organizations. But these responses were not universal. Some were drawn to the newly fashioned Palestinian Anne Frank and endorsed the artist's political point, which one blogger interpreted to mean that "the Zionists, in the name of Jewry, [were] doing to the Palestinians what was done to Jews in Europe."[9] This simplistic formula has become a staple in the rhetoric of contemporary anti-Zionism. The charge it makes is baseless, but it is rhetorically catchy and now routinely employed to smear Israel with the Nazi brush.

What plays well in certain political circles may not play well in business, however. Sensing, perhaps, that their company's image was at risk, Boomerang executives quickly switched to damage control mode. Their aggressively revisionist T-shirt version of Anne Frank now was said to present "an idyllic image of peace."[10] According to a company spokesman, it was meant, improbably, "to encourage people to reflect on a peaceful solution for Israel and the Palestinians."[11] But Boomerang's spin doctors never explained just how aligning the Holocaust's best known Jewish victim with the symbol of militant Palestinian nationalism could possibly create "an idealistic image in which both states exist alongside one another in peace."[12] The image is not only incongruous but offensive.

Yet contemporary political iconography has matched it with an image that is equally obscene: a drawing commissioned by the Arab European League, a Belgian-Dutch Islamic political organization headed by the popular leader Dyab Abou Jahjah, shows a wasted-looking young girl sinking desolately under the bed sheets, while propped up next to her, a bare-chested, swastika-laden Hitler triumphantly crows, "Write this one in your diary, Anne!" Above the head of the Führer's hapless victim, a wordless bubble registers the dark grief of the devastated girl. The fact that this graphic is vile has not kept it from being widely distributed by the Arab European League and other Islamist groups. In the wake of the Danish cartoon controversy, which infuriated many Muslims, Mr. Jahjah said he was offering payback, declaring that "Europe too has its sacred cows."

Indeed it does, but Europe's murdered Jews are not among them. Anne Frank, dead before she had turned sixteen, was no saint but rather one more addition to the mounds of anonymous corpses at Bergen-Belsen. One need not sacralize her memory in order to pay it a decent respect. Until recently, most have found it proper to do so, but in an age of resurgent antisemitism, respect for even the Jewish dead has become a dwindling commodity in some circles. Nothing exemplifies that moral erosion as dramatically as these tamperings with the image of Anne Frank.

There is more. In March 2004, a Dutch television crew visiting North Korea reported that Anne Frank's book had been adopted as a required text for secondary schools throughout the country—a surprising and, at first glance, encouraging development. Looking further, though, the Dutch team discovered that teachers in this strongly Stalinist state were using the diary to brainwash their pupils into believing that the experience of their country directly parallels that of the Frank family in hiding, that the Americans of this generation are the Nazis of the Hitler era, and the American president is as evil as Hitler himself. As interpreted in Pyonyang, the so-called "legacy" of Anne Frank is unambiguously clear. In the words of one North Korean youngster, "For world peace, America will have to be destroyed. Only then will Anne's dream of peace come true."[13]

Blatant misappropriations of the diary regularly appear in parts of the Arab world as well. In what is now commonly called the "Palestinian Holocaust," Anne Frank has become a ubiquitous point of reference, and a search for the "Palestinian Anne Frank" is, not surprisingly, being pursued quite deliberately. A recent story on the website aljazeerah.info presents the following plan.

Consider. A propaganda book [the reference is to Anne Frank's diary] that is designed to elicit sympathy for the Jewish people, via the mechanism of a young girl who is hiding from bad men is required reading in many USA schools. How many young growing children that do not understand propaganda and manipulation, read the story for what it is, a girl in hiding in trouble. They do not realize that subconsciously they are feeling sympathy for not just any girl but a Jewish girl. . . . That got me to thinking. If it works for Jewish people, why will it not work for someone else? If a Palestinian writer were to find a young Palestinian girl who had trouble. Maybe her brother was killed by a sniper. Or her parents were crushed by a bulldozer. Or her home was destroyed by Israeli explosives. If a Palestinian writer were to take his story and give it the same treatment and the same style as *The Diary of Anne Frank*, maybe the book would become as popular as *The Diary of Anne Frank*. Maybe it would bring home to average people exactly what life for this young Palestinian girl was like. Just like *The Diary of Anne Frank* brings home to regular people how life was for the young Jewish girl Anne Frank. . . . There must be literally thousands of young . . . Palestinian girls with stories of horror that will wrench the collective heart of the world. It would not hurt to try.[14]

There are writers who have been trying all along. In her diary entries about life in a Palestinian refugee camp, Muna Hamzeh implores, "Where are you Anne Frank? Where are you? Is this the reason you died for? So that your people can turn around and commit these pogroms against another people? You were so young and didn't deserve to die, yet you died because of your identity. The same reason they're killing us now."[15] Anyone familiar with the ongoing Arab-Israeli war knows that Palestinians are being killed, as are Israelis, but not because of their "identities" or anything else that bears resemblance to the motives behind the killing of Anne Frank. And yet, like her employment of the word "pogrom," Muna Hamzeh reaches into the lexicon of Jewish suffering to make Palestinian suffering indistinguishable from that of the Jews at its worst.

Others do the same. Reviewing Ghada Karmi's memoir *In Search of Fatima: A Palestinian Story*,[16] Muhammad Khan notes that Karmi's story of a "Palestinian girl forced out of her native country along with her family . . . instantly reminded me of the plight of Anne Frank and her family in Nazi Germany." He goes on to note that the picture of the young Karmi on the cover of her book is so strikingly similar to the picture of Anne Frank on the cover of her diary "that a non-suspecting reader would think that they were, in fact, sisters." The reviewer then continues:

> Soon after the Second World War ended, . . . European Jews, the victims of European anti-Semitism and Nazi persecution . . . move[d] into the heart of the Middle East and rapidly colonize[d] the country of an unsuspecting Palestinian people. This way, the one-time victims of mass persecution in Europe were overnight turned into the oppressors of another wholly innocent people in the historic land of Palestine. As soon as the story of Anne Frank, the beautiful German Jewish girl, came to an end, another tale, the tale of another unspeakable horror, indeed one of the worst crimes in the history of the modern era, was to be recorded and related to us by a Palestinian, who too was forced out of her native country as a young girl. That is the story of Ghada Karmi and the people of Palestine.[17]

For a number of years, the rhetorical trick of turning Jews into Nazis and Palestinians into Jews has been part of the Arab discourse on the Middle East conflict. Although the historical parallels are far fetched, a narrative of Palestinian victimization by Israeli Jews on a par with Jewish victimization under Hitler is now broadly accepted—and not only in the Arab and Muslim world, but among sizable numbers of people in Europe and elsewhere. The notion of a "Palestinian Anne Frank" fits into this context, although on closer inspection the fit reveals itself to be wholly fabricated. Since 1949, for instance, Ghada Karmi has lived in London, where decades ago she readily adopted British culture and assimilated into English society. Anne Frank, by contrast, never saw her sixteenth birthday and lies in some anonymous corpse mound in Bergen-Belsen. For all the obvious differences in their stories, though, in this instance and countless others, there has been a steady melding of Anne Frank's experiences with those of other young girls undergoing hardship of one kind or another.

The effort—patently a form of usurpation—is a regular feature of the Arab media. "Meet today's Anne Frank," writes Yusuf Agha in an article entitled "The Anne Franks of Palestine." The author then goes on to present several youngsters who are meant to be Palestinian stand-ins for Anne Frank and describes the first of these surrogates, Suad Ghazal, a seventeen-year-old Palestinian girl serving time in a Ramle prison in Israel, employing these lines:

> [T]he minute I was alone I knew I was going to cry my eyes out. I slid to the floor in my nightgown and began by saying my prayers, very fervently. Then I drew my knees to my chest, lay my head on my arms and cried, all huddled up on the bare floor. A loud sob brought me back down to earth. . . . I've reached the point where I hardly care whether I live or die. The world will keep on turning without me, and I can't do anything to change events anyway.[18]

This is not Suad Ghazal's voice in a Ramle prison cell, however, but the voice of Anne Frank in a rare moment of resignation. Although the experiences of the two girls are presented here as almost one and the same, in fact they are not at all comparable. Suad Ghazal ended up in an Israeli jail not for being a Palestinian, but for trying to stab to death an Israeli living on the West Bank; Anne Frank, on the other hand, was penned up in her Amsterdam attic as a Jew in hiding from her Nazi hunters. The Palestinian teenager has been imprisoned for attempted murder but will eventually be released. The Jewish girl had no chance of a reprieve from her sentence of being a Jew—a capital offense in the Europe of her time—and was murdered. For all of their differences, though, Suad is projected as an Anne Frank look-alike. "I am the Palestinian Anne Frank," she proudly declares, "and Israeli Hitlers who are all around me take pleasure in torturing me. . . . Though I am guilty of no crime, all the crimes in the world have been committed against me."[19]

It is impossible to know whether Suad Ghazal actually believes what she is saying, but it is easy to get trapped within hyperbolic rhetoric of this kind and to genuinely imagine oneself a victim on a par with the Jewish victims of the real Hitler.

The case of Binjamin Wilkomirski, the author of the notoriously fraudulent Holocaust "memoir" *Fragments*, comes prominently to mind as an admonitory example. In an age when victims have become valorized, though, it is both tempting and advantageous to project oneself as a target of extreme and unjust suffering. One solicits the world's pity and also neutralizes any sense of personal responsibility for one's situation. There is nothing opaque or subtle about the politics of such maneuvers, and depending on one's own political biases, one may agree or disagree with them. One should be fully aware, however, that rhetorical moves of this kind are inherently manipulative and transgress against historical memory and the integrity of truth itself. Appropriations of someone else's history, in this case that of Anne Frank, are inevitably misappropriations—the propagandistic use of one person's tragic experience to augment and promote that of another. No doubt Muna Hamzeh, Ghada Karmi, Suad Ghazal, and other Palestinian Arabs have led hard and unenviable lives, but it is deceitful to link their stories to that of Anne Frank—just as it is a distortion to idealize and sentimentalize Anne Frank's story and have it appear as a generalized symbol of oppression in a tyrannical world. If these trends continue unchecked, the Holocaust's most famous victim will still be remembered, but in ways that may put at risk an historically accurate and morally responsible memory of the Holocaust itself.

One further example, this one closer to home, will be cited to illustrate this trend. The Anne Frank Foundation in Amsterdam has created a large traveling exhibition of photographs entitled "Anne Frank in the World: 1929–1945," which has been shown in numerous countries over the years. The exhibition is a serious and generally effective undertaking, one of whose aims is to present the story of Anne Frank against the backdrop of historical developments in Nazi-occupied Europe. Another aim is to alert viewers to contemporary instances of antisemitism, racism, and other forms of discrimination and prejudice. Both are laudable aims, but inasmuch as local sponsors of the exhibition can augment the mounted photographs of Anne Frank and her times with lectures, films, publications, and other materials of their own, the balance between these two aims is not always kept steady.

For instance, one learns from *Legacy*, the newsletter of the Anne Frank Center USA, that "Anne Frank in the World: 1929–1945" was brought to Watsonville, California, by groups such as "the gay, lesbian and bisexual community, feminists, Japanese-Americans, Latinos, Native-Americans, the mentally-ill, the homeless, and people with AIDS." On first reading this, one is struck by the evident interest in Anne Frank among such a diverse group of people. As the report continues, however, one wonders about the intent of this broad coalition of program sponsors who, we learn, mounted "their own displays illustrating their experiences with discrimination. . . . Given the present day political climate in the United States, it was especially necessary to address existing prejudice and stereotypes about gays, lesbians, and bisexuals."[20]

Whatever the purpose of the people who brought "Anne Frank in the World" to Watsonville, California, a serious skewing of history is bound to occur when the crimes of the Holocaust are juxtaposed with contemporary American social problems. The latter are serious, but one cannot hope to understand them or resolve them if they are equated with genocide. Existing prejudice against gays, lesbians, bisexuals, and others is repulsive and dangerous, and it needs to be constantly exposed and actively fought, but enlisting Anne Frank in this fight today is hardly different from enlisting her as a partisan of the anti-war movement of the 1960s. In both cases, the aims may be admirable, but the means are tantamount to a kind of hijacking of history. Given such practices, one worries that the future memory of the Holocaust may become an increasingly tenuous matter. Indeed, since it has entered the domain of public speech, "Holocaust" has become a highly charged figure of speech and is commonly invoked in the debates that are raging about abortion, AIDS, civil rights, gay rights, the environment, health care, pornography, etc. These are serious debates, but they spring from a history that does not resemble the history that produced Auschwitz and Bergen-Belsen. They have nothing intrinsically to do with Anne Frank or the other victims of Nazi genocide, and we do no honor to Anne Frank's memory or the memories of so many others like her when we see ourselves as "victims" in their image. In fact, it is our good fortune that we are not Anne Frank's "sister" or "double," and we shouldn't pretend to be.

The writer Julius Lester recognized as much in his own reflections on Anne Frank, which stand in welcome contrast to the other contributions to *Testimony* cited above. Lester first came to learn about the diary as a senior in college, when he attended a lecture about Anne Frank given by a visiting Dutch scholar. The lecture obviously had an impact on the way he looked at the world and his own place in it. "I don't know how to live with the knowledge of such evil and such suffering," he realized. He continued to think about the nature of the new knowledge he had acquired and found some important clarifications in a revealing conversation he had with the poet Robert Hayden:

> "We think we know something about suffering," he
> [Hayden] says, referring to black people. "We don't know
> what suffering means. . . . Well, that's not entirely true.

Maybe it's a problem of language. . . . Maybe I'm not comfortable using the same word 'suffering' to describe what we have gone through and what the Jews went through. Do you know what I mean?"

I did. I had ridden at the backs of buses all my life, had read signs telling me where I could and could not eat, what doors I could and could not go through, what water fountains I could and could not drink from. I had been trained by my parents not to look at white women. Then I thought about living in an attic and gas chambers and furnaces into which human beings were shoveled like waste paper.

"I'm not saying that Jews have suffered more. How can you measure what a human being suffers? But there is a difference, and we need a word to make that difference clear. . . . That's what writing is, you know. Finding the right word."

I would like to be the one to find the right word. . . . But is there a word strong enough to hold naked bodies stacked in hills beneath a sunny sky? Being forced to ride at the back of a bus is not in the same realm of experience.

But Jews had to wear yellow Stars of David on their clothes to be identified as Jews. My star is my skin color. Yet I am alive. Anne Frank is not.[21]

With the simple acknowledgement of difference recorded in those last two sentences, Lester restores some much-needed balance to the issues under review here. One suspects, however, that his point of view may not be widely shared. We are living at a time when there are strong encouragements to flatten history into the shapes we would wish it to have, a revisionary process advanced by many people of all kinds to express a personal and collective sense of "oppression" and "victimization." There is a temptation to readily proclaim, "We are all Anne Frank." But, in fact, we are nothing of the sort, as Julius Lester is wise enough to know. Knowing enables him to recognize clearly what is distinctive about Anne Frank's story as well as his own. The two are both important, and each deserves to be widely known. It makes little sense to view them as competitive stories, or as stories of "comparative suffering," as Robert Hayden cautions, for each has a significant historical and moral claim upon us. In a cultural climate where historical memory is either reduced to popular entertainment or made subservient to strong assertions of personal and political will, however, it is not at all clear that either story will be remembered in the future with the integrity each one deserves.

SIX

Jean Améry:
The Anguish of the Witness

For me, being a Jew means feeling the tragedy of yesterday as an inner oppression. On my left forearm I bear the Auschwitz number; it reads more briefly than the Pentateuch or the Talmud and yet provides more thorough information.

—JEAN AMÉRY

To turn from a consideration of Holocaust victims to Holocaust survivors is to turn, one expects, from the dead to the living. In fact, though, the relationship of the living to the dead is less clearly defined within the troubled precincts of Holocaust memory. Far from encountering two sharply differentiated types—"victims" and "survivors"—one often finds an ontological status that is blurred and ambiguous. Lawrence Langer calls it *"death-life."* The term is awkward but points suggestively to a mental state that Langer posits may be a "neglected legacy of the Holocaust experience." Primo Levi exemplified it when, late in life, he confessed, "I had the sensation that I was living but without being alive."[1] In a wry allusion to Hamlet, Elie Wiesel puts it this way: "The problem is not: to be or not to be. But rather: to be and not to be."[2] The difficult experience of simultaneously living two existences—of being both here and still "there"—is familiar to Holocaust survivors. In the minds of many, the dead and those who have returned from the dead constitute a single, continuous, fated community.

The situation is also charged with paradox in another sense, for according to popular perception, some victims seem to attain a posthumous "survival" through the wide dissemination and ready embrace of their images—Anne Frank being the most famous example but by no means the only one—while numerous survivors become belated "victims" through the sufferings they continue to experience in the postwar years. In their most extreme manifestations, these sufferings sometimes even lead to a tragic self-victimization through suicide. Thus, in some cases, the actual victims of the Nazi crimes may seem to return from their graves in the form of powerfully resonant, "living" images, whereas the survivors may continue a tormented existence perilously close to the edge of obliteration and even succumb to the view that they really belong among those who perished.

To be sure, not all of those who managed to outlast the ghettos and camps of Nazi-occupied Europe continue to feel that they are victims. Some have apparently adapted to the new and better circumstances of their postwar existences and enjoy what looks like a familiar, unexceptional life.[3] Some survivors marry or remarry, have families, careers, and friends, bear normal responsibilities, and partake of common pleasures. What their dreams are like at night only they know, but unless they tell us otherwise, it would appear that such people have not only survived but have gone on to successfully rebuild their lives.

Others are less fortunate and continue to feel overwhelmed by forms of suffering that do not let up. Some suffer because they believe their stories about life in the ghettos and camps of Hitler's Europe have been largely ignored or have not truly "made a difference." They live with a sense of futility and failure and may come to the conclusion that the fault lies both with the larger "world" for not heeding them and also with themselves, for not being more faithful and effective spokesmen for the dead.

Witnesses who speak or write and are not listened to are sometimes beset by forms of anxiety, frustration, and forlornness that
can shadow their lives and sometimes lead to their deaths. It
hardly matters that they may be widely known or even publicly
celebrated as "survivors," for a private anguish tells them they are
still "there," in that "other country." Their situation is a heavily
burdened one and brings many complex matters to the fore, not
the least of which is the question: "What does it mean to bear
witness?" For those who set out to record and reflect upon their
wartime experiences, this question is often synonymous with the
related question: "What does it mean to write?"

In the conventional sense of modern authorial composition,
writing was hardly possible for most Jews in Nazi-occupied
Europe, and yet a good deal of writing in fact was done. It served
several functions, not the least of which was to defy the Nazi
aggressor by charting the course of his crimes. Given the power
and determination of the German army and auxiliary forces,
the persecutions of the Jews could not be effectively countered
in a military sense by the Jews themselves, but they could be
chronicled and remembered. And as remembrancers the Jewish scribes were as determined as their enemies. "It is difficult
to write," noted Chaim Kaplan in the important diary he kept
in the Warsaw ghetto, "but I consider it an obligation and am
determined to fulfill it with my last ounce of energy. I will write
a scroll of agony in order to remember the past in the future."[4]
Through detailed documentation of the degradation and mass
murder then in progress, writers, powerfully driven by the need to
record, dedicated themselves to diaries, journals, and other forms
of chronicle and reflection. Most knew they probably would not
survive the war, but neither would they be merely silent victims
of it. We tend to see their writings today as acts of spiritual resistance, although in the end such resistance had no chance at
all against the power of the German forces arrayed against the
beleaguered, unarmed Jews. In symbolic terms, the testimonial

literature produced in the ghettos of Warsaw, Lodz, and countless other places of entrapment survives as an expression of Jewish heroism, but the fact that it was destined to be a terminal
expression and a defeated heroism gives to this literature elegiac
qualities that can make any serious engagement with it almost
unbearable. One reads these books and suffers. Why, therefore,
read them at all?

A reasonable answer is that the knowledge to be gained from
the literature of the victims is essential for an understanding of the
fate of the Jews under Hitler. But beyond this obvious consideration there is another, more demanding one. Books like *The Warsaw Diary of Chaim A. Kaplan*, Emmanuel Ringelblum's *Notes
from the Warsaw Ghetto*, or *The Chronicle of the Lodz Ghetto*
are the invaluable but incomplete accounts of eye-witnesses to
a history that, their authors believed, was a crime like no other.
Apart from its genocidal aims, what distinguished the Nazi assault
against the Jews was the intent of the perpetrators to leave behind
no witnesses and, hence, no record at all. The destruction of the
Jews was to be a total, yet also a silent, deed—in the words of one
of its key agents, "an unwritten and never-to-be-written page of
glory."[5] The fact that Himmler's will in this regard has not prevailed is owing in the first place to the determination of his victims, who under almost impossible conditions found the courage
and the means to persist as recording witnesses. Today, it is owing
to the will of readers, who in a secondary but nonetheless important capacity serve as witnesses for the witnesses.

To read in this way is to do several complicated things at
once—to learn, to pay tribute, to suffer, to mourn, and to remember. It is to join as a secondary witness those who can no longer
stand in for themselves as primary bearers of testimony. Ultimately, it is to serve as an agent of historical memory—to preserve and transmit words about the horrors of history at its very
worst. "I write," Elie Wiesel has stated, "to wrench [the] victims
from oblivion. To help the dead vanquish death."[6] One can read

with a similar intention and, by so doing, help to keep the victims from being forgotten.

In addition to the writings that have reached us from those who perished in the ghettos and camps, there exists a large body of literature from those who were subjected to the Nazi terror but managed to survive it. For these authors, writing has also served as an act of testimony, although it has naturally sprung from other motives. Survivor-writers, mining torturous memories, have looked to writing largely as a means of retrieval, reflection, description, analysis, and commemoration. For some, writing is intended as an act of catharsis, an attempt to break free from the sufferings of the past. For others, it has served as protest or warning, rebellion or accusation. In all cases, and in whatever literary forms, the testimonial literature of Holocaust survivors contributes to a massive, still accumulating record of historical atrocity. Its aim is to chronicle the factual occurrence of this atrocity; probe its motives, development, and character; reveal the unprecedented human damage it has wrought; and, sometimes, and with no small amount of difficulty, reveal what life has been like in its traumatic aftermath. Thus, while often intensely personal, the memoiristic and essayistic writings of Holocaust survivors are historical in scope and purpose. Such writings testify that civilization is far more tenuous than was heretofore imagined: it has collapsed once, so these writers tell us, and could collapse again. In its most explicitly didactic terms, this literature tends to register a view of the world's near-demise in admonitory, sometimes even hortatory terms. It exhorts readers to take heed, to guard against the possibilities of a repetition, to learn and apply what are frequently called the "lessons of the Holocaust," and to do so "now, before it is too late."

There are also books of testimony by survivors that speak in other terms and more variegated tones — books that likewise solicit the attention of readers but acknowledge that the "world" would prefer to forget rather than remember. These books note, with no small degree of distress, that the anguished stories of the survivors have no necessarily binding claim on the attention of those living today and that it may already be too late for any "lessons" from the past, whatever these might be, to be learned and applied. Such testimony is graver and more ominous in what it has to tell us, for it holds out little consolation for the future; understandably enough, readers may be inclined to resist its dark visions of futility. And yet, it is precisely this more disconsolate literature that may convey some of the most profound truths of those who managed to survive the Nazi slaughter—truths that underline the painful fact that survivors can continue to be victims and that the particular victimization of survivor-writers may be owing, in part, to the sense that their writings carry so little weight with readers. For all the urgency of their testimony, such writers may come to feel that they have failed to find a truly responsive audience and, hence, have failed as agents of memory and moral conscience. Such a realization, when it occurs, can be perilous, as it was in the cases of Jean Améry and Primo Levi, two survivor-writers of the highest literary and historical significance.

Jean Améry is best known for his first book, available in English translation as *At the Mind's Limits: Contemplations by a Survivor on Auschwitz and Its Realities.*[7] In its original German edition, the book first appeared in 1966 as *Jenseits von Schuld und Sühne.* At the time of its initial publication, Améry was already fifty-four. The book was reissued with a new author's preface in 1977, one year before Améry's death. First published in English translation in 1980, *At the Mind's Limits* stands today as one of the most passionate and important works of reflection by a Holocaust survivor.

The author, of mixed Jewish and Catholic parentage, was born in Austria, as Hans Maier, in 1912. The anti-Jewish racial laws imposed soon after Hitler assumed power shocked him into full awareness of the death threat against the Jews, and he fled his native country for Belgium in 1938. Arrested by the Belgians in

1940 as a German alien and then again by the Gestapo in 1943 as a member of the anti-Nazi resistance, he suffered the war years as an inmate of German prisons and concentration and death camps, including Auschwitz, Buchenwald, and Bergen-Belsen. After liberation from Bergen-Belsen at war's end, he returned to Belgium in 1945, took up residence in Brussels, and began a career as a journalist and political and cultural critic, using the name Jean Améry. Although a resident in a predominantly French-speaking milieu, Améry chose to remain a German-language writer-in-exile. His favored literary form was the essay; his important subject, the sufferings of the victims of the Third Reich; his most revealing source of knowledge for the condition of victimization, himself.

At the Mind's Limits is a slim book that elicits a powerful effect. In its five essays, the author succeeds in describing and reflecting upon his experiences as a wartime victim of Nazism in a way that is highly personal and yet, at the same time, transcends the personal to speak revealingly about the torments and trauma of Holocaust victims in general. It is a book that draws upon autobiographical references to reach insights that are broadly representative in their moral, psychological, and historical implications. The "limits of mind" that Améry delineates in his writing help to define the limits of some of our most basic cultural assumptions about the individual and his place within the social order of modern political reality. One reads this author and learns anew the meanings of personal integrity and human vulnerability—the first, an essential condition of life that must be asserted no matter the cost; the second, the inevitable condition of life as it becomes devalued under the pressures of social meanness and degraded under a program of political barbarism. Améry, a militant exponent of the value of individual dignity, knew on his flesh the extreme difficulty of maintaining any semblance of dignity in a system such as that of German National Socialism. His writings speak forcefully on behalf of humanist values even as they testify to the massive failure of so many people of his time to uphold them.

The opening essays of his book tell of the ravages of body and mind brought on by the radical deprivation produced by the Nazi system. The title essay, "At the Mind's Limits," reveals how little remained to the prisoner who was deprived of the effective operations of his intellect, including those defensive operations that normally protect us against hostile threats from without. Améry's preoccupation in this essay is with the situation of the intellectual in the camp and specifically with the question of his chances for survival. He argues that de-intellectualization was an essential part of the Nazi program of dehumanization, for when the mind proved itself to be incompetent, the individual prisoner disposed to rational behavior was abruptly cut off from the most vital centers of his self and rendered helpless. "Beauty: that was an illusion. Knowledge: that turned out to be a game with ideas" (p. 19). Hence, spiritually disarmed and intellectually disoriented, "the intellectual faced death defenselessly." In Améry's memorable formulation, "No bridge led from death in Auschwitz to *Death in Venice*" (p. 16).

"Torture," the book's second essay, makes graphically, almost viscerally, clear the extent of one's loss when brutally deprived of the autonomy of one's own body. It is Améry's firm conviction that "torture was not an accidental quality of the Third Reich, but its essence," indeed, "its apotheosis" (pp. 24, 30). Torture defined and brought to a climactic point of realization the basically depraved and inherently destructive character of Nazism, an ideology "that expressly established . . . the rule of the anti-man . . . as a principle" (p. 31). Other regimes have been contaminated by this same nihilistic principle, but German National Socialism gave it a kind of purity. "The Nazis tortured, as did others, because by means of torture they wanted to obtain information important for national policy. But in addition, they tortured with the good conscience of depravity . . . : they tortured because they were torturers" (p. 31). Himself the victim of torture, Améry offers phenomenological reflections on the extremity of his own experience that find no parallel in the literature on this subject. With the onset of torture, a part of one's life ends, and "it can never again be revived" (p. 29). The violation is not only painful, it is permanent. And the traces of its destruction remain as a source of inner suffering that can grow worse with the years.

"How Much Home Does a Person Need?" changes the focus from the pains of torture to the pains of exile and alienation; in describing the forlorn sense of being deprived of one's place of origin, the essay also describes the concomitant loss of one's sense of self. "I was no longer an I," Améry comes to acknowledge, "and I did not live within a We" (p. 44). Like the experience of torture, that of exile is damaging in a permanent sense: the wound is not one "that will scar over with the ticking of time" but is more akin to "an insidious disease that grows worse with the years" (p. 57).

All three of these essays are vivid in their accounts of dispossession and the loss of essential human value. For the victims of the Third Reich, the most basic foundations of the self—mind, body, origins, and antecedence—all came under systematic attack. Deprived of the ordinary functions of the mind, one was unable to transcend the intolerable, threatening reality of the camps. Under torture, the reduction of all bodily sensations to the dominant sense of pain deprived one of the basic right to be at ease. Homelessness and exile removed the last vestiges of any sense of security—cognitive security fully as much as physical well being.

The point is made throughout these essays: such loss is not only radical, it is irrevocable. There is no overcoming it. Whatever future one might envision for oneself will not include the restoration of those essential elements of the self that were taken away years before. The damage to mind, body, and integrity is lasting. Trust in the world, Améry insists, once removed, is never regained.

These are exceedingly harsh conclusions, yet Améry sets them forth with such clarity and conviction that there is no denying them. The question that then comes to the fore is, how is it possible to live with them? The fourth essay in *At the Mind's Limits*, entitled "Resentments," conveys the emotional charge behind the author's motivations for writing as he does about such unbearable experiences. He feels a strong, understandable grievance against those who collaborated in reducing his humanity, in treating him as a despised Jew and a deprived, tortured human being, and, far from remaining silent about such treatment, he insists on his right to voice protest against his persecutors. As a part of this rebellion, he finds his way to some bold, new conclusions in the book's final essay, "On the Necessity and Impossibility of Being a Jew," where he spells out a highly personal and clearly defiant identity for himself as "a vehemently protesting Jew." By affirming himself in these terms, Améry sought to reattain the dignity that was denied him as a Nazi victim, when, as he wrote, to be a Jew was to be "a dead man on leave, someone to be murdered" (p. 86). By publicly proclaiming himself as a Jew, albeit a Jew "without positive determinants, [a] Catastrophe Jew" (p. 94), Améry defied his would-be murderers, past and present, and claimed for himself both the legitimacy and the dignity of one who will not be denied the right to live on his own terms.

In the preface to the first edition of his book, the author noted that in writing these essays he broke twenty years of silence to offer his readers what he called "a phenomenological description of the existence of the victim" (p. xxiii). He further noted that he was not writing for his "comrades in fate," for "they know what it is all about," but for "the Germans, who in their overwhelming majority do not, or no longer, feel affected by the darkest and at the same time most characteristic deeds of the Third Reich." He added, "I would like to relate a few things here that until now have perhaps not been revealed to them." He then concluded by expressing the idealistic hope that his writings might reach "all those who wish to live together as fellow human beings" (p. xxiv).

In 1977, Améry reissued his book with a new and important author's preface. Gone is any sign of hope for a better future. Instead, the preface begins on a despondent note and moves toward despair: "Between the time this book was written and today, more than thirteen years have passed. They were not good years. . . . Sometimes it seems as though Hitler has gained a posthumous triumph. . . . Given this, what is the good of my attempt to reflect on the conditio inhumana of the victims of the Third Reich? Isn't it all outdated?" (p. xvii).

A number of gruesome events had taken place in world politics in the years since his book first appeared, but what evidently troubled Améry the most was occurring within Germany itself: "When I set about writing, and finished, there was no antisemitism in Germany, or more correctly: where it did exist, it did not dare to show itself. . . . The tide has turned. Again an old-new antisemitism impudently raises its disgusting head, without arousing indignation . . ." (p. xix). Améry goes on to note that the danger this time lies on the Left and especially within segments of the politically active youth. He expresses concern that "the young people of the Left," entrapped within "ill-considered ideologies, . . . do not slip over unawares to those who are their enemies." The slippage, in fact, was already evident at so-called "anti-Zionist" rallies in German cities, where, Améry learned to his alarm, a familiar street cry was once again being heard among the self-styled "antifascist" German youth: "Death to the Jewish people." These brutal words brought Améry to declare in the clearest, most unequivocal terms: "The political as well as Jewish Nazi victim, which I was and am, cannot be silent when under the banner of anti-Zionism the old, wretched antisemitism ventures forth. The impossibility of being a Jew becomes the necessity to be one, and that means: a vehemently protesting Jew. Let this book, then, . . . be an appeal to German youth for introspection" (pp. xix–xx). Améry was appalled that he had to stand up against those whom he had always regarded as his natural friends and political allies, but he was not reluctant to assert himself forcefully. "I sound the fire alarm," he wrote. He had suffered too much, and had seen others suffer too much, to remain quiet in the face of what he obviously regarded as the possibility of a repetition: "What happened, happened. But that it happened cannot be so easily accepted. I rebel: against my past, against history, and against a present that places the incomprehensible in the cold storage of history and thus falsifies it in a revolting way" (pp. xx, xxi).

The falsification troubled Améry, as did certain other tendencies he observed in the political life of Germany in the years leading up to his death. As Sidney Rosenfeld, one of his American translators, described his mood:

> Especially toward the end, he was downcast by increasing manifestations of a right-wing authoritarian restoration in German public life, along with the resurgence of antisemitism; his estrangement from the New Left, in whom his hopes had rested for a democratic Germany, had grown still more acute; the absorption of the Nazi past in its singularity and irreducibility into a universal theory of fascism and totalitarianism, something he had foreseen in *At the Mind's Limits*, but in a still somewhat removed future, was becoming reality before his eyes. The grotesqueness of the Maidanek trial in Düsseldorf, where the witnesses, survivors of the Nazi death camp, were subjected to derision by reactionary defense lawyers, filled him with bitterness. His response to the debate on the Statute of Limitations was a terse, poignant request not to the parliamentarians but to German society not to condemn the last remaining victims by morally exonerating their former torturers and thereby vindicating the atrocities. He was beset by a feeling that he was speaking into the wind, and this led to a despondent anger, growing resignation, and finally indifference (p. 110).

This mood of despondency can be detected in the preface to the 1977 edition of *At the Mind's Limits*, where it mingles with a sense of urgency and outrage. The source of these intense, highly complex feelings is clear. In his reflections on the historiography of the Third Reich, Améry discounts the plausibility of any of the existing explanations of Nazism and describes it as a unique evil, "single and irreducible in its total inner logic and accursed rationality." Furthermore, he finds that nothing but obfuscation is to be gained by relativizing Nazism as part of a general theory of "fascism" or twentieth-century political barbarism. "It did not happen in a developing country, nor as the direct continuation of a tyrannical regime, . . . nor in the bloody struggle of a revolution fearing for its existence. . . . It happened in Germany. It issued, so to speak, through spontaneous generation, from a womb that bore it as a perversion" (p. xviii). One can try to describe the particular terror of German National Socialism, but one cannot satisfactorily explain it. Most of all, Améry argued, one must not attempt to explain it away through the application of ready-at-hand categories of conventional Enlightenment thinking: "Clarification would amount to disposal, settlement of the case, which can then be placed in the files of history. My book is meant to aid in preventing precisely this. For nothing is resolved, no conflict is settled, no memory has become a mere memory. . . . Nothing has healed, and what was perhaps on the point of healing in 1964 is bursting open again as an infected wound" (p. xxi).

Acutely aware that the social poison seeping out of such a wound had the potential to spread, Améry reissued his book at a time in his life, it is now clear, when an accumulation of outward events and inner troubles weighed heavily upon him. Absent from the preface to his 1977 edition of *At the Mind's Limits* is any appeal to "all those who wish to live together as fellow human beings." Instead, in a prose that alternately registers a sense of resignation with something approaching desperation, he declares his intention to continue to speak forcefully about the victims of the Third Reich, but he manifests no particular confidence that he will be heard where his words most need to be heard. "I can do no more than give testimony," he writes (p. xviii). He was dejected and evidently had reached the edge of his own, crucial limits. In October, 1978, during a visit to his native Austria, Jean Améry took his own life.

How does one read his testimony today? To what, indeed, does his book bear witness? Améry never claimed that his time in Auschwitz and the other camps in which he had been incarcerated had made him a better or more noble man, but he did believe that his experiences better equipped him "to recognize reality" (p. 101). What order of reality must he have recognized in the latter years of his life that led him to suicide? While such a question is unlikely to yield any certain answers, a sympathetic reading of his book can help one understand the source of some of the author's long-standing frustrations and most bitter feelings as a former victim of the Third Reich. More precisely, one comes to understand that in his case "former victim" was almost an oxymoron, an appellation that, like "survivor," made little sense. Améry had withstood the Nazi assault against him, had managed to outlast it, yet he was not able to look upon his victimization as a thing of the past but, in fact, saw it as ongoing. He who was tortured remains tortured, he insisted. As for the torturers and the nation that produced them, to them the suffering was largely a thing of the past. This radical disjunction between the victim's continuing ordeal and the abnegation of responsibility for it on the part of the victimizer was something that Améry could not easily abide in silence. It impelled him to write *At the Mind's Limits* and shows up with particular force in "Resentments," one of his most passionate essays and perhaps the one that most directly strikes to the heart of his sense of himself as a writer and witness.

The essay begins on a mock-pastoral note as the author recounts his journeys in summertime through an idyllic, unnamed country. Although the landscape is attractive, the cities clean and well run, the citizens tolerant and seemingly urbane, Améry confesses that he feels uneasy in this lovely land. He then states why: "I belong to that fortunately slowly disappearing species of those who . . . are called the victims of Nazism" (p. 63). Although he has still not mentioned the country by name, he admits that he bears a strong retrospective grudge against it, one that fills him with resentments that he does not entirely understand. Thus he begs the reader's patience (first and foremost, since he was writing in German, the patience of the German reader) as he sets forth to examine his resentments.

The very first thing he notes is that others judge and condemn him for continuing to bear his grudge. They resent his resentments, feel victimized by being reminded of his victimization. Moreover, in Germany, which he now explicitly calls by its proper name, he was their victim. That is too much for most of them to face, so they turn the tables on history and decide to see themselves as victims—"absolute victims" of a cruel war that caused them displacement, hunger, homelessness, and the dismemberment of their country. Unlike Améry and others who insist on retaining their status as victims of the war, however, the Germans manifest a will to "overcome" the misfortunes they suffered as a result of the Third Reich and get on with their lives. It is time to let bygones be bygones. As the author is told by a German businessman, with no irony intended whatsoever, "The German people bear no grudge against the Jewish people" and "no longer had any hard feelings toward the resistance fighters and Jews" (p. 67). Moreover, Germans had paid the Jews generously through a magnanimous policy of reparations. Why, then, should grudges be kept and public atonement demanded? After all, the allied powers that had fought against Germany in the war had long ago accepted her back into "the community of nations." As a result, the country had rapidly thrown off its pariah status, was intent on looking forward and not backward, and was busy rebuilding itself as a modern, democratic state. Indeed, as Améry notes, if anyone today were to be seen as a pariah, it would more likely be those who hold on to their resentments from the past and refuse to let go.

Améry sees himself as one of these retrogrades, bound far more to the past and its ruins than to the future and its promises. Whereas the criminals have now entered a new era, largely free of the taint of their crime, he, the victim, remains tied to the past by his resentments. Why, then, hang on to them? Because, as Améry discloses in his essay, such feelings keep alive the moral truth of the conflict between him and his torturers. He insists on reviving this truth even as most of his torturers have never acknowledged its existence in the first place: "The crimes of National Socialism had no moral quality for the doer, who always trusted in the norm system of his Führer and his Reich. . . . But my resentments are there in order that the crime become a moral reality for the criminal, in order that he be swept into the truth of his atrocity" (p. 70).

Nowhere in his writings does Améry idealize suffering, but he does insist that his own sufferings as a victim of Nazism are imbued with emphatic moral value and that the only way to understand the nature of his ordeal was to keep alive its memory in terms that stress its scandalous character: "The moral person demands annulment of time — in the particular case under question, by nailing the criminal to his deed. Thereby, . . . the latter can join his victim as a fellow human being" (p. 72). Given this view, which originated in a firmly held ethic of memory, any easy forgiving and forgetting was out of the question. Release from the iniquities of the past could be had, if at all, only by recognizing the gross moral trespass against the victims, but since those who had caused so much suffering were unwilling or unable to acknowledge it on their own, they might be prodded to do so by the surviving witnesses to their crimes. As Améry understood the continuing conflict between the Germans and those who had suffered so grievously under them during the Third Reich, therefore, resolution would only be possible if people like himself, acting out of their resentments, continued to protest against the injustices of the past. Aroused by such protest, the Germans, Améry averred, might finally awaken to "the fact that they cannot allow a piece of their national history to be neutralized by time, but must integrate it":

> [Germany] would then, as I sometimes hope, learn to comprehend its past acquiescence in the Third Reich as the total negation not only of the world that it plagued with war and death but also of its own better origins; it would no longer repress or hush up the twelve years that for us others really were a thousand, but claim them as its realized negation of the world and its self, as its own negative possession. . . . Two groups of people, the overpowered and those who overpowered them, would be joined in the desire that time be turned back and, with it, that history become moral. If this demand were raised by the German people . . . it would have tremendous weight. . . . The German revolution would be made good, Hitler disowned. And in the end Germans would really achieve what the people once did not have the might or the will to do, and what later, in the political power game, no longer appeared to be a vital necessity: the eradication of the ignominy (p. 78).

This passage represents a high point of hope in Améry's book, as it does in the literature of testimony at large. Améry was nothing if not a moral realist, however, and he recognized that if such an inner German cleansing were ever to take place, it could only be brought about by the Germans themselves: "This writer is not a German, and it is not for him to give advice to this people" (p. 78). He would speak—he had to speak—and then step back. But were there figures within the public life of the nation who were capable of stepping forward and, through their own voices, stimulating a desire for moral reversal on such a scale? Améry knew there were individual Germans of conscience who suffered the past inwardly and tried to make amends, but the struggle that he envisioned—a massive, unprecedented "negation of the negation"—had to occur on the national level if it were to be successful. He was calling for a radical turn of heart, nothing less than "the spiritual reduction . . . by the German people . . . of everything that was carried out in those twelve years" (p. 79). Did he believe the Germans were capable of such a redeeming act?

"Nothing of the sort will happen," he wrote. As he elaborates upon this negative view, his essay turns from the visionary to the sardonic and reveals in the most painful way that Améry expected nothing from the Germans in the future but the defeat of his own most passionate hopes:

> But what an extravagant daydream I have abandoned myself to! . . . All recognizable signs suggest that natural time will reject the moral demands of our resentment and finally extinguish them. The great revolution? Germany will not make it good, and our rancor will have been for nothing. Hitler's Reich will, for the time being, continue to be regarded as an operational accident of history. Finally, however, it will be purely and simply history, no better and no worse than dramatic historical epochs just happen to be, bloodstained perhaps, but after all a Reich that also had its everyday family life. The picture of great-grandfather in his SS uniform will hang in the parlor, and the children in the schools will learn less about the selection ramps than about an astounding triumph over general unemployment. . . . What happened in Germany between 1933 and 1945, so they will teach and say, could have occurred anywhere else under similar circumstances, and no one will insist any further on the trifle that it did happen precisely in Germany and not somewhere else (p. 79).

What Améry feared most but also, as is evident, what he expected to occur over time, was a gradual normalization of Nazism, a process of historical revisionism that would have the inevitable effect of blurring and ultimately denying the reality of his own experience. As it happened, a self-chosen death spared him from having to witness further signs that the revisionism he foresaw was gathering momentum, as illustrated all too clearly by the grotesque spectacle at the Bitburg military cemetery in the spring of 1985, by some of the arguments that accompanied the German *Historikerstreit* that began shortly thereafter, by the ominous appearance of German neo-Nazis in the streets of German cities and the violent assaults against Turks and other "foreigners," and by other analogous events that have regularly punctuated the political culture of Germany over the past few decades. These developments would have added to Améry's distress and deepened his pessimism. But he already had seen enough in his lifetime to reach some sorrowful conclusions about what was taking place in Germany and his own situation vis-à-vis the Germans: "I bear my grudge for reasons of personal salvation," he wrote. As for its effect on the others: "Our resentments . . . have little or no chance at all to make the evil work of the overwhelmers bitter for them" (p. 80). The bitterness was his to swallow; his persecutors would have none of it. If anything, Améry knew that a perpetual pointing of the finger at the Germans would only turn them indignant and might, in the end, turn some of them aggressively against the victims and those identified with the victims. He would continue to feel bound to the moral truth of what he continued to call "the conflict," but for most others there was no longer any such "conflict." In their view, the war was over. Whatever misfortunes may have accompanied it were to be regretted and then put behind them. Acknowledging this painful gap between himself and his potential reading audience in Germany and finding no way to bridge it, Améry, in effect, threw up his hands. "Resentments" ends on a bitter, mordant note, which pointed to nothing ahead for its author but grimness: "We victims must finish with our retroactive rancor, in the sense that the KZ argot once gave to the word 'finish'; it meant as much as 'to kill.' Soon we must and will be finished. Until that time has come, we request of those whose peace is disturbed by our grudge that they be patient" (p. 81).

One comes away from a reading of "Resentments" feeling downcast, for this is writing that seems to testify to the futility of testimony itself. One admires Améry for the clarity and moral stringency of his thinking, but one recognizes, as he himself recognized, that his complaint was not widely shared and was not likely to ever have the salutary effects he once envisioned it might produce. That would not keep him from declaring his truth, to be sure, for he believed that what he had to say was not only for his own good "but also for the good of the German people." He responded with evident disappointment, however, to the way German readers had taken him up: "No one wants to relieve me of [my grudge] except the organs of public opinion-making, which buy it. What dehumanized me has become a commodity, which I offer for sale" (p. 80). Despite the caustic nature of this remark, however, Améry continued to write and publish his work for German audiences.

What kept him writing was something other than sales. Committed to the heuristic as well as ethical dimensions of literature, he wrote because he wanted to understand the nature of his own extreme experience and also because he was convinced others should learn of it. In his lifetime he was more successful in the first instance than in the second, but there is no reason to confine his ultimate importance to his own epoch. His mature writing career was brief—a mere twelve years—but produced work whose significance should be recognized well into the future.[8] There is, it is true, a price to be paid for reading a book like *At the Mind's Limits*, which projects an order of experience that is nothing if not distressing, but there is a far higher price to be paid by foregoing an author such as Jean Améry, and that is the diminution of historical and moral consciousness itself. Améry was irrefutably right in his insistence that we recognize reality for what it is, by which he meant not only that we acknowledge that "what happened, happened" but also that we refuse to assent to the acceptability of what happened. Normalization of the Third Reich, he feared, might be taken as a prelude to its acceptance. Such a development, the early signs of which he already saw, had to be opposed. Améry's rebellion against the past, therefore, was fundamentally a moral rebellion—in his own terms, the require-ment that reality include a basic component of justice. Anything short of that he regarded as unreasonable and cause for vigorous protest. Hence, his rancor and resentments were not sustained for their own sake but rather employed in the service of a large and pressing demand: the insistence that "reality is reasonable only so long as it is moral."[9] In Améry's case, indeed, this formula applied. It did not finally matter, therefore, whether his protest drew a large number of followers, for protest was for him a neces-sary means of bearing witness, the form his testimony took at its most impassioned. And testimony—as he offered it: credible, cor-rective words about an otherwise incredible, unacceptable order of experience—was not to be denied no matter what its chances of gaining an immediate effect:

> It is certainly true that moral indignation cannot hold its
> ground against the silently erosive and transformative effects
> of time. It is hopeless, even if not entirely unjustified, to
> demand that National Socialism be felt as an outrage with
> the same emotional intensity as in the years immediately fol-
> lowing the Second World War. No doubt there exists some-
> thing like historical entropy: the historical "heat gradient"
> disappears; the result is a balance with no order. But in view-
> ing historical processes we should not foster this entropy; on
> the contrary, we should resist it with all our power, if only for

the reason that even distribution of the historical molecules would no longer permit us to discern a coherent picture of history. More decisive for humane concerns, however, is the demand that the study of history contain a component of moral judgment, as do the historical events themselves.
. . . Seen in this way, the myth of the Third Reich as a myth of radical evil is truer to fact than an alleged objectivity that does not oppose the evil and already by its indifference alone becomes the advocate of this very evil.[10]

Améry wrote in opposition to the old evil and in protest against any future attempts to rehabilitate it. The moral stance he took up as a witness against the crimes of the Third Reich was uncompromising. He was a fighter, but he must have felt worn down by the fight and reached the point where he became convinced that continuing it was futile. And so, during a return visit to his native country, in the loneliness of a Salzburg hotel room, he opted to put an end to his struggles once and for all. Whether one regards his suicide as a final act of protest or as an act of despair, it confirms a harsh truth, known by other Holocaust survivors as well, which Jean Améry made terrifyingly clear: after Auschwitz, to be a Jew, he was convinced, "means feeling the tragedy of yesterday as an inner oppression. . . . To be a Jew [means] . . . to be a dead man on leave" (p. 94, p. 86).

SEVEN

Primo Levi:
The Survivor as Victim

After Auschwitz everything returns us to Auschwitz.
— ELIE WIESEL

The suicide of Jean Améry, like that of numerous other Holocaust writers, raises troubling questions about the possible links between the lingering effects of Holocaust trauma and a self-inflicted death. Literary scholars, social scientists, psychiatrists, and writers themselves have made serious inquiries into the roots of suicide among those who survived the camps, wrote about their experiences, and later took their own lives. Their analyses differ significantly and offer no definitive answers. Given the range of motives behind such deaths, this absence of consensus is no surprise. In some cases, suicide seems impulsive — a rash and sudden act; in others, it may have a more rational, premeditated character. Acute depression is often a contributing factor, as are the pains that accompany old age, illness, and bodily decrepitude. Apart from rare instances where suicide is deliberately chosen as a form of political protest — the death of Shmuel Zygielbojm is a prominent example — in the majority of cases, it is unlikely that the etiology of such death can be traced to a single cause. As Primo Levi noted in his late reflections on Améry, included in *The Drowned and the Saved*, "Jean Améry's suicide, which took place in Salzburg in 1978, like other suicides, admits of a cloud of explanations."[1]

But while these may have been Levi's last words on Améry's death, they were not his only ones. Writing in *La Stampa*, on December 7, 1978, soon after learning of Améry's death, Levi was more expansive and also more self-assured in his comments:

> It is particularly difficult to understand why a person kills himself [but] . . . the suicide of Jean Améry [is] . . . absolutely comprehensible. . . .
>
> No, the death of Jean Améry is not a surprise. . . . It is unbearable to think that while the torture that Améry suffered weighed down on him right to his death, indeed was for him an interminable death, it is more than likely that his torturers are sitting down in an office or enjoying their retirement. And if they were interrogated (but who is there to interrogate them?), they would give the same old answer with a clear conscience: they were only following orders.[2]

Levi's comments on Améry's death are striking for several reasons. One is that they are not in the least tentative: while Levi acknowledges that, in general, the motives for a self-inflicted death are typically difficult to decipher, he is certain why Améry killed himself. He offers a brief history of the Austrian writer's anguished wartime experiences and then quotes the following lines from Améry's writings, which, he says, read "like an epitaph": "The man who has been tortured remains tortured. . . . Whoever has suffered torment will no longer be able to find his way clearly in the world, the abomination of annihilation will never be extinguished. Trust in humanity . . . can never be regained."[3]

Levi was sure that the accumulation of inner pain that Améry carried with him from his time in the Nazi camps ultimately killed him. Especially in the absence of any cathartic sense of justice, which Améry long sought among the Germans but never found, memory of the sufferings inflicted on him as a Jewish victim of Nazi cruelty led "inevitably to [his] death."[4] Whether or not Levi's analysis of Améry's violent ending is correct, his words seem ominously self-referential and are hard to put out of mind when considering the author's own unexpected end.

News of the death of Primo Levi in April 1987 brought with it a sense of loss and dismay that has not entirely receded to this day. Levi's death was reported to be self-inflicted, reason enough to feel more than just saddened by the passing of an exceptionally fine writer. Inevitably, the names of others came to mind: Paul Celan, Tadeusz Borowski, Piotr Rawicz, Jean Améry. As a writer who reflected continually on the crimes of the Third Reich, Levi belonged in the company of these writers, but one was reluctant to place him among them as a fellow suicide. How could he, whose books were distinguished by such measured temperament, emotional balance, and rational control, how could *he* of all writers take his own life? Did he, in fact, kill himself or, as some claimed, did he fall accidentally to his death?[5] However one views it, Levi's passing was tragically premature and was mourned as an enormous loss to the world of letters. Beyond that, if his was indeed a death by suicide, the implications are all the more troubling, for Levi's violent end raises once again the awful possibility that the Nazi crimes might continue to claim victims decades after Nazism itself had been defeated. As in the case of Jean Améry, one is driven to ask a question that transcends the personal and becomes deeply psychological and broadly cultural in its implications: is there latent within the memory of these crimes a peril that, years later, might overwhelm those who seemingly had managed to escape them? And not just escape them but, as appeared to be true in Primo Levi's case, prevail over them?

Among all those who had survived the death camps and gone on to write about them, Levi seemed to be one of the few who had achieved some permanent measure of artistic control over his experience. His writings never shrank from a direct confrontation with the horrors of Nazism, but at the same time they were conspicuously free of outrage or self-pity, of overt expressions of bitterness, emotional fury, or uncontained rage. "My personal temperament is not inclined to hatred," he wrote. "I regard it as bestial, crude, and prefer on the contrary that my actions and thoughts, as far as possible, should be the product of reason."[6] Hatred and vengeance are passions that simply do not appear in his writings, and even anger is rare.

Although he had plenty to be angry about, Levi had reached an unusual level of intellectual and moral poise in his books. It seemed indeed that he had come through his ordeal and, in his person as well as in his writings, showed that it was possible for the civilized values of intelligence and humane feeling to survive the Nazi assault against them. This sense of Levi as stalwart survivor was badly shaken by the news of his death. To be sure, it was not the case that his writings were suddenly invalidated or meant less than they had before but finally that they were not strong enough to shield the author from the lacerating memories of personal and historical extremity that they recorded. Worse still was the real possibility that by keeping these memories alive and by returning to them in book after book, Levi may have prolonged and even intensified the trauma that had so cruelly marked his earlier years. He was a survivor but, by right of his intense absorption in the past, was he not also increasingly a victim? His books are both testimony and reflection, a vivid evocation of, and continuing meditation on, the past by a survivor-witness. Is it necessary for us now to regard that status, that self-chosen vocation, as fraught with high risk and, for some, ultimately a vocation of doom?

At the very beginning of his last book, *The Drowned and the Saved*, Levi quotes a revealing passage from Simon Wiesenthal's *The Murderers Among Us*. The speaker is an SS militiaman; his address is made in cynical, taunting fashion to prisoners in one of the camps:

However this war may end, we have won the war against you; none of you will be left to bear witness, but even if someone were to survive, the world will not believe him. There will perhaps be suspicions, discussions, research by historians, but there will be no certainties, because we will destroy the evidence together with you. And even if some proof should remain and some of you survive, people will say that the events you describe are too monstrous to be believed: they will say that they are the exaggerations of Allied propaganda and will believe us, who will deny everything. We will be the ones to dictate the history of the Lagers.[7]

Levi comments that "this same thought ('even if we were to tell it, we would not be believed')" was shared by all of the prisoners in the camp. He adds that "both parties, victims and oppressors, had a keen awareness of the enormity and therefore the noncredibility of what took place in the Lagers . . ." (p. 12). To overcome this unbelievability by telling their stories and, thereby, to convince others that the incredible actually occurred is a large part of the task of Holocaust testimony.

It is a task that Levi shared with others who had undergone analogous experiences and likewise understood themselves as writer-witnesses. One of these writers was Améry, who had been incarcerated in Auschwitz-Monowitz at the same time as Levi. In the title essay of *At the Mind's Limits*, Améry refers to Levi by name.[8] Levi, in turn, wrote about Améry at length in *The Drowned and the Saved*. In "The Memory of the Offense," Levi explores the nature of traumatic memory and sees it as "an injury that cannot be healed." To reinforce his point that "the memory of a trauma suffered or inflicted is itself traumatic," he quotes lines from Améry's powerful essay on "Torture" that by now will be familiar:

It is not without horror that we read the words left us by Jean Améry, the Austrian philosopher tortured by the Gestapo because he was active in the Belgian resistance and then deported to Auschwitz because he was Jewish: "Anyone who has been tortured remains tortured. . . . Anyone who has suffered torture never again will be able to be at ease in the world; the abomination of the annihilation is never extinguished. Faith in humanity, already cracked by the first slap in the face, then demolished by torture, is never acquired again."

Levi went on to note that "torture was for him an interminable death: Améry . . . killed himself in 1978."[9] In light of his own death less than a decade later, these words take on a special poignancy. They point, if not directly to a premeditated, self-willed death, then certainly to the sense, common to both authors, that survival for those who had been in the camps could mean an intermittent death-in-life, an affliction of consciousness triggered now and again by what Levi called "the memory of the offense." Levi concluded, "Once again it must be observed, mournfully, that the injury cannot be healed; it extends through time, and the Furies, in whose existence we are forced to believe, not only rack the tormentor . . . but perpetuate the tormentor's work by denying peace to the tormented."[10] While it is obviously not the case that every survivor suffers in the manner described here, there can be little doubt that Levi himself knew the Furies all too well and must have felt himself punished by them in no small measure. Memory, the very source of his genius as a writer, was also the source of much of his pain.

Out of necessity, one learns to live with such pain, to disguise it or suppress it or otherwise evade a direct confrontation with it, but these maneuvers work at best to tame the inner suffering, not eliminate it. Werner Weinberg, another keenly perceptive survivor-writer, speaks of learning "to live and function with an unexorcisable piece of the Holocaust within me."[11] Primo Levi learned to live that way as well, but at a cost to himself of a punishingly high order.

Among other things, he was troubled by a deep and lingering sense of injustice, a subject that came to the fore often in his writings and did so in an especially curious way in his reflections on Jean Améry and suicide. Levi recounts an episode from Améry's essay "On the Necessity and Impossibility of Being a Jew," in which Améry describes trading blows with an aggressive Polish foreman in Auschwitz. The latter would willfully strike at Jews under his command and one day, for no apparent reason, hit Améry in the face. In a rare moment of revolt, Améry struck him back with a punch to the jaw. That blow by a rebelling Jew served to bring on a worse beating by the violent Pole, but all the same it was a deed that had to be done: dignity demanded it. In commenting on this episode, Levi expresses appreciation for Améry's courage, but he remarks that he himself never would have been capable of striking back. "I have never known how to 'return the blow,'" he writes. "'Trading punches' is an experience I do not have, as far back as I can go in memory." He then says something about this episode that is not easy to grasp. While he respects Améry's action as "a reasoned revolt against the perverted world of the Lager," he implicates it directly in Améry's suicide. Here is the crucial passage: "Those who 'trade blows' with the entire world achieve dignity but pay a very high price for it because they are sure to be defeated. Améry's suicide . . . like other suicides admits of a cloud of explanations, but, in hindsight, that episode of defying the Pole offers one interpretation."[12]

Precisely what was it that Levi saw in Améry's moment of rebellion that led him to believe he had understood the nature of Améry's violent death? The American writer Cynthia Ozick believes that it was rage. *"The Drowned and the Saved,"* Ozick writes, "is a book of catching-up after decades of abstaining. It is a book of blows returned by a pen on fire." This long-suppressed rage was simply too much for Levi, in Ozick's view: "Levi waited more than forty years; and he did not become a suicide until he let passion in, and returned the blows. . . . I grieve that he equated rage with self-destruction."[13]

The Drowned and the Saved is a more forceful book than any Levi had published previously, but in my reading of it, it does not, in fact, show us the author enraged. There is an emphatic note of grievance that runs through the essays in this collection, but there is also more than a little self-criticism. Levi is hard on himself in this book, indeed, much too hard. While he is highly critical of the Germans, he also feels the need to defend himself for his previous writings about them. "Améry," he writes, "called me 'the forgiver.' I consider this neither insult nor praise but imprecision. I am not inclined to forgive, I never forgave our enemies of that time. . . . I know no human act that can erase a crime; I demand justice, but I am not able, personally, to trade punches or return blows."[14] "I am the way I was made by my past," he writes, "and it is no longer possible for me to change."[15] It was an honest way for him to account for his own relative passivity in contrast to Améry's more openly rebellious nature. But were his actions, or, more precisely, his inaction, an adequate reply to the injustices he was made to suffer?

Almost certainly not. He seems to have felt himself doubly violated—first, by the dehumanizing experiences of his time in Auschwitz; and second, by the troubling accusation, which may have been, in part, also a self-accusation, that he did too little to back up his demand for justice with concrete actions. What comes through his extended reflection on Améry and suicide, therefore, has far less to do with any rage directed against his former persecutors than with intense self-criticism and, along with that, possibly a serious loss of personal dignity. These are matters that Levi regarded with the utmost seriousness and described in grave tones in writing about Améry: "In order to live, an identity—that is, dignity—is necessary. . . . Whoever loses one also loses the other, dies spiritually: without defenses he is therefore exposed also to physical death."[16] This passage, too, seems revealingly self-reflexive and points to a difficult moment of spiritual crisis in Levi's own life.

Werner Weinberg provides insight into the inner life of survivors that may be applicable here. "There are wounds that defy healing," he has written, "and the reason is that they must not be allowed to heal."[17] The reference is to spiritual wounds, memory-wounds, the very same that Primo Levi had in mind when he spoke of "the memory of the offense." Levi demanded justice, but on some deep level he knew that justice would not be forthcoming. And so he turned in his writings to an ever more anguished analysis of the problematic itself: to an examination of the motivations and actions of those who defined, organized, and carried out unprecedented acts of injustice and to an examination of himself and others who had been in the camps, the victims of extreme injustice. At the same time, and out of a sense of increasing necessity in his latter years, he examined the quality of his own witness by looking at himself as a chronicler and anatomist of injustice. As he proceeded to think and write along these lines, his books show that he was driven to reflect more and more on the value of life itself and to ponder what it is that brings some to put an end to life through suicide.

Prior to the war, Primo Levi had completed his formal studies in Italy, but, as he often remarked, his true university was Auschwitz.[18] Thus in important, even transformative, ways, it might be said that Levi also received a "German" education. It was to be a continuing one, for from the age of twenty-five until the end of his life he remained endlessly curious about Germany and the Germans. By his own count, he visited the country at least fifteen times in the postwar period,[19] spent several years studying the German language, and from his first book to his last did his best to ponder the people and the culture that constituted the German nation. He was driven to do so, as he said repeatedly, not out of hatred and not in order to exact vengeance upon his former persecutors, but in an effort to figure them out. That proved to be no easy task.

Levi's reflections on Germany and the Germans are dispersed throughout his writings. A careful reading of this material yields numerous insights, most of which center on the author's attempts to grasp the essence of the peculiar education he had received at the hands of the Germans in Auschwitz.

It was, as he relates it in his first book, an education in the processes of dehumanization, or, as he put it more memorably, in "the demolition of a man."[20] *Survival in Auschwitz* portrays dehumanization on several different levels, but if one were to search Levi's first book for a primal scene of basic human reduction—one in which the author portrays himself as having been the victim of a fundamental act of degradation—one could hardly do better than to return to the chapter entitled "Chemical Examination." There Levi recounts a memory of offense that showed him just how vulnerable he was to the indignities and diminishments of injustice. Trained as a chemist in Turin, Levi volunteered in Auschwitz to join a chemical unit; if accepted, he could count on the relative security of an indoors job and, thus, hope to prolong his life a little longer. In order to become a member of this unit, however, he first had to pass a chemistry examination. Under ordinary conditions such an examination would have posed him no special problems, but as a Jewish inmate of Auschwitz his conditions were anything but normal. Here is how Levi describes coming before Doktor Pannwitz, his examiner:

> Pannwitz is tall, thin, blond; he has eyes, hair, and nose as all Germans ought to have them, and sits formidably behind a complicated writing table. I, Häftling 174517, stand in his office, which is a real office, shining, clean, and ordered, and I feel that I would leave a dirty stain whatever I touch. When he finished writing, he raised his eyes and looked at me. From that day I have thought about Doktor Pannwitz

many times and in many ways. I have asked myself how he
really functioned as a man; how he filled his time, outside
of the Polymerization and the Indo-Germanic conscience;
above all, when I was once more a free man, I wanted to
meet him again, not from a spirit of revenge, but merely from
a personal curiosity about the human soul. Because that look
was not one between two men; and if I had known how completely to explain the nature of that look, which came as if
across the glass window of an aquarium between two beings
who live in different worlds, I would also have explained the
essence of the great insanity of the third Germany.[21]

Levi left Doktor Pannwitz not knowing if he had passed the
chemistry examination, but the memory of his strange ordeal of
standing in his prison rags before his German examiner never
left him. Precisely who or what was he in the eyes of the other?
That question, in one version or another, remained with Primo
Levi for the rest of his life. If he could have answered it, as he
remarked, he would have been able to explain the essence of
Nazism itself.

Levi had been taken to the chemistry examination by a Kapo
named Alex, a crude, delinquent type. This same Kapo escorted
Levi back to the camp. On the way they had to climb across
some dirty steel barriers. Alex got himself soiled in the process
and cursed his grease-blackened hand. Here is Primo Levi's
description of what followed:

Without hatred and without sneering, Alex wipes his hand
on my shoulder, both the palm and the back of the hand, to
clean it; he would be amazed, the poor brute Alex, if someone told him that today, on the basis of this action, I judge
him and Pannwitz and the innumerable others like him, big
and small, in Auschwitz and everywhere.[22]

One can find scenes of dehumanization that are more unnerving in their depictions of human degradation than the one just cited. It is typical of Levi's genius as a writer, however, to reveal the large offense in the ostensibly small act—in this case, to show the reduction of a fellow human being by turning him into a convenient rag. To be sure, during his time of incarceration in Auschwitz Levi was to go on to know far greater horrors, but those alluded to in "The Chemical Examination"—the disarming inequality and basic absurdity of his audience with Pannwitz and the abuse he suffered at the hands of Alex the Kapo—these two constituted primary acts of injustice that he never forgot. Both prompted in him a lifelong desire to understand the Germans and were at the root of his becoming a writer. Here is how he put it to his first German translator:

> I cannot say that I understand the Germans. And what one cannot understand forms a painful void; it is a thorn, a constant urge that demands fulfillment. . . .
>
> When I think about my life and the various goals that I have set for myself, then I recognize only one as clearly defined and conscious, and it is this: to bear witness, to allow the German people to hear my voice, and to "answer" the Kapo who wiped his hand on my shoulder [and] Dr. Pannwitz. . . .[23]

He was convinced, as he stated in *The Periodic Table*, that "every German must answer for Auschwitz,"[24] but the more he probed into the nature of the Nazi crimes and into what he generally regarded as a failure among Germans of the postwar period to do the same, the more forlorn he tended to become. He regarded German silence during the time of the Third Reich as inexcusable: "Most Germans didn't know because they didn't want to know. Because, indeed, they wanted *not* to know."[25] As for German silence in the years following the end of the war,

"The 'I don't know' or 'I did not know' spoken today by many Germans no longer shocks us."[26]

It was a failure that he foresaw intuitively in some of his earliest writings and can be illustrated by the following passage from *The Reawakening*, his second book. In it Levi describes the sensations he felt when, in October 1945, as part of his long, circuitous repatriation to Turin, he suddenly found himself in Munich. It was his first time ever in Germany:

> We felt we had something to say, enormous things to say, to every single German, and we felt that every German should have something to say to us; we felt an urgent need to settle our accounts, to ask, explain, and comment. . . . Did "they" know about Auschwitz, about the silent daily massacre, a step away from their doors? . . .
>
> I felt that everybody should interrogate us, read in our faces who we were, and listen to our tale in humility. But no-one looked us in the eyes, no-one accepted the challenge; they were deaf, blind, and dumb imprisoned in their ruins, as in a fortress of willful ignorance, still strong, still capable of hatred and contempt, still prisoners of their old tangle of pride and guilt.
>
> I found myself searching among them . . . for someone who could not but know, remember, reply; who had commanded and obeyed, killed, humiliated, corrupted. A vain and foolish search; because not they, but others, the few just ones, would reply for them.[27]

The Drowned and the Saved, Levi's last book, was written some two decades later, but it concludes on a similarly disconsolate note and for many of the same reasons: in Levi's view, the Germans, with only few exceptions, had chosen to remain willfully ignorant about the crimes of the Third Reich. The older generation of Germans remained by and large as he had seen them in Munich in the fall of 1945: deaf, blind, and dumb. As for the younger people, accounts such as his own seem to speak to them, if at all, of a world that is "distant, blurred, 'historical.'" Levi was generally not a cynical or fatalistic writer, but toward the end of his life he felt himself to be anachronistic and increasingly irrelevant when it came to the Germans. His final words on the subject carry uncharacteristically forceful tones of bitterness and of something approaching despair:

> Let it be clear that to a greater or lesser degree all were responsible, but it must be just as clear that behind their responsibility stands that great majority of Germans who accepted in the beginning, out of mental laziness, myopic calculation, stupidity, and national pride the "beautiful words" of Corporal Hitler, followed him as long as luck and the lack of scruples favored him, were swept away by his ruin, afflicted by deaths, misery, and remorse, and rehabilitated a few years later as the result of an unprincipled political game.[28]

On the evidence of these words one would have to conclude that Levi had more or less given up on the Germans. In his "Letters from Germans" he reports that most of the people who wrote to him from Germany either tried to whitewash the past or expressed a sincere but helpless guilt over its worst aspects. Moreover, many responded to Levi's plea to understand the Germans by confessing that they could not understand them themselves.

Evidence of Germany's lingering ambivalence about the past surfaced in especially prominent ways in the two years leading up to Primo Levi's death. The Bitburg affair, in the spring of 1985, for instance, was an event that Levi looked upon as a personal affront to the victims of Nazism as well as a national scandal.[29] He regarded the *Historikerstreit*, a highly publicized debate among historians about German guilt and responsibility, which began soon after, as a troubling form of historical revisionism and criticized it sharply in print.[30]

These tendencies and others like them undermined Levi's earlier hope of having some kind of honest encounter with the Germans. As becomes clear from his last book, when he had first learned that *Survival in Auschwitz* was being translated into German, he had felt uneasy; but then he welcomed the prospect of a German edition, for at last, as he put it, he would be reaching "them," his work's "true recipients, those against whom the book was aimed like a gun." As a result of the translation, he wrote, "Now the gun was loaded."[31] This is an unusual, powerfully aggressive metaphor, and it highlights the strength of Levi's feelings as he anticipated his encounter with a German readership. It was an encounter long in the making and finally would give him the opportunity to reestablish the proportions between him and those who had sought to diminish him. In fact, though, he came to see that the response to his book in Germany had been relatively weak, and he doubtless was disappointed that in his battle against the attenuation of historical memories of the Nazi oppression his best shot had carried so little echo. Did he then do the desperate thing and, in keeping with the language of his metaphor, begin to anticipate a time when he might turn his loaded gun against himself?

"Suicide," Primo Levi wrote, "is a meditated act."[32] Like all other acts of consequence, it has a history behind it, including, in the case of most writers, a literary history. A careful reading of all of Primo Levi's writings reveals an intermittent fascination with sudden endings, violent explosions, drownings, and acts of self-destruction. Apparent as well is a concern with the psychological and spiritual components of what Levi called "the survivor's disease"—the diminution of energy, a wearing away of vitality, the heavy burdens of guilt and shame, a slow but certain collapse of the will to live. Levi did not center his major writings on such preoccupations as these, but they appear often enough in his books to signal at least an underlying concern with the possibility, if not also the desirability, of a self-willed death.

One finds explicit references to such death in Levi's expository reflections on Améry, Trakl, and Celan, but his most interesting treatment of suicide appears in the author's more imaginative writings—in the stories "Versamina" and "Westward," collected in *The Sixth Day and Other Tales*, in "Lorenzo's Return," collected in *Moments of Reprieve*, in passages of *The Periodic Table* and *The Monkey's Wrench*, and in such poems as "Pliny" and "The Girl-Child of Pompei."

"Pliny," for instance, portrays the dangers that accompany a fascination with the power of natural eruptions. The poem's narrator, based on Pliny the Elder, who died in the year 79 CE from venturing too close to Mt. Vesuvius, is a passionate observer who will not be restrained from following his desire to investigate the explosive sources of destruction. A student of "ash," Pliny appears to be a mask for Levi himself, even as his determination to launch himself forward into the heart of danger seems at odds with the commonly held perception of Levi as a basically poised, non-impulsive figure.

PLINY

Don't hold me back, friends, let me set out.
I won't go far; just to the other shore.
I want to observe at close hand that dark cloud,
Shaped like a pine tree, rising above Vesuvius,
And find the source of this strange light.
Nephew, you don't want to come along? Fine; stay here and
    study.
Recopy the notes I gave you yesterday.
You needn't fear the ash; ash on top of ash.
We're ash ourselves; remember Epicurus?
Quick, get the boat ready, it is already night:

Night at midday, a portent never seen before.
Don't worry, sister, I'm cautious and expert;
The years that bowed me haven't passed in vain.
Of course I'll come back quickly. Just give me time
To ferry across, observe the phenomena and return,
Draw a new chapter from them tomorrow
For my books, that will, I hope, still live
When for centuries my old body's atoms
Will be whirling, dissolved in the vortices of the universe,
Or live again in an eagle, a young girl, a flower.
Sailors, obey me: launch the boat into the sea.[33]

In contrast to the fatal impetuosity portrayed in "Pliny," cau-
tion, skepticism, and control characterize the scientific investiga-
tors of "Westward," but the compelling theme is once again self-
destruction. In this story two scientists set out to study the death
instinct by investigating the suicidal behavior of lemmings. As they
proceed with their study, they are given to ponder the value of life
itself and the option of freely choosing to put an end to life. Their
dialogue is inquisitive and demanding and pushes rational inquiry
to the limits: "Why would a living being want to die?" one asks.
The other answers, "And why should it want to live? Why should
it always want to live?"[34] The questions are insistent, and the conclusions reached are often of a downcast nature: "Life does *not*
have a purpose; pain always prevails over joy; we are all sentenced
to death, and the day of one's execution has not been revealed; we
are condemned to watch the end of those dearest to us; there are
compensations, but they are few."[35] There are numerous reflections of this kind in "Westward," most of which turn on negative
assessments of the ability of the life instinct to sustain itself against
the inevitability of decline and the wasting power of death. The
story ends with a reference to the Arunde, a people that is said to
attribute "little value to individual survival, and none to that of
the nation."[36] Once the members of this tribe sense the onset of

decline, they freely choose death. Given the opportunity to prolong life through the aid of medicines, the Arunde declare: "We
prefer freedom to drugs and death to illusion."[37]

Such a preference apparently was also Lorenzo's, as Primo
Levi described it in "Lorenzo's Return." As readers of *Survival
in Auschwitz* know, Lorenzo was a figure of crucial importance
to Levi during his time in Auschwitz. An Italian civilian worker
at the camp, Lorenzo faithfully brought extra food to Levi, thus
enabling him to sustain hope in human goodness as well as to
satisfy his physical hunger. Levi looked upon Lorenzo as a simple, thoroughly decent man, and he felt that his own survival
owed in no small measure to Lorenzo's numerous acts of kindness and generosity. In a place overwhelmed by the omnipres-
ence of death, Lorenzo stood on the side of life. Thus it grieved
Levi greatly when, at war's end, he discovered that Auschwitz
had taken a far greater toll on Lorenzo than he had imagined:

> I found a tired man, . . . mortally tired, a weariness without
> remedy. . . . His margin of love for life had thinned, almost
> disappeared. . . . He had seen the world, he didn't like it, he
> felt it was going to ruin. To live no longer interested him. . . .
> He was assured and coherent in his rejection of life. . . . He,
> who was not a survivor, died of the survivor's disease.[38]

In pondering such passages and the others that have been
cited above, the question naturally arises: did Levi himself die of
"the survivor's disease"? We shall never know for certain, but his
writings point toward such a possibility. They show us an author
increasingly beset by preoccupations with pain, guilt, shame,
self-accusation, futility, and failure—in sum, struggling with the
anguish of his own survival. This struggle finds forceful expression
in Levi's last book, which is, in its mode, as painfully aggrieved a
meditation on the sorrows and torments of survivorship as any in
the whole corpus of Holocaust literature.

The grievance is manifold in nature and is sharply inner-directed as well as focused on forces from without. As already noted, more than a little of Levi's sense of grievance was bound up with his feelings about Germany. He remained tormented by traumatic memories from his time in the camp, but the people who belonged to the nation of his oppressors were relatively untroubled in the years after Auschwitz and, in his encounters with them, gave him little if any solace. Had he been able to settle his accounts with the likes of Dr. Pannwitz or Alex the Kapo, perhaps he might have been able to put to rest some of his more turbulent feelings, but no such settlement was to be his. Instead, the perpetuation and intensification of traumatic memories determined that he who had been tortured remained tortured.

A writer in such a condition naturally seeks refuge and relief in his work. Levi was no exception. He was fond of quoting the Yiddish saying "*Ibergekumene tsores iz gut tsu dertseylin*" ("Troubles overcome are good to tell"),[39] and there is no doubt that he looked to writing as a means of overcoming, as well as representing, his troubled past. However, while it is the case that Primo Levi's writings show a high degree of analytic precision and representational power, they generally lack cathartic effect. They are masterly in depicting the physical and moral character of the sufferings they record, but in only rare instances do they resolve such suffering or point to a less anguished future that might lie beyond it. Indeed, in writing as he did about his experiences in the camp, Levi may have deepened his sense of trauma rather than found relief from it. In this respect he faced a dilemma of a particularly demanding and ultimately exhausting kind. Immersed as he was in memory and what he understood to be its obligations and demands on him as a writer, Levi returned time and again to the past, which was the site of his worst and also his richest experiences. Initially, he had looked upon writing as a means of inner liberation, and he had actually begun his first book while still a prisoner in Auschwitz.[40] He saw himself then as a chronicler of a historic crime like none other, and, as both a victim and a witness of that crime, he had dedicated himself to assuring that others would know of its enormity. To the question posed in his first book about whether "it is necessary or good to retain any memory of this exceptional state,"[41] therefore, the only conceivable answer for the author of *Survival in Auschwitz* was an emphatic *yes*.

It is doubtful whether the older writer could have replied with such confidence in the saving powers of memory. Indeed, by the time he came to write the sometimes bitter, sometimes brooding chapters of *The Drowned and the Saved*, Levi evidently had experienced second thoughts, and he shows serious reservations about the quality of his own witness. "Have we—we who have returned—been able to understand and make others understand our experience?" he queries.[42] His answer, implicit in the question itself, is hardly affirmative: "Human memory is a marvelous but fallacious instrument," he writes. "Even under normal conditions a slow degradation is at work, an obfuscation of outlines, a so to speak physiological oblivion, which few memories resist. ... [Therefore] an apology is in order. This very book is drenched in memory; what's more, a distant memory. Thus it draws from a suspect source and must be protected against itself."[43] This is a powerful, revisionary turn, and it reveals that the young Levi who had lived, as he put it, "in order to tell"[44] is succeeded by an older, sadder author who evidently came to doubt the accuracy and the efficacy of his own tellings.

The younger Levi spoke of "the liberating joy of recounting [his] story,"[45] and narrated it with the self-confidence of an author who felt himself in full command of his expressive powers. The older Levi, however, showed himself to be increasingly uneasy about the testimony of survivors and even about the reliability of memory itself. "The greater part of the witnesses," he notes, "have ever more blurred and stylized memories."[46] Moreover, in his view they have written their accounts out of only partial knowledge. Those who knew the full horror of Nazism either did not survive their ordeals or were so incapacitated by them as to be rendered all but speechless. Thus in his last years Levi seems to have faced the melancholy conclusion that the fundamental reality of his life—the full truth of Auschwitz itself—might never be accurately known.

Levi devoted his last book to extended analyses of the causes and implications of this disturbing prospect. *The Drowned and the Saved* exhibits a pronounced anxiety about the drift and distortion of memory and consequently about the obfuscation and falsification of the past. Levi attributes this worrisome development in part to those who would choose to forget the past or those who manipulate it in intentionally dishonest ways, but a substantial part of his worry seems self-directed and points to the troubling implication that he may have come to regard himself as a compromised witness. The theme of moral ambiguity that he develops with such forcefulness and precision in "The Gray Zone" is one from which he did not absent himself, and while there is no evidence that points to Levi's actual complicity as an inmate of Auschwitz, he nevertheless appears to have seen himself as in some way complicit: "An infernal order such as National Socialism exercises a frightful power of corruption, against which it is difficult to guard oneself. It degrades its victims and makes them similar to itself, because it needs both great and small complicities. To resist it requires a truly solid moral armature."[47] "The Gray Zone" clearly indicates that Levi did not believe there were very many who possessed such moral defenses or who, in the depraved condition of the camps, could manage to keep them intact. "We are all mirrored in Rumkowski," he wrote; "his ambiguity is ours, it is our second nature."[48] He includes himself in this judgment: "I had also deeply assimilated the principal rule of the place, which made it mandatory that you take care of yourself first of all."[49] This realization introduces into his last writings a note of self-indictment and, with it, a burden of shame that must have been excruciating for him to bear.

Misery, anguish, exhaustion, guilt, and shame—these were part of the legacy of the Lagers for many of those who survived them. Liberation brought physical but not necessarily psychological freedom. "One suffered," Levi wrote, "because of the reacquired consciousness of having been diminished."[50] In addition, one suffered from tortuous feelings of guilt. "What guilt? When all was over, the awareness emerged that we had not done anything, or not enough, against the system into which we had been absorbed. . . . [The survivor] feels accused and judged, compelled to justify and defend himself." Defend himself against what? "Self-accusation, or the accusation of having failed in terms of human solidarity, . . . of having omitted to offer help, . . . a human word, advice, even just a listening ear."[51] Guilt also accompanied the troubling suspicion that one survived in place of another—"of a man more generous, more sensitive, more useful, wiser, worthier of living than you. You cannot block out such feelings: you examine yourself, you review your memories. . . . No, you find no obvious transgressions, you did not usurp anyone's place. . . . [Nevertheless, shame] gnaws at us; it has nestled deeply like a woodworm; although unseen from the outside, it gnaws and rasps."[52] The late poem "The Survivor" expresses the agony of the former camp inmate haunted by these corrosive feelings, but their sharpest elaboration is found in the essay "Shame," from which I have been quoting. Like nothing else in Levi's work, it shows us the author turning against himself in a manner that was harsh to the point of being self-punishing:

> The "saved" of the Lager were not the best, those predestined to do good, the bearers of a message: what I have seen and lived through proved the exact contrary. . . . The worst survived, the selfish, the violent, the insensitive, the collaborators of the "gray zone," the spies. . . . The worst survived, that is, the fittest; the best all died. . . .
>
> I must repeat: we, the survivors, are not the true witnesses. . . . We . . . are not only an exiguous but also an anomalous

minority: we are those who by their prevarications or abilities or good luck did not touch bottom. Those who did so . . . have not returned to tell about it or have returned mute, but they are . . . the complete witnesses, the ones whose deposition would have a general significance. They are the rule, we are the exception.[53]

If one takes this passage as indicative of Levi's final sense of himself and his work, the conclusions one draws are extremely unsettling. On both moral and literary grounds, the author of *The Drowned and the Saved* seems to call into serious question the value of the testimony offered in his earlier books. The survivors are not the true witnesses, Levi comes to acknowledge, but "speak in their stead, by proxy." The story they have to tell is "a discourse 'on behalf of third parties,'" not the narrative of an experience personally lived through. Those who touched bottom remained submerged, their stories unspoken and unheard; as for those who survived and have attempted to speak for them, "I cannot see any proportion," Levi concluded, "between the privilege [of surviving] and its outcome. . . . We who were favored by fate tried . . . to recount not only our fate but that of the others, the drowned; but . . . the destruction brought to an end, the job completed, was not told by anyone."[54]

On the evidence of these words, it seems clear that in writing his last book Levi suffered from a belated sense of his own inadequacies as a survivor-witness. Was he moved as well to call into question the value of his survival itself? We shall probably never know for certain. The testimony offered by his friends is often contradictory and inconclusive. One searches for definitive answers in the author's published writings and does not find them. It would be useful if there were other sources that might hold clues to the nature of Levi's thinking in the final period of his life and perhaps illuminate his end, but to date no such sources have turned up. And so the question—as crucial as it is troubling—remains open.

It was my privilege to be a friend of Primo Levi in his later years, and I carried on an active correspondence with him from 1980 until just days before his death in April 1987. These exchanges with him cannot by themselves resolve the matter of his death, but some of these letters are helpful for what they might tell us about one troubled side of Primo Levi's life in his last years.

In a letter to me of September 15, 1985, Levi referred to his "essay-book" in progress in these terms: "Its title will be I SOM-MERSI E I SALVATI (The Drowned & the Saved), a silent quotation from Dante (Inf. xx: 3), to be understood ironically: the Saved are not the ones that deserved salvation in the theological sense, but rather the shrewd, the violent, the collaborators." Levi himself was not a brutal or cunning man and does not belong in this ironic category of the undeserving "saved," but he did manage to outlast Auschwitz and later in life came to suffer for it. The suffering was compounded by the anguish of intermittent depressions. When I saw him in Italy in the spring of 1981 he was in good spirits, but when I proposed a second visit a year and a half later his condition had altered. In a letter of January 14, 1983, he wrote as follows:

> Your proposal to come and see me in the next months has moved me, but has caught me off-balance. I hope, I *do* hope, to be soon in a condition to meet you and to speak with you, but I am suffering now from an episode of depression (not my first one; I suppose they are a heritage from the Lager). I hope you never experienced such an alteration of the soul; it is painful and thought-hampering, it prevents me not only to write but also to drive or to travel. Naturally I am under medi-cal care, but I cannot tell how long it will last. . . . Will you excuse me? Perhaps when you are in Europe I'll be OK again, but I cannot foresee anything nor make programs.

It is generally known that Levi suffered from episodes of depres-sion, but I know of no other document in which he associates this affliction with his time in the camp. Precisely how he understood this connection is unclear, but it is significant that, some four decades after his liberation, Levi saw Auschwitz as continuing to have such an overwhelmingly negative, debilitating effect on his life.

Whatever the benefits of the medical treatment he received, the condition of lassitude and creative paralysis that Levi describes did not pass quickly. On April 23, 1983, he wrote me: "My condition of general tiredness has slightly improved, but I am not yet satisfied. I experience a difficulty in concentrating, and especially in writing. Rarely did I wish something so intensively as to recover quickly my normal condition." This particular episode of depression lasted for some seven months and then, at the end of May, lifted. He wrote me on August 3, 1983: "One feels as [if] re-born! Although I live now quite normally, I am short of ideas, and for the moment my activity is reduced to a desultory collaboration with the local newspaper."

Shortly afterwards Levi began writing the essays that would constitute *The Drowned and the Saved*. He worked well and by September 1985 had completed six of the ten or twelve essays he had originally scheduled for the book (letter of September 15, 1985). He added two more pieces (the published volume actually was to include a total of eight essays) and, on January 16, 1986, he wrote me in generally buoyant spirits, "Exactly today I have handed to Einaudi my book of essays." Levi originally intended this book as a sociology of camp life (letter of May 8, 1985), but however we may value that aspect of it, we are moved to read his last book today in other terms—as a profound self-portrait of a Holocaust survivor as well as testimony of the author's farewell to writing. In the same letter in which he mentioned that he had just submitted the manuscript to his publisher, Levi typed out for me an English translation of his poem "The Survivor." The opening lines, from Coleridge's *The Rime of the Ancient Mariner*, stand as an epigraph to *The Drowned and the Saved*:

Since then, at an uncertain hour,
That agony returns:
And till my ghastly tale is told,
This heart within me burns.

There is no doubt that Levi identified with the Ancient Mariner. The figure of the spectral storyteller who searches about passionately for listeners epitomized for him the writer as a survivor-witness bound to recount his experience of extraordinary events. The syndrome of the survivor who is a compulsive narrator, however, is a highly problematic one, for it repeatedly returns the storyteller to the memory of his traumatic past without relieving him of it. It also exposes him to the peril of urgently telling a tale that others may not want to hear. Such a writer faces a triple jeopardy: through his tellings and retellings, he may exhaust the propellant charge of his narrative impulse; or he may become exhausted by its demands on him; or he may suffer the rebuff that comes with the sense that he is not reaching his intended listeners. To some degree, Levi suffered at the end of his life from all three of these consequences. In addition, he suffered from a guilt that only other survivors can properly understand.

Levi must have written *The Drowned and the Saved*, at least in part, to quiet this guilt, but it was not to be quieted. He thought he had written a "harsh" book and did not expect it would reach a broad audience (letter of June 30, 1986), but in fact it found a sizable and receptive readership in Italy. Nevertheless, Levi was disquieted by what he took to be the futility of his efforts. As he wrote his friend Dan Vittorio Segre, "The trouble is that the people who read and understand this book don't need it and those who need it don't understand." In contemplating these words after Levi's death, Segre thought that "his end, the manner of his end, came either because he could not speak anymore, or could not be understood."[55]

There were other complicating factors—too many to shoulder easily. Levi described some of these to me in a letter of July 30, 1986: "Our family situation has suddenly worsened. Last Monday my mother had a stroke, and now she is in hospital. . . . The future is completely obscure, but, at her age (91) the hopes of a recovery are practically null." He concluded the letter with these words: "Forgive my brevity. Hope to be more tranquil and extensive next time, if things clear."

Things did not clear but, on the contrary, evidently worsened. Several months passed without any word reaching me from Italy. Then I received the following letter, dated March 29, 1987:

Dear Alvin,

Thank you for your letter of March 13, and for the fine essay enclosed. Yes, in fact we have been out of touch for a while: it is my fault, or at least mine was the missing link. My family has been struck twice, and things at home are going pretty badly: my mother, 92, is in a bed paralyzed for ever, I came home yesterday from a hospital where I underwent a serious surgical operation; but mainly, as a consequence of all the above, I am suffering from a severe depression, and I am struggling at no avail to escape it. Please forgive me for being so short; the mere fact of writing a letter is a trial for me, but the will to recover is strong. Let us see what the next months will bring to all of us, but my present situation is the worst I ever experienced, Auschwitz included.

Best wishes for your summer trip in Europe, and warmest regards to all your dear family and to you.
Primo

This letter reached me on April 9, 1987. Two days later I learned that Primo Levi was dead.

The death of a great writer leaves a gap in consciousness that we do not know how to fill. We pay tribute to the dead and offer other forms of personal testimony and public respect, but whatever the ceremonial and therapeutic value of these gestures, we recognize that they do not suffice. When, as in this case, the death appears to have been self-inflicted, we are moved as well to search for explanations. Primo Levi anticipated such a move and, in *The Monkey's Wrench*, provided a cautionary warning against it: "When a person dies . . . afterward everybody says they saw it coming. . . . After the disaster they all had to speak their piece. . . . Obviously, if a person dies . . . there has to be a reason, but that doesn't mean there was only one, or if there was, that it's possible to discover it."[56]

During his lifetime Primo Levi accumulated a surplus of pain, and it would be unwise to attribute his death to any single cause. There is no doubt that as a result of his wartime experiences he suffered the torment of traumatic recollections and that through his writings he sought both clarity and relief. It is evident today that he found more of the former than the latter. In terms of his literary achievements, the results of his efforts were enormous and are sure to be lasting. In terms of the cost to his spiritual and psychic well being, there are few among us with imaginations large enough to understand the extent of his inner suffering. In the end, the pain and anguish of his life were simply too great and apparently overwhelmed him. His books remain—an unmatched record of troubles encountered and overcome and of still other troubles too vast for the survivor to withstand.

EIGHT

Surviving Survival:
Elie Wiesel and Imre Kertész

Our stay there planted time bombs within us. From time to time one of them explodes. And then we are nothing but suffering, shame, and guilt. . . . One of these bombs will undoubtedly bring about madness. It's inevitable. —ELIE WIESEL

As should be clear from the preceding chapters, a close reading of Jean Améry and Primo Levi shows a significant strain of authorial doubt regarding the efficacy of Holocaust testimony. Both writers produced exceptionally important work about the nature and impact of the Nazi crimes against the Jews. At the end of their careers, however, Améry and Levi both came to believe their writings lacked decisive effect, if not, indeed, were fated to fail altogether. Other survivor-writers have recorded similar moments of doubt but ultimately have avoided becoming despondent. This chapter will focus attention on two of these writers—Elie Wiesel and Imre Kertész—and inquire into what has kept them from succumbing to the sense of futility that oppressed Améry and Levi and has enabled them to continue writing into their eightieth year and beyond.

Elie Wiesel's dedication to preserving and transmitting memory of the Holocaust has been fundamental to shaping his life's work as a writer, teacher, and public intellectual of global reach.

Wiesel's contributions to the literature of testimony are so seminal as to make it virtually impossible to consider this body of writings without attending to his books and essays. Central to the author's large and still growing corpus are the figure of the witness and the imperative to remember: ". . . our deep conviction," he writes in "Art and Culture after the Holocaust," is "that anyone who does not commit himself to active remembering is an accomplice of the executioner, for he betrays the dead by forgetting them and their testimony."[1] It was out of such conviction that the young Wiesel wrote his now famous memoir of Auschwitz and Buchenwald and that the mature author has produced most of the books that have followed it. In "Why I Write," he declares: "The only role I [have] sought is that of witness. . . . I knew the story had to be told. Not to transmit an experience is to betray it; this is what Jewish tradition teaches us."[2] More than anything else, fidelity to this tradition, and especially to its injunctions to remember, has animated and defined Wiesel as a writer and a Jew (in his case, the two are inseparable).

At the same time, Wiesel, like Améry and Levi, has experienced moments of dejection, stemming from the belief that the public at large is simply not interested in absorbing what he has had to say. One hears that downcast note in many of his writings, including, astonishingly, his very first book, which includes these lines at its close: "Today, ten years after Buchenwald, I realize the world forgets. . . . The past has been erased, buried. . . . Books no longer command the power they once did. Those who yesterday held their tongues will keep their silence tomorrow."[3] Most readers of *Night* will not know these lines, for they do not appear in the English translation of *Un di velt hot geshvign* (originally published in Yiddish). Those who read this text will discover that, even as he was writing a book that was destined to assume canonical status within the corpus of testimonial literature, Wiesel expressed, right from the start, a sense of pessimism about the efficacy of such writing. Some of that pessimism was rooted in personal doubts about his abilities as a writer. Were his literary powers sufficient to describe the extremity of experience he had known? It troubled him that they might not be. His gravest doubts, however, concerned his audience: for even if he were to prove capable as a writer, how many people would really care to hear his tale? Not nearly enough, he feared.

"Was it not a mistake to testify," he asks in "One Generation After." He answers, rather forlornly, "Nothing has been learned; Auschwitz has not even served as warning."[4] The conclusions that Wiesel then draws from these melancholy thoughts parallel similar conclusions one finds in the late writings of Améry and Levi: "If the witness happens to be a storyteller, he will be left with a sense of impotence and guilt. He was wrong to have forced himself upon others, to have badgered a world wishing to take no notice. He was wrong to have thrown open the doors of the sanctuary in flames; people did not look. Worse: many looked and did not see. Thus, writing itself is called into question."[5]

These are sober, dispiriting thoughts and inevitably lead to the question: what, in fact, has kept Wiesel writing over the years? No doubt a number of things, but four in particular stand out as critical. One, no doubt, is temperamental and is a consequence of Elie Wiesel being who he is—an individual who thinks and acts as he does as a result of a particular intellectual bent, emotional makeup, and spiritual disposition. Another stems from the fact that he is, by training, loyalty, and commitment, a learned and religiously observant Jew and understands reality within Jewish historical and conceptual frameworks. A third involves his aesthetic choices. And a fourth involves his particular audience and the nature of their response to his work.

The temperamental, or personal, factor is reflected almost everywhere in Wiesel's oeuvre. One can see it, for instance, in the novel *The Testament*, when the book's central character, Paltiel Kossover, declares, "I am writing because I have no choice."[6] Wiesel also has had no choice. Given his inherent need to write, along with his particular history as a Holocaust survivor, he knows he has been charged to testify about the nature of his experiences under Nazi rule and, thereby, to combat forgetting. In this regard, there is little to distinguish him from Améry and Levi. In one crucial respect, however, Wiesel stands out from these other authors: unlike them, he has located the source of this charge to write within Jewish religious traditions and identifies his vocation as a writer with the imperatives of Judaism itself. In his own words: "To be a Jew . . . means: to testify. To bear witness to what is, and to what is no longer. . . . For the contemporary Jewish writer, there can be no theme more human, no project more universal."[7]

Améry and Levi would not have put it in these terms. For while each identified as a Jew, they were far more the products of secular Enlightenment culture than of Jewish culture, and the largest questions they asked regarding the Nazi crimes pointed to a crisis in the rationalist and humanist traditions of Western modernity, which had shaped them. In their own ways, each reflected sensitively on what Améry called "the necessity and impossibility of being a Jew,"[8] but neither felt a sustained need to plumb their wartime experiences for deep Jewish meaning. Their attention was directed elsewhere: to the causes and consequences of Nazi terror, to its political, cultural, and psychological origins and ramifications, to questions of individual and collective guilt and responsibility, to complex issues of moral compromise and ethical collapse: in sum, to the many ways that Hitler's Germany undermined the foundations of Western civilization as they knew it and valued it. These authors felt both damaged and diminished by what they had suffered in the murder camps and feared the damage was permanent. It might be mitigated but only if those responsible for the Nazi crimes owned up to their culpability and thereby helped the victims of those crimes find a necessary degree of intellectual clarity and inner peace. As the late writings of Améry and Levi reveal, both authors required and actively sought understanding and justice, which they felt could only be obtained through a difficult but necessary engagement with people in Germany who would truthfully confront their country's past. Yet they were disappointed and even brought to the point of despair by what they saw as postwar Germany's unwillingness to engage in such a reckoning in a forthright way.

These concerns appear in Wiesel's work as well, but at least in his strongest writings, they are not primary. Rather than seeking redress from the Germans, Wiesel's most sustained and impassioned quarrels have been with the God of Israel, whose ostensible absence during the years when the people of Israel was being subjugated and slaughtered has been an inexplicable mystery and an intolerable affront. To pierce that mystery and reply to that affront has been among his life's major goals. Such theological issues play virtually no role in the writings of Améry and Levi, both of whom were basically not religious and sought explanations for their wartime experiences within the major categories of European thought. They failed to find them, for Auschwitz defied and subverted the rational and ethical traditions of the culture that had formed them. In Améry's memorable formulation, "no bridge led from death in Auschwitz to *Death in Venice*."[9]

Wiesel's cultural formation has been markedly different. It is true that from his postwar years in France until today, he has absorbed influences from European literature and philosophy, as well as from some of the sacred writings of Hindu religious thought, but in his soul of souls Wiesel is fundamentally the product of another world—Hungarian hasidism and its traditions of learning and piety—and consequently he has framed the challenges posed by the Holocaust in radically different terms. The crisis he has faced is not, in the first place, one of thought, at least in modern or Cartesian terms, but of belief. It arises not so much from the silence of the Germans but from the silence of God. In book after book he has sought to probe that silence and make audible the spiritual pain and dilemmas that accompany it. His quest has taken him on a broad search through Jewish religious texts and has enabled him to discover within those texts a language to carry on an impassioned, at times confrontational, engagement with God. It has been a demanding and difficult quest, but it has energized and directed him as a writer for almost six decades now.

It has also taught him he is not alone, for the questions he has been driven to ask situate Wiesel within a tradition of God-seeking and God-wrestling that dates back as far as the story of the *Akedah* and the torments of Job. "Everything seems to bring me back to Jewish memory," he acknowledges. "Everyone I meet is an old acquaintance."[10] Hence Wiesel has discovered options as a writer that were largely closed off to Améry and Levi, such as the turn to midrash, which has enabled him to interpret later experience against earlier. His questions remain, and he may still conclude that "if God is the answer, it must be the wrong answer," but he knows that in asking the question, he is keeping alive a tradition of interrogation that validates who he is: "To me, the Jew and his questioning are one."[11]

As here, Wiesel has made certain aesthetic choices as a writer that set him apart from the other writers we have been considering and provided him with resources to continue that they lacked. Both Améry and Levi tried their hand at fiction, for instance, but their major work was done in the more personal forms of memoir and essayistic reflection. They excelled in these forms, but in using them they could gain little, if any, distance from themselves. If they wrote about trauma, for example, it was their trauma, and writing about it to some degree must have retraumatized them all over again. When Améry declares, and Levi repeats, that "he who has been tortured remains tortured,"[12] he is referring to his own experiences as a victim of Nazi atrocities, even as his insights into the phenomenology of torture extend beyond to all who have been subjected to such cruelty. What makes such writing so vivid, but also so costly to the writer, is precisely the subjective or autobiographical element. Because it is directly rooted in personal experience, writing of this kind can achieve a level of testimonial authority that other kinds of writing may not readily reach. But it does so at a high price to the writer. "After Auschwitz, everything brings us back to Auschwitz," as Wiesel has put it.[13] That is especially true for those who write about their camp experiences in personal, highly confessional modes.

As a first-person memoir, Wiesel's first book was written in such a mode, but in his later works he has often turned to fiction and thereby found a means to develop many of the same themes that first appeared in *Night* by using voices other than his own. The advantages gained by writing in less personal literary genres can be saving. Human pain may still be forcefully registered, but it is imagined now as someone else's pain: Elisha's in *Dawn*, Gregor's in *The Gates of the Forest*, Elhanan Rosenbaum's in *The Forgotten*, and so on. Like so many of Wiesel's books, these novels are rooted in aspects of the author's personal history, but in refracting that history in fictional, and not autobiographical, terms, they rely on the development of literary characters, who are no less true for being imagined.

Wiesel's protagonists are often intent on searching out ways to return to life after a prolonged and punishing encounter with death. Engaged in missions of retrieval, they pursue traces of their former lives, seeking to rescue, if only for memory, whatever might remain of a past they cherished but know has been destroyed. Along the way, they frequently intermingle with, and sometimes begin to resemble, madmen and mystics, beggars and dreamers, poets and mutes, children and grave-diggers. What virtually all of these figures have in common is that they are largely pre-rational or post-rational types—"messengers of God," as Wiesel sometimes calls them. By populating his fictional worlds with these figures, and investing them with deep intuitive insights, Wiesel has opened his writings to a range of imaginative intensities—madness, obsession, revery, fantasy, parable, paradox, and prayer—that comprise a spiritual vocabulary basically unknown to Améry and Levi. One prizes these latter writers for the lucid and disciplined ways they described and attempted to understand Auschwitz, but lucidity could take them only so far, and at some point they reached the mind's limits, beyond which they could not advance. Add to this cognitive impasse the discouragements they felt in believing their intellectual and literary efforts simply did not matter to the people who most needed to hear them, and one can understand how they came to assess their work as ultimately irrelevant. Of course, we know it was anything but that, and we hold them in esteem for their writings, without which our understanding of Auschwitz and its aftermath would be greatly diminished. Nevertheless, in their last years Améry and Levi both felt extraneous to the younger generations in Europe and believed themselves to be anachronistic, marginal figures, who tried their best but, in the end, went largely unheard.

As noted earlier, Wiesel has also experienced a sense of futility about his work and has sometimes expressed remorse for writing at all: "The survivor . . . has tried to bear witness; it was all in vain," he confesses at one point. And at another: "The witnesses would speak," but "to no avail."[14] At such times, Wiesel has been tempted to forego speaking and writing altogether. To give in to silence, however, would be to surrender his obligation to speak for the dead and thereby let the executioner have the last word. That would be an act of both betrayal and despair, and "to be a Jew means not to despair, even when it seems justified."[15] What has kept Wiesel going, then, is bound up with his particular spiritual orientation toward both his Jewish identity and his writing. "Ultimately to write is an act of faith,"[16] he has said, and through the exercise of this faith, he has maintained a conviction that "the call of the dying will be heard; if not today, then tomorrow. . . . A testament is never lost."[17] That belief runs deeper than doubt in Wiesel's work and has given him his charge as a writer-witness.

Following that commitment to making his testimony heard, Wiesel has had an uncommonly productive career, publishing some fifty books over the past half a century and presenting hundreds of public lectures to audiences around the world. It is no exaggeration to say that, in these and other ways, he has probably done more than any other single writer of the postwar period to educate vast numbers of people about the Jewish fate under Nazi rule. The winner of the Nobel Prize for Peace and numerous other international honors and awards, it is also no exaggeration to say that Elie Wiesel enjoys a degree of global recognition and public acclaim unrivaled by that of any other Jew alive today. This prominence is the result of a number of factors. One is the fact that Wiesel years ago decided to settle in America and has won his fame, in no small part, as a consequence of the openness of people in his adopted country to a broad range of cultural representations of the Holocaust—an openness that he himself has helped to create and sustain.

While Americans, on the whole, may know less about the history of the Holocaust than Europeans, they have been far less resistant than people in Europe to recognize the Holocaust as a catastrophe that specifically targeted Jews. And with respect to the Jews, Americans are less burdened by a guilt-laden history than most Europeans. Many are also more closely identified with their Christian faith and consequently are moved by writers whose struggles with questions of religious belief resonate powerfully with them. For these and other reasons, they have embraced Elie Wiesel more fully than Europeans have embraced most Jewish writers who survived the Nazi death camps and remained on the continent after 1945 to write about their wartime experiences. This question of national reception may be one more means to help explain why some writers have come to feel a heavy sense of futility about their work whereas others have kept their sense of authorial purpose and meaning alive. Numerous factors lift or depress a writer's self-image and creative powers; acceptance or marginalization by one's country is surely one of these.

Consider the following. Jean Améry, born in Austria, continued to write in his native German while living as an exile in French-speaking Brussels. His books originated in radio broadcasts heard in Germany, but he never won as broad a reception among Germans as he had hoped for; and, especially in his later years, he came to the melancholy conclusion that his testimony had failed to reach those who most needed to confront it. In his later years, Primo Levi won considerable fame in Italy and beyond, but he, too, came to believe that what he had to say was growing more and more distant from the concerns of the younger generations. Toward the end, he felt negligible, out of sync, unheeded. In the cases of both of these authors, Elie Wiesel's remarks about suicide seem sorrowfully apt: "Nothing makes a survivor despair more than knowing that he is useless."[18] Sadly, at the end of their lives, Améry and Levi felt they had been rendered more or less useless.

And what of Wiesel? No one who had been in the Nazi camps and survived to tell about it has shown more tenacity or greater productivity as a writer than he. Given his remarkable literary output, which has won him world-wide acclaim, he has not at all been marginalized or made to feel useless. And yet a brooding sense of dejection and even of despair sometimes registers in his books. These low feelings typically come to the fore in Wiesel's work when speech is threatened by silence and memory by oblivion. The tensions between these opposite pulls produce characters who are memorable for the linguistic impairments that often afflict them.

Consider, for instance, Elhanan Rosenbaum, in *The Forgotten* (1992).[19] A survivor of the horrors of the war in the Carpathians, he is living in New York as a retired professor. Deeply melancholy and chronically depressed, Elhanan is the victim of a past that continues to trouble him. He is also the victim of a strange brain disorder that is eroding his memory. "What is man deprived of memory?" he asks. "Not even a shadow . . ." (p. 247). A witness to atrocities that he is unable to reconcile with his moral beliefs as a Jew, he is strongly committed to the idea that "to forget is to abandon, to forget is to repudiate" (p. 3); nevertheless, he is forgetting, and he seems unable to prevent the progressive attenuation of the past.

In an effort to save whatever he can of his former life, Elhanan urges his son Malkiel to return to Feherfalu, his native village in Transylvania, and learn what he can about events there during the war years. By immersing himself in his father's past, Malkiel becomes an agent of memory and also a would-be healer of memory's wounds. In fact, though, he comes to learn that "a memory transfusion" (p. 151) from father to son is impossible: Malkiel can no more make his father's past his own than he can save him from the disease that is destroying his mind. What he can do is link himself to his ancestral origins through discoveries he makes about the wartime experiences of his father and grandfather. As he brings to light truths about his family's history that he never knew before, Malkiel emerges more fully as the elder Rosenbaum's son—not the incarnation his father's memory but, in his own right, a witness for the witnesses who are either already gone or are fast becoming mute.

As in many of his books, Wiesel is intent in *The Forgotten* on exploring the urgency and moral efficacy of Jewish storytelling. His aim is to give a voice to the voiceless, to tell the story of the dead and to get others to listen. It is unclear, however, whether he believes this is an aim he can actually fulfill. Does he have the power to give the dead their voice, and, if he does, are there those who truly want to hear it? This question appears as early as Wiesel's first book, *Night*, and over the years has become an increasingly urgent one. It is represented in *The Forgotten* through the book's two most memorable characters. One of them is Hershel, the last remaining Jewish gravedigger of Feherfalu, whose gift for telling stories is a result of his proximity to the dead. Hershel has forgotten nothing of the past. Indeed, the dead are his extended family, and his intimacy with them enlivens his memory and animates his voice. Elhanan, by contrast, represents post-Holocaust Jewish consciousness in its most brooding aspect—the storyteller anxiously caught on the edge of narrative incapacity. Unable to bridge the gap between the demands of memory and the impoverishments of his language, Elhanan is a despairing figure. Progressively enervated by the dead who inhabit him, he wonders whether "forgetting would be worse than dying?" (p. 113).

There are virtues to forgetting, as Nietzsche knew and as this novel makes clear in its climactic moments, but it is unlikely that the author of *The Forgotten*, whose entire literary corpus is a testament to memory, has now become a Nietzschean and wishes to embrace such virtues. Rather, one recognizes in Wiesel's work concerns of the kind that Primo Levi expressed in *The Drowned and the Saved* when he wrote about a slow degradation of the historical sense and the "physical oblivion which few memories [can] resist." Elhanan prays that his own memories be spared such oblivion; but by book's end it is apparent that his prayer will not be answered and that his story will only be preserved, if at all, through the intellectual and spiritual labors of his son. That is to put an exceedingly heavy burden of responsibility on the generation of the sons, however; and, as *The Forgotten* reveals through the note of inevitability sounded in its very title, it is far from certain that the successor generation will be able or willing to preserve a past that it may not feel to be its own.

What, then, will ultimately come of Jewish memory? More than any other, it is this question that seems to lie anxiously at the core of Elie Wiesel's writing. Indeed, if one had to identify a unifying concern that runs throughout his copious and diverse oeuvre, it would be a preoccupation with memory—its historical power and necessity, its moral and ethical obligations, but also its frailties, weaknesses, and vulnerability to distortion and exploitation. More than most writers, Wiesel has seen it as his task to keep the past alive, both as a tribute to the dead and as a warning to the living. "If there is a single theme that dominates all my writing, all my obsessions," he has remarked, "it is that of memory—because I fear forgetfulness as much as hatred and death."[20] This obsession and the fears that attend it are taken up once again in *A Mad Desire to Dance* (2009), the author's most recent novel.[21]

Although not a Holocaust novel as such, *A Mad Desire to Dance* carries familiar echoes of Wiesel's earlier Holocaust-related books. And yet in at least two significant respects, it marks a notable departure from some of his previous work: the lean, reticent style of narration of *Night* and some of the author's other early books gives way in this novel to non-stop, at times manically expansive talk; and the talk is propelled far more by therapeutic imperatives than testimonial ones. Thus, while the narrative often returns to the experiences of the war years, it does so chiefly to seek relief from the torments of traumatic memory and not primarily to advance the broader aims of historical and moral awareness. The primary focus is on the main character's quest for personal healing and consolation.

A Mad Desire to Dance is overwhelmingly a talk novel. And much of the talk is about madness. On the first page alone, "mad" or its noun counterparts appear twelve times. Two pages later, the same words are cited ten times. Their variations—"crazy," "disturbed," "insane," "nuts," "unbalanced," etc.—recur throughout the novel. As the reader quickly learns, the protagonist, Doriel Waldman, "takes refuge in madness" and seems unable or unwilling to escape it. His talk—to himself, his psychotherapist, various people he meets on his travels, to the God whom he ardently wants to understand—is frequently overwrought and not always intelligible. Doriel's talk is the product of unsteady nerves, and the reader needs steady nerves to absorb it.

Explorations of madness appear in many of Wiesel's previous books, but not in the extended, clinical way they do in this novel. One is therefore moved to ask: Who is Doriel Waldman, and what ails him? Doriel doesn't know himself, but as we learn over the course of his therapy sessions with his psychoanalyst, Thérèse Goldschmidt, he is about sixty years old, single, a loner, doesn't work, can't sleep, is anxious, touchy, suspicious, nervous, frightened, often angry and out of sorts, and generally unwell. Though attracted to women, he is also afraid of them, and normal erotic desires seem to elude him. As for fathering a child: "I always believed that my past and the state it left me in don't allow me to beget life" (p. 226).

Born in 1936, Doriel survived the Holocaust by hiding with his father in a small Polish village. His mother, whom he barely knew, was an active member of the resistance and rarely saw her family during this period. Doriel's brother and sister were murdered in Poland. Though his parents survived the war, they died soon after in a car crash. Brought to America as a young orphan by a faithful uncle, Doriel looks to make a new start in the new land, but he suffers from causes that he cannot decipher, is basically dysfunctional, and so seeks the professional guidance of Dr. Goldschmidt. He hopes that she can help him understand "the language and logic of my illness" (p. 259).

Elaborate reports on Doriel's therapy sessions with his analyst and her extended notes are artfully developed and give the novel much of its formal structure and thematic interest. During his often contentious meetings with Dr. Goldschmidt, Doriel uncovers long-submerged family secrets, including one about an illicit affair his mother may have had with a fellow resistance fighter. This formerly repressed information, he comes to understand, has contributed to his emotional problems and hampered his relationships with women. Once disclosed, the insight proves liberating. Following termination of his therapy, Doriel comes more confidently into his own, courts and marries a woman, changes his name, and at book's end learns he is about to father a child. In the concluding line, this once joyless, inhibited man even expresses "a mad desire to dance" (p. 274).

Inasmuch as this book is largely a narrative about the mind turned in on itself, struggling with the psychic burdens of guilt, shame, solitude, and fear, recourse to remedial talk comes as no surprise. In our age, after all, scores of novelists have looked to the methods of psychoanalysis to illuminate human experience. But because Wiesel has tended to concentrate on the spiritual and moral dimensions of tormented souls rather than the clinical or psychological ones, this novel is startling for the emphasis it places on the therapeutic. It sends the reader in search of a sub-text that might help to explain what is going on in the supertext.

Here is a clue worth following. When Doriel engages Dr. Gold-schmidt for therapy sessions, he says, "Doctor, I'm confused. I'm your patient and you're my only hope. All my real-life or imaginary stories, all these burdens full of remorse and guilt—it is to you that I show them. Tell me what I should do with them" (p. 225). Wiesel is a master storyteller, and in past books his characters have typically known what to do with their tales. They search out sympathetic listeners for them; or, failing to find such listeners, they address them to God; or, failing to find a way to God, they retreat into silence. Far from being seen as a form of illness in Wiesel's copious oeuvre, madness is often related to muteness, an existential condition imposed from without on a witness to atrocity who tells his story but is not listened to. The etiology of such pain was more clearly conveyed by the original Yiddish title of Wiesel's memoir—*Un di velt hot geshvign (And the World Was Silent)*—than by the more abstract English title, *Night*.

Doriel's "madness" is characterized by many years of silent suffering, which is then broken by a superabundance of nervous talk. The novel suggests that his disturbance is primarily rooted in repression of some version of the Freudian family romance and therefore amenable to treatment by a capable analyst. But buried within the book is a brief but telling vignette that offers another explanation:

Let's go back to the last survivor in my town. Do you know why and how he lost the power of speech? When he returned from the camps, he decided to roam the world and tell people about the unspeakable; he hoped to lift the world from its torpor and from an indifference that could lead to its own annihilation. He spoke, he spoke everywhere, to the point of exhaustion. . . . At first people listened to him. . . . Then they turned their backs on him. . . . And since then, he has never uttered another word. (pp. 249–50)

The utterer of too many words, Doriel is the mirror image of this man, who is referred to as "the last Jew." As a young boy hidden in a small Polish town, Doriel was spared the massacres that overtook so many others, but the wounds he bears in the postwar years are similar to those of other survivors. As such, these are not merely psychological wounds, but indicative of what Primo Levi knowingly called the "survivor's disease." As Wiesel has shown in some of his other books, this much more encompassing affliction is a wound to human definition itself, for which proven therapies are still to be devised.

From the publication of *Night* until today—a span of half a century—Wiesel has explored the nature of Holocaust victimization and survivorship more persistently and more fully than any other living writer. He sometimes says that he has not yet gone far enough into the complexities of his subject, that still deeper probings need to be undertaken: "I am still tormented by the same anguish: notwithstanding all the books I have written, I have not yet begun."[22] His creativity is at least partly fueled by this dissatisfaction and the urge to do more. Given time, he no doubt will attempt further explorations of the survivor's experiences, even as he questions whether his words will be strong enough and true enough to ever make them fully understandable to others. He has given us much, and yet he is not free of concerns that call the efficacy of writing itself into question, and he worries to this day that, in the end, "the messenger [will be] unable to deliver his message."[23]

Wiesel's disquiet is shared by others, including the Hungarian-Jewish author Imre Kertész who wonders "who is interested in the real survivors and the true problems of surviving?"[24] The problem of living with the "survivor's disease" is often bound up with problems of language: "Consider what happened to language in the twentieth century, what became of words. . . . The first and most shocking discovery made by writers in our time was that language, in the form it came down to us . . . had simply become unsuitable to convey concepts and processes that had once been unambiguous and real."[25] This concern, too, is a shared one. In some of his novels about survivors, for instance, Wiesel reveals just how acute such problems can be by interfering with the speech patterns of his narrators. Elhanan Rosenbaum, anxious about his fading memory and afflicted by aphasia, fears the loss of his ability to speak altogether. Never far from madness, Doriel Waldman suffers intense bouts of paraphasia, causing strange breaks in his thought patterns and making his words seem disjointed and out of control. In these two cases and others, Wiesel's recourse to failing or otherwise impaired speech is meant to be mimetic, conveying by means of linguistic incapacity the idea that normative language is simply inadequate to express the extreme abnormalities suffered by the victims of the Holocaust. Those who survived such experiences and feel impelled to impart them to others often find themselves stymied or blocked. Either they lack the verbal resources to speak effectively or they manage to tell their tales only to find that most people are unwilling to hear them or grant them credence. As they accumulate, these frustrations can begin to feel like terminal failures. If unrelieved, they worsen the "survivor's disease" and intensify the inner sufferings that accompany it. At such moments, the question of how to survive one's own survival brings to the fore the most perilous of all questions: why continue to live at all?

Among those who have reflected most deeply and perceptively on these problems, and also sought new ways to incorporate them in their writing, Imre Kertész stands out. As he reminded an interviewer, "Albert Camus once said that suicide is the only philosophical problem." He added, "I tend to agree. . . . You constantly, constantly think about the idea of suicide—especially if you live under a dictatorship."[26] It was Kertész's misfortune to live under two dictatorships—that of Nazi-occupied Hungary and also that of postwar Hungary under communist regimes. It is a sign of his resilience as a man and his genius as a writer that he not only survived such oppression but found ways to creatively transform it into some of the most stringently honest, if also most demanding, meditations on life under the brands of Hitlerian and Stalinist rule. To his credit, he managed to keep from succumbing to both tyrannies and even to turn the social, psychological, and political disfigurements they caused to high art. But at a cost: "In 1944, they put a yellow star on me, which in a symbolic sense is still there; to this day, I have not been able to remove it."[27]

In recognition of his achievements as a writer under the sign of this star, Kertész was named the recipient of the 2002 Nobel Prize for Literature. And yet despite the fame bestowed upon him, he still remains a relatively unread and underappreciated figure. At the time of his receiving the Nobel award, probably few Americans had ever heard of this Hungarian writer, let alone read his books. Only two of Kertész's novels, *Fatelessness* (1975) and *Kaddish for a Child Not Born* (1990), had been issued in English (both in relatively limited editions by a small academic press). But in Western Europe—and especially in Germany, where he lives most of the year and where all of his books are available in translation—he has enjoyed a wider readership. In his native Hungary, by contrast, Kertész's reception has been mixed. This is partly due to the notion among some of his more nationalistic countrymen that a Jew who writes so frequently and passionately about Auschwitz cannot be a genuine "Hungarian." Indeed, an imposed marginality has shadowed the author for years, and the feelings of rejection, solitariness, pain, and vulnerability that accompany it are indelible aspects of his personal biography as well as recurring themes in his work:

The proletarian dictatorship disliked any mention of the
Holocaust; and since it disliked it, it suppressed such voices
or channeled them into conformist euphemistic clichés. If
anyone was bold enough to think that Auschwitz was the
greatest event for Man since the Crucifixion . . . , and if he
wanted to approach these questions with proper seriousness,
well, then he had to reckon with being condemned to total
loneliness and isolation. His books were printed in a limited
number of copies, if at all, and himself banished to the margins of literary and intellectual life, into the deaf silence of
controlled criticism as into a solitary cell; in other words, his
work was then condemned to death just as he himself had
been condemned to death at one time.[28]

Kertész does not name himself as the author in question in this
passage, but his words clearly reflect bitter personal experience. It
is little wonder, then, that when he is abroad, he feels like a different man: "In foreign countries, I feel at home while, at home, I act
like a stranger."[29] Although Kertész continues to reside part-time
in his native Hungary, his words here and elsewhere echo those
of the exiled writer in search of a coveted but unreachable home-
land. So, like many other European-Jewish writers of his generation, Kertész has looked chiefly to literature for asylum. Whether
he can ultimately find it there remains an open question.

Kertész was born into an assimilated Jewish family in 1929
in Pest. In 1944, he was deported to Auschwitz and then sent to
Buchenwald and Zeitz, a small auxiliary camp of Buchenwald.
He was not yet fifteen years old. His father had already been
pressed into a compulsory labor squad and was killed during a
forced march. His maternal grandparents, and the parents of his
first wife, were murdered by the Nazis. His paternal grandparents
were forcibly relocated and, as a consequence, perished under
the rule of Mátyás Rákosi's communist government.

Following his liberation from Buchenwald, young Kertész returned to Budapest. In the early 1950s, he served in the Hungarian Army for two years prior to trying his hand at journalism. To earn a living, he also wrote for the theater and did librettos for a variety of light operas. Chiefly, though, he has worked as a freelance writer and literary translator over the past half century, during which time he has devoted himself to refining his skills as a fiction writer and essayist, focusing his most serious work on exposing and explaining the sufferings imposed on the individual by totalitarian systems. He sees these regimes as part of a continuum of political oppression, which, far from ending with the defeat of Nazi Germany, extended its reach in the postwar period under Stalinism. Alert to the daily restrictions on life imposed in communist-ruled Hungary, Kertész harbored no illusions about his post-Auschwitz fate. In critical ways, he remained a captive, as did the nation in which he lived. These sober understandings bred in him a skepticism that may have saved him from the fate of those survivor-writers who, he believes, took their lives as a consequence of severe personal disillusionment: "For some time now I have given much thought to the fact that the Holocaust reached its intended victims not only in the concentration camps but also decades later. The liberation of the camps merely postponed the verdict which then those selected for death executed on themselves." He specifically names Paul Celan, Tadeusz Borowski, Jean Améry, and Primo Levi:

> If I confront my fate with theirs, . . . I have to think that I had been helped to get over the past decades obviously by a "society" that after Auschwitz, in the form of the so-called Stalinism, proved that there was no possibility for liberty, liberation, great catharsis, etc. — everything that in more fortunate climates intellectuals, thinkers, philosophers not only spoke of but also obviously believed in; that guaranteed a continuation of a prisoner's life for me. . . . This is clearly the reason

why I had not been affected by a wave of disillusionment that those with similar experience living in freer societies had fled from and which reached their feet first, and however much they tried to speed up their steps, it slowly reached up to their throats.[30]

Living without any illusions of revived freedom, Kertész took it upon himself to write about Auschwitz and Buchenwald in the present tense and to do so as far as possible using a literary language that would reflect the collapse of the pre-Auschwitz humanistic worldview. While writers in Western countries might seek to retrieve or replace that worldview, Kertész has held to a more severely deterministic position: "Nothing has happened since Auschwitz that could reverse or refute Auschwitz."[31] Much of the challenge of Kertész's work is to discover a language that might effectively inscribe that stark vision and, while holding faithfully to it, also find grounds to keep on living.

His first novel, *Sorstalanság* (1975), was retranslated into English and appeared in 2004 under the title *Fatelessness*. The same year saw the publication, also in a new translation, of *Kaddis a meg nem született gyermekért* (1990), now called *Kaddish for an Unborn Child*, and of the novel *Felszámolás* (2003), or *Liquidation*. These three books comprise a fictional trilogy on the trials of living through and after Auschwitz and can be taken as a series of intense meditations on "the situation of a survivor who has tried to survive his own survival."[32]

Kertész insists that *Fatelessness*, which was published in Hungary when he was forty-six years old, is not autobiographical. Since the novel narrates the story of a fifteen-year-old Hungarian Jewish boy's incarceration in Auschwitz, Buchenwald, and Zeitz, though, it clearly draws on personal experience. The narrator, György Köves, an innocent, guileless youngster, tries to accommodate himself to a world whose strangeness he can hardly decipher. Early in the novel, he comes to understand that he is persecuted for his "race," or "Jewishness," but, like other assimilated Hungarian Jews, he "doesn't even know exactly what 'Jewish' is" (p. 35). He believes it is not inherent, a "difference carried within ourselves" (p. 36), but, like the yellow star he is forced to wear, a stigma imposed from without. In any event, it seals his fate and is the cause of his arrest and incarceration in Auschwitz, Buchenwald, and Zeitz. The rest of the novel is unsparing in its description of his sufferings and rapid deterioration in these three camps and focuses on his attempts to make sense of it all. The perspective is unusual, that of a young, baffled teenager who feels he has been "dropped slap in the middle of some crazy play in which I was not entirely acquainted with my role" (p. 57). Phrases like "as best I could tell," "from what I could make out," "from what I could hear," pervade the narrative and reveal the boy's groping efforts to move beyond the strangeness and perplexity of his experience and figure out the nature of his fate. "Who can judge what is possible or believable in a concentration camp?" he asks. No one, he concludes, "even if you mustered the totality of your knowledge." In the end, all he knows is that "what had happened had happened" (p. 257) and that, being fateless, his only choice is to "continue my uncontinuable life" (p. 262).

Whether autobiographical or not, much of Kertész's subsequent work might usefully be seen as attempts to meditate further on the experiences described in *Fatelessness* and those the author himself confronted in repressive postwar Hungary. The linkages between past and future are constant and confirm György Köves's hard-won awareness that "we can never start a new life, only ever carry on the old one" (p. 259). It is a difficult assignment, and yet Kertész has held to it faithfully.

Kaddish for an Unborn Child is a slim but infinitely sad and tormenting book. The narrator, referred to merely by the initial B., ruminates non-stop on his tortured childhood, his unsuccessful writing career, his failed marriage, his refusal to father a child. There is little storytelling of the conventional sort and almost no dialogue. Rather, from first page to last, the reader is in the grip of a compulsive monologue, ostensibly addressed to B.'s never-to-be-begotten progeny, although possibly also to his ex-wife. The relentless talk often has a hallucinatory effect. Some sentences go on for almost a full page, and paragraphs run from a single line or two to almost sixty pages. Every paragraph—there are seventeen in all—begins with an impassioned "No!" What drives this determined negativity is the same specter of terror and inescapable death that drives Paul Celan's famous poem "Todes-fuge," cited throughout the novel.

Even though the narrator survived the camps, the past is not over with and will not leave him alone. His postwar life is lived "under the mark of Auschwitz," which is "not quite living, and indisputably not quite a life" (p. 58). So he talks and writes, despite his realizing that to write is "in essence nothing other than to dig, to keep on digging to the end, the grave that others have started to dig for me in the air" (p. 30). His grim view of life and its continuing threats prompt him to liken his century to an "execution squad on permanent duty" (p. 75). He rejects his wife's wishes for him to father her child. "No!" he exclaims repeatedly, and with his passionate refusal he advances the only project that strikes him as reasonable in the absurd, punishingly harsh world he inhabits: his self-liquidation.

As its title indicates, the novel *Liquidation* continues and deepens the themes introduced in *Kaddish for an Unborn Child*. It, too, tells the story of B. (more often referred to here as Bee), a Hungarian-Jewish writer born in Auschwitz, who manages to outlast the camp and settle in his family's native Budapest, only to later commit suicide. He has written a play, found among his papers, called "Liquidation," full of gloomy reflections about life as "one enormous concentration camp" (p. 57) and revealing, not surprisingly, a preoccupation with suicide.

The writer's death shakes his friends. One in particular, King-bitter, is driven to search for an explanation among Bee's papers, where he suspects he may turn up the manuscript of an unpublished novel that would provide the key to Bee's death. What he discovers instead is devastating: in accordance with Bee's orders, the manuscript has been burned by the author's ex-wife. Nevertheless, in conversations with her and some others, Kingbitter is able to reconstruct much about Bee's life and the dark thoughts that led to his death. A sample: "We are living in an age of disaster; each of us is a carrier of the disaster. . . . Disaster man has no fate, no qualities, no character. For him there can be no return to some center of the Self, a solid and irrefutable self-certainty; in other words, he is lost . . ." (pp. 55–56).

Bee's deep pessimism is rooted in several different sources, chief among them the unyielding pressure of his time in the Nazi death camp. As one of his friends remarks, "Bee himself lived Auschwitz here, in Budapest, not of course an Auschwitz comparable to Auschwitz itself, but a voluntarily accepted, domesticated Auschwitz, though one in which it was just as possible to perish as in the real one" (pp. 109–110). A sizable part of the narrative involves Kingbitter's efforts to probe and explain this line of thought. There is an "Auschwitz mode of existence" (p. 110), he concludes, that continues to claim victims decades after the Nazi death camps themselves were destroyed. For many who were in those places, the peril lives on. It is no wonder, then, that Bee's personal philosophy crystallizes in utterly pessimistic terms— "Evil was the life principle" (p. 43)—and leads to his final act of self-destruction. In this brief but hugely troubling novel, as in much of his other work, Kertész brings to a point of summarizing clarity a truth that is as tenacious as it is terrifying: "No one can revoke Auschwitz. Auschwitz is irrevocable" (p. 123).

A large corpus of writings by and about Holocaust survivors now exists. Rarely, however, does one encounter in this literature books as harrowing, but also as strikingly innovative, thoughtful, and challenging as *Fatelessness*, *Kaddish for an Unborn Child*, and *Liquidation*. For sanity's sake, one would like to believe that what Levi called "the Auschwitz disease" is not incurable, but a long list of writers who took their own lives indicates that effective antidotes are not always at hand. What is available, thanks to writers like Tadeusz Borowski, Paul Celan, Jean Améry, Primo Levi, Elie Wiesel, and Imre Kertész, is an important body of writing that reveals the possibilities, but also the perils, of life after Auschwitz. As these writers make clear, one cannot properly speak about "life after Auschwitz" without being alert to its punishing legacy. In most cases, there has been no closure, and the suffering continues. So do the hatreds that brought on so much of the suffering. In Kertész's view, even in ostensibly free countries, there exists today a post-Auschwitz form of antisemitism that draws inspiration from Auschwitz and desires to reproduce it: "Our age is not an age of [classic] antisemitism, it is of Auschwitz. And the anti-semite of our age no longer loathes Jews; he wants Auschwitz."[33] Does the return of antisemitism and the genocidal fantasies that accompany it indicate that the end of the Holocaust might presage the arrival of a new Holocaust? As we will see, Kertész is not the only writer who thinks it does.

NINE

The End of the Holocaust

The day came when nobody wanted to listen to them anymore,
and another day, when the last of them had vanished. . . .
The era of the survivor has come to an end.

Werner Weinberg's downcast prognosis, taken from his exceptionally thoughtful but barely known book, *Self-Portrait of a
Holocaust Survivor,*[1] says more than his words seem to say at first
glance. Most Holocaust survivors are already gone, and those
who remain are now in their eighties or older. Weinberg, however, expressed his lament over the closing of the era of survivors almost thirty years ago, so he clearly had in mind more than
the diminishments that belong to human mortality and naturally come with the passing of time. He was troubled by losses
of a more grievous kind—memory losses—those stemming from
what he and others have seen as a general indifference to the testimony of Holocaust survivors and an unwillingness to learn from
them. What he did not foresee and would have been shocked to
see is the emergence of attacks on Holocaust memory, culminating in calls for the "end of Auschwitz."

According to Imre Kertész, such an ending is impossible:
"The real problem with Auschwitz is that it happened, and this
cannot be altered."[2] With respect to the indisputable facticity of

the Nazi death camps, Kertész, of course, is right. With respect to the memory of those places—of those who built and ran them and those who suffered and died in them—alteration of various kinds has been occurring all along. In looking at the evolution of such change over time, one can find ample grounds to support Weinberg's sad assessment of what will be lost with the passing of his generation of survivors.

Holocaust remembrance is sustained by multiple sources— educational, cultural, religious, and institutional—and will not quickly fade, but it vies with a range of contrary and often contentious sources that facilitate forgetting. Manfred Gerstenfeld has compiled an extensive sample of these more inimical trends in *The Abuse of Holocaust Memory: Distortions and Responses.*[3] Gerstenfeld's analysis of this material confirms what the preceding chapters of this book have sought to demonstrate: far from being fixed, the memory of the Holocaust is beset by an array of cultural pressures that challenge its place as a pivotal event in modern European and Jewish history. There are those who deny the Holocaust ever happened, minimize its magnitude and consequences, appropriate and instrumentalize the power inherent in its words and images, or invert, distort, deflect, and trivialize its meanings. Others are more positive, even idealistic, in their wish to make meaning of this history and apply what they take to be its "lessons" to contemporary social problems, but their efforts to universalize the Holocaust sometimes result in overlooking or diluting its distinctive features. Still others, exhibiting signs of Holocaust fatigue and Holocaust resentment, have simply had enough of talk about the Holocaust and want greater distance from it. And then there are those who employ Holocaust references polemically in a bitter, ongoing ideological and political struggle against the State of Israel (they have their counterparts in certain defenders of Israel who also invoke the Holocaust recklessly and irresponsibly). Taken together, these ways of treating the catastrophe visited upon the Jews have the effect of altering the representational shapes and moral weight of Holocaust memory. Two or three generations from now, it is likely that the term "Holocaust" will still be in circulation, but as a historical referent it may no longer bring so vividly to mind the events that it still is capable of conjuring today, especially among those who were subjected to its horrors and survived to tell about them.

As should be clear by now, late in their lives a number of the most compelling survivor-writers suffered an anguished sense of futility regarding the value and impact of their work. Some recent trends, described below, would add to their gloom. They lend credence to the notion that something like "the end of the Holocaust" is beginning to come into view.

In January 2010, just days before the observance of International Holocaust Remembrance Day, a prominent Polish bishop was quoted as stating that "the Holocaust, as such, is a Jewish invention." In an interview published on an Italian Catholic website, www.pontifex.roma, Tadeusz Pieronek, former head of the Catholic bishops' conference, added that the Jews shaped memory of the Holocaust to their own advantage and exploited it for selfish ends: "Undoubtedly, the majority of those who died in the concentration camps were Jews, but also on the list were Poles, Gypsies, Italians, and Catholics. So it's not right to expropriate this tragedy to make propaganda." Bishop Pieronek reportedly said that special memorial days should be held for the "victims of communism, for Catholics, for persecuted Christians, and so on." He added, "The Jews enjoy good press because they have powerful means behind them, enormous power, and the unconditional backing of the United States, and this favors a certain arrogance that I find unbearable."[4]

Shocking in themselves, these words, spoken just before the onset of special ceremonies to mark the sixty-fifth anniversary of the liberation of Auschwitz, instantly provoked protests from Jewish groups. They also caused embarrassment to the Catholic Church, which was still contending with equally repellent statements made a year earlier by a dissident bishop, Richard Williamson, who claimed there had been no gas chambers in the Nazi death camps and that the total number of Jewish dead was no more than 300,000. Under pressure, Bishop Williamson offered a brief apology for embarrassing the Church (although he did not retract his bogus charges). Bishop Pieronek refused to apologize but, predictably, claimed his remarks were taken out of context and distorted. Yet in an age of instant global communication, the bishop's ugly words had already been widely disseminated, and the damage was done.

Or was it? Within Western society, outright Holocaust denial has long been considered beyond the pale of acceptable opinion, and the reprehensible views of Bishops Pieronek and Williamson are not likely to win broad approval either within the Roman Catholic Church or without. Nevertheless, both men quickly found supporters among those who take malicious pleasure in denying or minimizing the Holocaust and decrying what they insist is Jewish exploitation of the catastrophe for personal and communal gain. For decades following the end of World War II, these Holocaust negationists, or revisionists, have propagated their implausible views, but mainly from positions on the margins of society. From what one could tell, the impact of their propaganda tracts has been slim. In more recent years, however, and especially with the advent of the internet, their opinions are readily available to much larger numbers of people, some of whom seem to be susceptible to the notion that a Jewish plot, or "Holocaust industry," has foisted on a guilt-ridden Western society a massive lie about Jewish suffering or willfully exaggerated and manipulated the extent of such suffering for venal and political ends.

These pernicious views can easily be refuted, but they have appeal among some people and are unlikely to soon fade. Almost twenty years ago, the American historian Deborah Lipstadt exposed the mendacious character of Holocaust denial, chiefly among people on the far end of the political right.[5] More recently, the Israeli philosopher Elhanan Yakira has convincingly demonstrated that people on the far left are not immune to such perverse thinking either. Especially within France, their extreme views on the Holocaust have gained a degree of respectability. Through detailed analysis of the work of such figures as Maurice Bardèche, Paul Rassinier, Pierre Guillaume, Robert Faurisson, and Serge Thion, Yakira has shown that a small but influential number of intellectuals on both the radical left and radical right have had an effect on mainstream opinion by "turning denial into a legitimate point of view and making it into a central issue in France and elsewhere." Their success, Yakira argues, is owing to their systematic use of the Holocaust—including but not restricted to its denial—in what they see as a critical ideological struggle against Zionism and Israel:

> Both in Rassinier and in his faithful followers on the radical French left one can find this syndrome: one must not allow the crime that was committed at Auschwitz, as it were, to blind us to the main thing, which is the suffering of those who are truly exploited—the workers, people of the Third World, the Palestinians. What happened at Auschwitz was, in the last analysis, just another instance, among many, of the true sources of all crimes: colonialism, imperialism, capitalism, and Zionism. Thus, one cannot avoid the conclusion that nothing unique happened at Auschwitz. Its uniqueness can be negated by the claim that there was no systematic, planned extermination of Jews or, alternatively, by the claim that systematic, planned extermination, real or symbolic, is what the Israelis are doing to the Palestinians.[6]

We will look further at the political dimensions of Holocaust denial and distortion later in this chapter. For now, suffice it to say that Yakira's analysis of the ideological motivations of such maneuvers seems correct. It finds both confirmation and extension in Matthias Küntzel's precise and chilling formulation, "Every denial of the Holocaust contains an appeal to repeat it."[7]

In addition to those who deny, minimize, or exploit the facts of the Holocaust, some acknowledge that the Jews were indeed persecuted and slaughtered in large numbers, but they dislike being reminded of it so often. An opinion poll that the Anti-Defamation League conducted in 2009 in seven European countries (Austria, France, Germany, Hungary, Poland, Spain, and the United Kingdom) found that 44 percent of respondents believed that Jews talk too much about the Holocaust. In three of these countries—Austria, Poland, and Hungary—55 percent or more of respondents registered this negative opinion.[8] A subsequent poll released by the University of Bielefeld in Germany, surveying opinions among individuals in eight European countries, found that almost 42 percent of respondents believe that "Jews exploit the past to extort money."[9] The implications of these findings are clear: sixty-five years after the end of World War II, a sizable part of the European population has heard all they want to hear about the tribulations of the Jews. Sometimes expressed as irritation, sometimes as resentment, an attitude of impatience with the Jews and rejection of stories about their victimization is now palpable, and not only on the margins.

One expression of this resentment at its crudest can be seen in the proliferation of Holocaust jokes. Tasteless and mean-spirited, some of these have become part of the repertoire of popular stand-up comedians. By ridiculing and mocking Jewish suffering, comics like France's Dieudonné, Norway's Otto Jespersen, Ireland's Tommy Tiernan, and their counterparts in other countries look to laugh away Hitler's Jewish victims by deriding them. A review of Holocaust jokes available on the internet brings up far more of these than one can easily stomach. A random sample includes such obscenities as these: "'What is the difference between a ton of coal and a thousand Jews?' 'Jews burn longer.'" "'How many Jews can you fit into a Volkswagen Beetle?' '1004, 2

in the front seats, 2 in the back seats, and 1000 in the ashtray.'"
"'What do you call the murder of 6 million Jews?' 'A good start.'"

The impulses that give rise to this degenerate humor are hard to fathom. It is well known that during the period of the Nazi persecutions itself, a kind of gallows humor circulated among Jews in the ghettos and camps. Its function, as best we can tell, was to enable people to better cope with the hardships they faced by lightening these somewhat. By calling Hitler "Horowitz," for instance, one might cut the major villain of Nazi terror down to size and make him seem less threatening. Today's Holocaust humor, by contrast, has no such function and seems merely cruel. "What's brown and hides in the attic? The Diarrhea of Anne Frank." "I feel sorry for Anne Frank. First she gets her diary published, which is every girl's worst nightmare, but on top of that she doesn't get any money from it, which is every Jew's worst nightmare." These so-called "Anne Frank jokes," and there are many more of them, comprise an especially vile subset of this odious strain of humor. To expose oneself to it is to be instantly soiled. And yet one ought not to dismiss these "jokes" as being of no consequence, for they indicate that a point has been reached where, at least for some people, it is now acceptable to reduce the horrors of the Holocaust to sick jokes and then throw the foul remains back at the Jews.

Others are not prone to mock and make fun of the Jews, but they claim too much attention to the Nazi Holocaust has resulted in too little attention to other victim groups and even other "holocausts." In certain European countries today, most prominently but not only in the Baltic republics, one finds a growing tendency to equalize the crimes of Hitler and Stalin and a call for the creation of new institutions and public ceremonies to jointly remember the victims of both dictators. The "Prague Declaration on European Conscience and Communism," of June 3, 2008, sets forth a rationale for recognizing "Communism and Nazism as a common legacy" and argues for "reaching an all-European understanding" that the "crimes committed in the name of Communism" should be assessed and remembered "in the same way Nazi crimes were assessed by the Nuremberg Tribunal." The Prague Declaration has been a significant spur for such thinking, and parallel proposals have been presented to the political bodies of other east European countries. The effect is to redefine genocide so that it will apply more broadly, if less precisely, to people other than just the Jews. On April 2, 2009, more than 400 members of the European Parliament voted in favor of setting aside August 23, the date in 1939 when the Ribbentrop-Molotov pact was signed between Nazi Germany and the Soviet Union, as "European Day of Remembrance for Victims of Stalinism and Nazism."[10] If successfully instituted, such a day would render Holocaust Remembrance Day superfluous and, in a relatively brief time, no doubt would lead to its dissolution.

The eminent Israeli historian of the Holocaust, Yehuda Bauer, decries these developments. While recognizing that the many victims of Soviet tyranny should be remembered through appropriate memorials and special commemorative events, Bauer sees these moves towards equivalence as a "mendacious revision of recent world history," which seriously distorts the character of both Nazi Germany and the Soviet Union and "trivializes and relativizes the genocide of the Jews perpetrated by the Nazi regime."[11] Dovid Katz, an American scholar who resides in Vilnius, comes to similar conclusions. Katz points to a "newly energized European movement to confuse, recombine, or equalize phenomena that are empirically and conceptually unequal, in service of the effort to obscure, relativize, minimize, or delete entirely 'the Holocaust as such' from European history and consciousness."[12] The Lithuanian philosopher Leonidas Donskis rues these developments within his own country and sees them as examples of a "general inflation—and hence devaluation—of concepts and values," including the concept of genocide. He concludes that, "Whether we like it or not, the Holocaust was the one and only bona fide genocide," and he affirms that attempts to rewrite the history of World War II by equalizing the fate of the Jews with that of other Europeans seriously distorts the reality of what actually occurred.[13]

Donskis's locution, "Whether we like it or not," is telling, for as he knows, many of the author's fellow countrymen decidedly do *not* like it and are setting about to change the perception that the Jews and the Jews alone are entitled to special attention. Their counterparts elsewhere in Europe are doing the same. If they succeed, "International Holocaust Remembrance Day" may, in time, be eclipsed by a more generalized "European Day of Remembrance for Victims of Stalinism and Nazism." If this happens, the particular features that defined Nazi crimes against the Jews henceforth may be blended into some more generalized concept of totalitarian or tyrannical criminality.

In milder forms, some movements toward equivalence are observable in America as well, although to date they have largely been confined to debates within the academy and certain cultural institutions and have not been a factor in serious discussions at the political level. For example, several colleges and universities that house institutes originally established for the study of the Holocaust have redefined the mandates of these institutes and have focused them on a wider range of historical and social problems. Clark University, in Massachusetts, for instance, calls its former Center for Holocaust Studies the Center for Holocaust and Genocide Studies. The University of Minnesota, in Minneapolis, has done likewise. Following the same pattern, California's Claremont McKenna College now boasts a Center for the Study of the Holocaust, Genocide, and Human Rights. In a still broader expansion of program mission, Chico College in California has a Center for Excellence in the Study of the Holocaust, Genocide, Human Rights, and Tolerance; the University of Nevada has a Center for Holocaust, Genocide, and Peace Studies; in New York one finds the Suffolk Center on the Holocaust, Diversity, and

Human Understanding; in Cincinnati, Ohio, there is the Center for Holocaust and Humanity Education; and at Western Washington University, one finds the Center for Holocaust, Genocide, and Ethnocide Education. Numerous other centers with names like these exist elsewhere. In addition, some institutes that began as Holocaust museums are now guided by mandates that include the "defense of human rights," "tolerance training," "working toward a society which fosters dialogue among all ethnic, political, and religious groups," "fostering tolerance, inclusion, social justice, and civic responsibility," and "exploring peaceful avenues for human improvement."[14] Admirable in themselves, these goals originate in contemporary American social and political agendas that look to the Holocaust chiefly for pragmatic and didactic reasons, as a catalyst for moral education and social action. The idea, a recognizably American one, is to use the Nazi genocide of the Jews for programs that will derive some good from all that bad. The aim may be commendable, but in working to attain it, will the overwhelmingly destructive history of the Holocaust be accurately remembered and still at the center of concern?

To some within the American academy, this is the wrong question. As they see it, a preoccupying concern with the Holocaust has left too little space for other people's concerns to be effectively addressed. It is time, they believe, to "de-center the Jewish Holocaust from the ubiquitous discussions of genocide, reparations, and U.S.-Israel relations. . . . The Jewish Holocaust, citing its supposed uniqueness, cannot continuously be used as the yardstick or point of reference for all incidents of genocide and xenophobia. . . . The Jewish Holocaust's hyper-visibility inherently stifles our understanding of [other] . . . national and more generally genocidal histories."[15]

These words appeared in a "Call for Papers" circulated in November 2002 by David Leonard, a Washington State University professor, who wanted to organize projects that would "challenge the hegemonic position of the Shoah within American life." Taking his cue from the work of Norman Finkelstein and Peter Novick, this scholar blamed "the Jewish Holocaust" and "the accompanying 'Holocaust Industry'" for deflecting attention from "those discourses and debates within the United States that are not exclusively the domain of Jewish or Holocaust Studies." In short, he had heard all he cared to hear about Jewish victims of the Nazi genocide and wanted attention focused on "the genocide of Native and African Americans."

He is not alone. The literary scholar Walter Benn Michaels asks, "Why is there a federally funded U.S. Holocaust Memorial Museum on the Mall in Washington, D.C.?" and offers an answer that turns this ostensible question into an indictment: "The commemoration of the Nazi murder of the Jews on the Mall [is] in fact another kind of Holocaust denial, or, more precisely, the denial of another Holocaust." In his view, too much public attention to the Holocaust has served to block public remembrance of the history of black slavery and the oppression of Native Americans.[16] As Michaels sees it, privileging the Holocaust of Europe's Jews as "the paradigmatic hate crime" has impeded long-overdue acknowledgement of hatred directed against others closer to home.

In line with this view, if less polemical in tone, Marianne Hirsch and Irene Kacandes, the editors of *Teaching the Representation of the Holocaust*, argue that because scholars who teach the Holocaust in the United States do so as part of "a people with its own troubled history of suffering, persecution, and genocide," an "acknowledgment of the relation of Holocaust representation and memorialization to the representation of slavery and Native American genocide is fundamental to any Holocaust course taught in the United States." In support of their argument, they cite the work of the historian Eric D. Weitz, who maintains that "on the larger canvas of school and university curricula and of research, the singular focus on the Holocaust no longer suffices."[17]

Why it no longer suffices is never made clear. Most American scholars who offer courses on American slavery and the fate of Native Americans, after all, feel no obligation to focus their curricula along comparative lines but treat their subjects as fully sufficient unto themselves. But if they are right to do so, why is a focus on the Holocaust deemed to be *insufficient?* And why is there a supposed need to encompass study of the Nazi crimes against the Jews within an American context that will expose students to what Hirsch and Kacandes call "the workings of racism and prejudice that we can find within our own culture?" Racism and prejudice are well-established facts of American national life, but to date they have not culminated in anything remotely like the Warsaw Ghetto or Auschwitz. To situate study of the Nazi crimes against the Jews within a specifically American framework, therefore, will inevitably distort the histories of both the Nazi Holocaust and the American experience, including that of racism. The imperative to reorient Holocaust studies in this way is but one more illustration of a growing impatience with the place of the Holocaust in American life, which mirrors similar, even more strongly expressed, feelings of dissatisfaction with Holocaust history and memory in parts of Europe and throughout much of the Muslim world.

As voiced in the United States by a number of scholars and writers, this dissatisfaction calls into question what is now commonly, and sometimes pejoratively, called "Holocaust consciousness" and the motives of those who seek to perpetuate it. Before looking at those who denigrate the diffusion of Holocaust awareness, though, it is important to note that some scholars affirm it. In contrast to the polemical arguments of Norman Finkelstein, Peter Novick, and others to be discussed below, the work of Jeffrey Alexander, Michael Rothberg, and Daniel Levy and Natan Sznaider refutes claims that Holocaust consciousness invariably leads to inattention to other groups' histories of suffering.[18] On the contrary, the authors show that an awareness of the fate of the Jews in Hitler's Europe frequently helps to direct attention to injustices committed against others, albeit in terms that sometimes detach the Holocaust from its historical base and universalize it as a signifier of generic evil broadly conceived.

Thus, in a much-discussed essay, "The Social Construction of Moral Universals," Jeffrey C. Alexander, a cultural sociologist at Yale University, argues that, whereas the Holocaust may originally have been known as "a specific and situated historical event," it has in recent years become "transformed into a generalized symbol of human suffering." In contrast to such critics as Lawrence Langer and Berel Lang, who deplore such transformations as exploitative, Alexander strongly affirms them on moral and political grounds. In his reading of these developments, the widespread adoption of the genocidal crimes against the Jews as an accessible metaphor for evil "has created historically unprecedented opportunities for ethnic, racial, and religious justice, for mutual recognition, and for global conflicts becoming regulated in a more civil way."[19] In short, through "symbolic extension" of the Holocaust as a "bridge metaphor," the memory of the Nazi crimes can help advance the causes of human rights, human solidarity, and a greater degree of moral responsibility and justice worldwide.

While it is hard to recognize in the real world a great deal of progress toward fulfilling these idealistic goals, Alexander is correct in noting that, on a global scale, the Holocaust is being universalized as a moral-political myth that can be readily appropriated by others who claim a history of victimization. No longer restricted to the persecution and mass murder of the Jews, "Holocaust," as he notes, has become "a *worldwide* point of reference and comparison for crimes against humanity" as such.[20] As a consequence, various states and social groups now want to see their own "holocausts" recognized. Thus, the famine in the Ukraine in the 1930s, brought on by Soviet collectivization policies that devastated agriculture and resulted in the deaths of millions, is now sometimes referred to as the "Ukrainian Holocaust." Some gay rights advocates would like the Nazi persecution of homosexuals during the Third Reich to be known as a "Homocaust."[21] And the State of Israel is routinely accused of committing "genocide" and even of enacting a new "Nazi-like Holocaust" against the Palestinians. Alexander does not refer to any of these examples, but he sees the widespread invocation of "progressive" Holocaust references as indicating an enlargement of the moral imagination, which he believes is bound to have a humanizing impact on social and political life. What he fails to sufficiently acknowledge is that every such appropriation of Holocaust memory is likely to be a misappropriation. For with the broad diffusion and adaptation of the Holocaust as a metaphor, the Nazi genocide of the Jews becomes reduced to the status of an abstractly universal, generic phenomenon, a trope available to all who feel aggrieved over past or present abuses. Its distinctive features are then diminished and its power to shock and disrupt is reduced. As one of Alexander's critics notes, by subordinating the history of the Nazi crimes against the Jews to its "coding" as a form of "sacred-evil," "the hard factuality of the events recedes."[22] According to another critic, the "paradox of this process lies in the disconnect between the signifier and the signified: what happened has forgotten its name and the name has forgotten what happened."[23] Thus, while Alexander affirms the spread of Holocaust awareness as an instrument for curbing future genocides, he gives too little historical weight to the genocide that actually was.

Others see bad faith and manipulation in the promotion of Holocaust consciousness and denounce its agents fiercely. The most vehement of these critics, Norman Finkelstein, seeks in *The Holocaust Industry* to indict "The Holocaust" as an ideological representation of history that he claims has been fraudulently devised and "sold" to the American public in order to revive a faltering Jewish identity and to "justify criminal policies of the Israeli state and US support for these policies." Beyond these motives, Finkelstein charges, those who run the so-called "Holocaust industry" are embarked on a multi-billion dollar scheme of extortion.[24] While these ideas are presented in *The Holocaust*

Industry in an especially harsh and aggressive way, Finkelstein's book, for all of its extremism, is representative of a polemical engagement with the Holocaust that has been building over the years in the work of a number of other writers, many of whom employ terms that resemble those delineated by Finkelstein, even if they do not use his inflammatory tone. As a result, Holocaust memory at the outset of the twenty-first century finds itself embattled on several fronts.

The issues on which the arguments typically turn have less to do with the Holocaust as an historical event than with accusations about the manipulative use of it as an exaggerated element of contemporary Jewish identity. What is at stake in these increasingly bitter debates, in other words, is a version of the politics of memory, according to which American Jews allegedly use the moral advantages that are supposedly theirs as privileged "victims" to advance parochial aims and partisan political agendas. The "centering" of the Holocaust in Jewish consciousness and general public awareness, it is charged, not only distorts Jewish identity and deforms Jewish life but produces a seriously adverse effect on others, whose own histories of persecution and suffering have been marginalized and all but forgotten as a consequence of the overwhelming emphasis that has been placed on Jewish suffering. As it has been advanced in America by a "substantial cadre of Holocaust-memory professionals"—the term is Peter Novick's[25]—Holocaust consciousness serves the purposes of Jewish self-aggrandizement and prevents other victimized peoples from receiving a proper share of public attention and sympathy. For these and related reasons, it is deemed to be the proper function of critics to expose the "Holocaust industry" for what it is and thereby loosen the hold that Holocaust memory has had on the Jewish and general American imagination.

These charges have become more overt and impassioned in recent years but, in milder form, versions of them appear in a variety of American Jewish journals as far back as the late 1970s.

Over the last two decades, though, these criticisms have become more expansive and have taken on tones of disparagement and derision that seldom appeared in earlier years. Michael Goldberg, in *Why Should Jews Survive?* (1995), decries the emergence of Holocaust consciousness as something that "mutilates Jewish self-understanding" and insists that "the challenge to Jews today is not outliving Hitler and the Nazis but overcoming the life-threatening story created in their aftermath." The Holocaust, according to Goldberg, had become a "cult," with its own "tenets of faith, rites, and shrines," presided over by a "High Priest," Elie Wiesel. Goldberg criticizes Wiesel for the cultic powers he allegedly wields, the lecture fees he demands, and his supposed failure to sensitize his followers to the sufferings of others, most especially the Palestinians, who were "beaten, tortured, and worse" during the first intifada. Goldberg is so convinced of the pernicious effects of Holocaust consciousness that he concludes his book by stating that "Jews cannot long remain Jews while holding a Holocaust-shaped story" and "neither can humankind stay human."[26]

Goldberg, a rabbi, opposes the "Holocaust story" because he believes its negative emphases subvert religious faith and, thereby, the very ground of Jewish existence. Philip Lopate, a prominent essayist who refers to himself as being a "secular, fallen Jew," finds other grounds to oppose what he sees as an excessive Jewish preoccupation with the Holocaust. The very term "Holocaust" is objectionable to him and has a "self-important, strutting air." Those who insist on the term's exclusivity "diminish, if not demean, the mass slaughter of other people": "Is it not possible for us to have a little more compassion for the other victimized peoples of this century," he asks, "and not insist quite so much that our wounds bleed more fiercely?" Like Goldberg, Lopate singles out Elie Wiesel as the one most responsible for this supposed Jewish chauvinism. Wiesel, he says, heads up the Holocaust as if it were "a corporation." Lopate acknowledges that millions of Jews were murdered by the Nazis, but he knows that multitudes of Bengalis, East Timorese, and Ibos have also been murdered, and "when it comes to mass murder, I can see no difference between their casualties and ours." Finding no justification in Jewish "extermination pride," and having no taste for "tribal smugness," Lopate argues that the most authentic stance toward the Holocaust today is one of resistance. As he puts it, "just because someone has suffered a lot doesn't mean you have to like them."[27] Lopate's angry essay represents, as does Goldberg's diatribe, a strain of Jewish rejection detectable among others as well, who also feel they have reached a point of satiety with being fed "too much Holocaust."

These critical voices—and there are many more like them—must be understood against the development of Holocaust consciousness in America over time. For a number of years after the end of World War II, the majority of Americans were probably unable or unwilling to face up to the full horrors of the Nazi period. Many simply knew little about them. Commemorative services and other memorial programs took place within American Jewish communities,[28] but "the Holocaust," as the Nazi genocide later came to be popularly known, was not a significant factor within mainstream American culture as such. Owing to a number of factors, this situation underwent significant change in the 1960s. Beginning with Israel's abduction and 1961 trial of Adolf Eichmann, and intensifying in June 1967, when the State of Israel seemed threatened with destruction, American Jews and others came into a greater awareness of the full significance of the Holocaust. Following Israel's victory in the Six-Day War and continuing after the perilous situation that Israel faced in the 1973 Yom Kippur War, there was an outpouring of writing about the Holocaust, an exceptional effort by Jews to educate themselves and the public at large about the Nazi crimes. This was an understandable and legitimate goal, and it succeeded in bringing the Holocaust more prominently into the mainstream culture. That success, however, perhaps made it inevitable that Holocaust consciousness would become subjected to the compromises and abuses that always accompany the popularization, commercialization, and politicization of history. Inevitable, though, does not mean desirable, and it is salutary that critical attention has been drawn to some of the more dubious ways in which the stories and images of the Holocaust have circulated in the public sphere.

Less admirable are the glib, caustic, and often mean-spirited attitudes that some of these critics have shown towards those they accuse of "selling" the Holocaust or otherwise promoting it for pecuniary or parochial ends. Attacks against the so-called "purveyors" of Holocaust consciousness often carry exaggerated claims about a Jewish "obsession" with the Holocaust, a Jewish "hegemony" over news about mass suffering, the elevation of the Holocaust as American Jewry's substitute "religion," and the like.[29]

In virtually all of these cases, Holocaust consciousness is taken to be the cause of developments that almost certainly have their origins elsewhere. Nevertheless, it is not unusual for rabbis to lament that attention to the Holocaust is distracting American Jews from their religious duties, just as it is common for avowed secularists like Peter Novick and Philip Lopate to charge that too much Holocaust on the brain is eroding the social consciousness of American Jews and hardening their hearts to the sufferings of others. If, as Novick claims, American Jewry has turned "inward and rightward in recent decades," it is owing to the "centering of the Holocaust in the minds of American Jews,"[30] a claim for which Novick can offer nothing but conjectural arguments. Taking this line of thinking to its next level of crudeness, Lopate contends that "the Jewish preoccupation with the Holocaust" has made American Jews "uncharitable, self-absorbed, self-righteous—and pushy."[31] Had he seen fit to add "venal," he would have rounded out the profile of the Ugly Jew in classic antisemitic fashion (Norman Finkelstein has done that for him through his brutal sketches of the opportunistic, money-grubbing Jew).

The Holocaust, in short, is blamed for much of what is said to ail American Jews. Traditionalists hold it responsible for distorting Judaism and replacing religious observance with a new civil religion that enshrines Jewish victimization, and not God, at its core. And liberal-minded thinkers call it to account for narrowing the Jewish political vision and replacing a broad-based universalism with a chauvinistic particularism. Almost every deviation from what is held to be normative or desirable — the growing disidentification of American Jews with Judaism, an alleged indifference to the pain and sufferings of other people, an apologetic attitude to what some regard to be Israeli "atrocities" on a Nazi-like scale — is placed at the doorstep of those who have worked to perpetuate Holocaust memory.

To make matters worse, one now commonly hears that Jewish Holocaust advocates are responsible, in no small measure, for what ails others as well. Accused of being proponents of a radically ethnocentric view of history, "certain Jewish scholars and their acolytes" insist that the Holocaust is an unprecedented crime that bestows upon the Jews a preeminence of suffering.[32] This "cult" of "zealots" with "powerful friends in high places" has managed to win broad sympathy for the Jews through a "self-serving masquerade of Jewish genocide uniqueness," and anyone who raises questions about this "deception" is "immediately in danger of being labeled an anti-Semite." Nevertheless, writes one author unintimidated by this alleged Jewish strategy of coercion, "Not only is the essence of their argument demonstrably erroneous, the larger thesis that it fraudulently advances is fundamentally racist and violence-provoking. At the same time, moreover, it willingly provides a screen behind which opportunistic governments today attempt to conceal their own past and ongoing genocidal actions." Among these governments, the State of Israel has been able to use the Holocaust as "justification for [its] territorial expansionism and suppression of the Palestinian people," a crime that for too long has gone unacknowledged as a result of the "hegemonic product of many years of strenuous intellectual labor by a handful of Jewish scholars and writers."[33]

I am quoting from David Stannard, a scholar of Native American history and one of several figures to emerge in recent years who have taken earlier arguments against Holocaust consciousness to new levels of polemical attack. With their work, the politics of resentment enters the critical literature on the Holocaust with an angry roar and introduces a rhetoric of aggression against Jews that until now has rarely been seen outside of antisemitic literature.

This note is forcefully sounded as well in Ward Churchill's *A Little Matter of Genocide: Holocaust and Denial in the Americas, 1492 to the Present*. A now largely discredited scholar of Native American history, like Stannard, Churchill is convinced that too little attention has been paid to the fate of indigenous peoples in the "American Holocaust" because too much attention has been paid to the Jewish victims of the Nazi Holocaust. He charges that victims of other genocides have been virtually erased from history because a "substantial component of Zionism . . . contends . . . that no 'true' genocide has ever occurred other than the Holocaust suffered by the Jews . . ." The politics of what Churchill and Stannard condemn as a militant form of ethnic chauvinism are clear for all to see: Jewish "exclusivism" serves to "compel permanent maintenance of the privileged political status of Israel, the Jewish state established on Arab land in 1947 as an act of international atonement for the Holocaust." It also seeks to "construct a conceptual screen behind which to hide the realities of Israel's ongoing genocide against the Palestinian population whose rights and property were usurped in its very creation."[34]

Both Stannard and Churchill accuse Jewish scholars of the Nazi Holocaust of "denying" other "holocausts." Stannard goes so far as to charge the "Jewish uniqueness advocates" with being the equivalent of Holocaust deniers, even claiming that they "almost invariably mimic exactly the same assertions laid out by the anti-Semitic historical revisionists."[35] Churchill denounces these scholars in similar terms: "The techniques used by proponents of Jewish exclusivism in presenting their doctrine of 'uniqueness' [are comparable] to those of the neo-Nazi revisionists." And he carries the accusation one step further: "The proponents of 'Jewish exclusivism' represent a proportionately greater and more insidious threat to understanding than do the Holocaust deniers," for in denying that other peoples have been the target of genocidal crimes, they have marginalized the sufferings of countless others and rendered them inconsequential. They have, he says, peddled a "mythology" about history that "dovetails perfectly with the institutionalized denials of genocide" put forth by numerous governments intent on seeing to it that their own "hidden holocausts" remain hidden. For the sheer invidiousness of their work, therefore, the Jewish scholars—Churchill names Steven Katz, Yehuda Bauer, Elie Wiesel, Lucy Dawidowicz, Leni Yahil, Yisrael Gutman, Michael Marrus, Deborah Lipstadt, and Martin Gilbert—are placed in a class by themselves: "Those who would deny the Holocaust, after all, focus their distortions upon one target. Those who deny all holocausts other than that of the Jews have the same effect upon many."[36] Stannard and Churchill are clearly guilty of the same fallacy that mars the work of some of the Jewish critics referred to above. While it is true that for many years the history of Native American peoples was neglected, the fault lies not with scholars of the European Holocaust but with generations of American historians and political leaders who, for their own reasons, have not focused on some shameful chapters of America's past. The omission is a serious one, but, chronologically, it long predates the Holocaust and therefore cannot reasonably be explained by pinning the blame on proponents of "Zionism" or "Jewish exclusivism." Castigating scholars of the Nazi Holocaust for neglecting the history of Native American suffering would be equivalent to condemning scholars of Native American history for diverting attention from the immense sufferings of African slavery, the massacres of Armenians, or the murder of millions of Cambodians. Each of these histories obviously deserves serious attention, but each has unique features, and those who write about them are justified in recognizing as much and pursuing their research and teaching accordingly. It is faulty logic, therefore, to claim that by focusing scholarly attention on one nation's sufferings, they "deny" the sufferings of others. Nevertheless, Stannard and Churchill place blame overwhelmingly on the work of those who have devoted themselves to scrupulous study of the Nazi Holocaust in all of its ramifications. In their view, attention to historical "distinctiveness" equals "denial" of the history of others; and the "Jewish uniqueness advocates," in consciously aiding and abetting "the willful maintenance of public ignorance regarding the genocidal and racist horrors that have been and are being perpetrated by many nations," are in "murderous complicity with both past and present genocidal regimes."[37]

These are serious accusations, and they have moved well beyond the sphere of academic Native American studies. The charge is now commonly made that Jews use their own past history of suffering as a pretext to inflict suffering on others or to divert attention from the oppression of other peoples. The State of Israel is constantly and harshly singled out, an Israel whose image has been transformed into that of an aggressor state, shielded by the protective cover of Holocaust memory. No less a major media figure than *New York Times* columnist Thomas Friedman wrote, during the first intifada, that "Israel today is becoming Yad Vashem with an air force."[38] At the same time, but in less colorful language, sociologist Zygmunt Bauman reiterated the notion of an aggressive Israel that manipulates Holocaust memory for self-serving ends: "The Jewish state [has] tried to employ the tragic memories [of the Holocaust] as the certificate of its political legitimacy, a safe conduct pass for its past and future policies, and above all as the advance payment for the injustices it might itself commit."[39] Bauman's words are favorably cited by Stannard, Churchill, Novick, Finkelstein, and others, for whom it is now a given that the Holocaust has been cynically used by the Jews, and especially by the Jewish State, as a matchless resource against its foes.

Inasmuch as it defines Holocaust memory as little more than a tool of Jewish empowerment, the political logic of this thinking is evident. In the name of Auschwitz, the Jewish State is said to be brutally oppressing another people, so much so that the former victims are now routinely described as present-day perpetrators on a par with Nazis, and their victims are portrayed as the new "Jews." This grotesque role reversal finds no basis in reality, but the rhetorical power of this charge is evident, and it is now frequently cited as if it were true. No less extreme are the means proposed by some to restore the Holocaust to its proper historical perspective and the Jews to what is considered to be their authentic ethical vocation by proclaiming an "end to Auschwitz." This critique of Holocaust consciousness, in other words, links an appeal to disengage from the Holocaust with an appeal for Jews to disengage from the exercise of political power by disconnecting from the State of Israel.

No one has stated this case as clearly as Marc Ellis, a Jewish theologian and professor of religion at Baylor University. From his standpoint, "Jews are essentially a diaspora people" and one that does not require a state organization to support its religious life and communal affairs. For them to live freely and ethically among the peoples of the world, the Jews should recognize the need for the "deabsolutization of Israel," which, Ellis reasons, entails at the same time "deabsolutizing the Holocaust":[40]

> *Auschwitz has become a burden to the Jewish future.* . . . To continue Auschwitz as a central overriding memory is in a sense to postpone . . . the explosive realities within our community as they relate to power and injustice. . . . Thus, to end

Auschwitz is to admit that we are no longer innocent and that Israel is not our redemption. . . . "Ending Auschwitz" would also allow us, or perhaps even compel us, to think the unthinkable—that our future is bound up in an essential solidarity with those whom we have displaced, a solidarity with the Palestinian people. . . . The only way for the renewal of Palestine in the Jewish imagination to take hold is through ending Auschwitz; or, put another way, ending Auschwitz and the renewal of Palestine are bound together.[41]

The theological/political argument Ellis makes is predicated on the belief that "Auschwitz was in fact killing us as a people long after the crematoria were destroyed,"[42] and that in the name of Auschwitz, Jews have felt at liberty to humiliate, oppress, and kill another people. Avishai Margalit describes the same connection even more cynically: "Against the weapon of the Holocaust, the Palestinians are amateurs . . . As soon as operation 'Holocaust Memory' is put into high gear, . . . the Palestinians cannot compete."[43] It is no doubt due to this perceived linkage of the Holocaust and the State of Israel that the media in Arab countries are so intent on erasing the Holocaust or exposing its history as a "myth," and that the most passionate critics of Israel are so moved to deride the "Holocaust industry" and put an "end to Auschwitz."

The notion of a "Holocaust industry" has been popularized by Norman Finkelstein, not Peter Novick, but in his influential book, *The Holocaust in American Life,* Novick writes in roughly similar terms.[44] Through his repeated references to the work of well-placed Jewish influentials—they include a "substantial cadre of Holocaust professionals," a "growing cadre of Holocaust professionals," Jews who "occupy strategic positions in the mass media" and project images of the Holocaust "through the culture at large"—Novick comes close to positing a Holocaust industry in all but name. His book, a determined critique of the politics of Holocaust memory, stresses many of the same themes that one finds in the writings of Stannard, Churchill, and others and foreshadows the full-blown attack that came with the work of Norman Finkelstein.[45]

Novick aims to expose Holocaust consciousness as a deliberate construct of American Jewish organizations and institutions, most of them alleged to be working on behalf of the State of Israel. The leaders of these organizations, he says, recognized that Jewish identity in America was weakening, focused on the Holocaust as "the one item in stock with consumer appeal," and set about shoring up flagging Jewish commitment by creating "a Holocaust-centered Jewish identity." They also worked to spread Holocaust awareness in order to "mobilize support for a beleaguered Israel, pictured as being in a kind of pre-Holocaust danger." They were aided in these efforts, claims Novick, by a powerful Jewish presence among the "media and opinion-making elites"—the Jews who "play an important and influential role in Hollywood, the television industry, and the newspaper, magazine, and book publishing world." Through the dedicated work of these people—and Jews are "not just 'the people of the book,' but the people of the Hollywood film and the television mini-series, of the magazine article and the newspaper column, of the comic book and the academic symposium"—the Holocaust was repositioned from the margins to the very forefront of American consciousness. In short, if the Holocaust has come to assume a prominent place in American life, it is largely owing to a massive Jewish presence within the media, if not quite full Jewish media control. In staking out this position, Novick draws uncomfortably close to those who are quick to spot a Jewish "hidden hand" in international finance, politics, the media, the entertainment world, and other sources of power in the modern state. In Novick's case, though, the influential hand is not hidden at all but overt. As he sees it, in a culture that has come to valorize victims, Jews established primacy of place for the Holocaust and have reaped the benefits that come with such success. Not to be outdone in the high-stakes arena of "comparative atrocitology," the Jews now "possess the gold medal in the Victimization Olympics."[46]

Norman Finkelstein shares Novick's cynical evaluation of the cultural and political underpinnings of Holocaust memory but wants to put an end to the matter altogether by exposing it as a total fraud. Drawing, in part, on the work of earlier critics of Holocaust consciousness—in addition to Peter Novick, he cites Arnold Jacob Wolf, Jacob Neusner, David Stannard, Boas Evron, and others—Finkelstein is intent on mounting a full-scale indictment of "The Holocaust," which he sees as little more than "the Zionist account of the Nazi holocaust."[47] Finkelstein deplores the soft categories that Novick employs—"'memory' is surely the most impoverished concept to come down the academic pike in a long time"—and prefers to think in terms of "power," "interests," and "ideology." In making the shift from the "bland" categories of cultural analysis to the more "robust" categories of political analysis, Finkelstein is convinced that he has discovered the real culprits—not just the Holocaust memory manipulators but those he excoriates as Holocaust racketeers and extortionists. He has nothing but contempt for these people, whom he denounces as shakedown artists whose corrupt practices are "the main fomenter of anti-Semitism in Europe." It is they who run the Holocaust industry, and it is they whom Norman Finkelstein is determined to run out of business so that "those who perished . . . [can] finally rest in peace."[48]

Among the many bizarre features of Finkelstein's persona as an author is that of the indignant son of Holocaust survivors. A fierce opponent of the "exploitation of Jewish suffering," Finkelstein shamelessly exploits the fact that his father and mother had been in Hitler's camps and were the sole members of their family to survive. His book, he piously avers, is an attempt to "represent my parents' legacy," but whatever that legacy might be, his book is, more than anything else, a tirade of abuses against a Judeo-Zionist conspiracy that exists solely in the author's head. Since he is self-credentialed as the son of survivors, however, Finkelstein feels a crusader's entitlement to wage warfare on anyone and everyone who has dealt with the Holocaust in ways that he dislikes.

These people—described as bogus Holocaust scholars, Zionist ideologues, Israeli aggressors, Jewish influence peddlers, phony survivors, and other assorted Jewish politicos and mercenaries—make up the "Holocaust industry," a corrupt, ruthlessly exploitative bunch that has used the Holocaust to acquire personal wealth and political power and to gain immunity for those in the Zionist and American Jewish camps who are busy "lording it over those least able to defend themselves." In describing those who have manipulated the Jewish catastrophe under Hitler for their own purposes, Finkelstein presents an unredeemably shameful picture of human behavior at its craftiest. There is a bit of light in this otherwise dark picture, though, for rising above the machinations of this morally bankrupt crowd is the figure of the author's mother, who is cited more than once for her moral probity and worldly wisdom. Here is a sample. Instead of exploiting Jewish suffering for selfish ends, Finkelstein writes, "the time is long past to open our hearts to the rest of humanity's sufferings. This was the main lesson my mother imparted. . . . In the face of the sufferings of African-Americans, Vietnamese and Palestinians, my mother's credo always was: We are all Holocaust victims." Or again: "'If everyone who claims to be a survivor actually is one,' my mother used to exclaim, 'who did Hitler kill?'"[49]

Much of the moral tenor of Finkelstein's argument rests on simple-minded dicta of this sort, when it does not rely on high-decibel denunciations of both a personal and political kind. As a consequence, one is tempted to set aside this book as so much sentimental drivel or bullying rant. That would be a mistake, though, for while Finkelstein is not taken very seriously in America, he has found an attentive audience abroad. His book, now available in numerous foreign language translations, is widely discussed and, in some circles, also lauded. The notion that "we are all Holocaust victims" appeals to people who have had enough of the Jews as victims and find it intolerable that the Jews are so often singled out for special sympathy. In addition, Finkelstein's argument that crafty "Holocaust hucksters" are pumping up the numbers of Holocaust survivors in order to cash in on Jewish suffering wins sympathy among those who are inclined to see a predatory hand in the much publicized Holocaust-related litigation. If the figures on Holocaust survivors are being artificially inflated, then it follows that many of these "survivors" may themselves be little more than a figment of the Jewish imagination or, more damningly, a concoction of Jewish financial scheming.

In developing the notion of an enterprising and manipulative "Holocaust industry," Finkelstein's thought moves recklessly in many of the same directions already charted by the worst of the Holocaust deniers. These people may not be his natural allies but, like them, he has vilified Israel and "organized American Jewry" in relentless fashion and held "The Holocaust" up for scorn. It is not surprising, therefore, that his book is touted among people in right-wing circles in Europe and the United States. There is concern in Germany that the fantasies that Finkelstein has let loose will lend encouragement to some of the more troubling elements in that country, who find in Finkelstein's book confirmation of a Jewish conspiracy to exploit German historical guilt for selfish ends. In fact, the author's "Holocaust industry" is as much an ideological construct as neo-Nazi constructions of a Holocaust-that-never-was. But that hardly matters, for to people who are weary of hearing about Hitler and the Jews, Finkelstein's impassioned "exposé" of an elaborate Holocaust extortion racket is a welcome, long overdue gift. As one German reviewer wrote soon after the German publication of Finkelstein's book, reading *The Holocaust Industry* "is like opening a window for a sudden gust of fresh air."[50]

In fact, Finkelstein has not so much opened a window as thrown a stack of bricks through it. Many applaud him for doing so. While dismissed by most historians as being without any scholarly merit, *The Holocaust Industry* has enjoyed a popular success abroad, owing, no doubt, to the opportunity it affords readers to observe the angry son of Jewish Holocaust survivors attacking Israel as a Nazi-like state and accusing American Jews of exploiting the Holocaust for their own ends. For those who might relish the spectacle of this kind of Jew-on-Jew assault, *The Holocaust Industry* obviously has appeal, and Finkelstein's book has sold hundreds of thousands of copies worldwide. The German translation's initial print run of 50,000 quickly sold out, and, for a time, *The Holocaust Industry* topped the German best-seller list for nonfiction with 150,000 copies in print in 2001 alone.[51] In a poll taken by the prestigious Emnid Institute soon after the German translation appeared, sixty-five percent of Germans questioned agreed, either fully or partially, that Jewish organizations exaggerate Holocaust-related compensation claims in order to enrich themselves.[52] In Norman Finkelstein's deeply flawed work, they now have what looks to them like a certifiable proof-text.

The Holocaust Industry is the most sustained attack yet made against Holocaust memory, but it does not come out of nowhere. Finkelstein's allegations that most of the attention paid to Jewish suffering is not serious but is driven instead by "hucksters" intent on "Holocaust booty" is a cruder version of Arnold Jacob Wolf's allegation that "the Holocaust is being sold—it is not being taught."[53] Indeed, Finkelstein quotes Rabbi Wolf's very words as a prefatory inscription to his book. His conviction that Jews stress the unique features of their suffering for political and pecuniary motives—"unique suffering confers unique entitlement"[54]—is of a piece with earlier attacks on the so-called "Jewish uniqueness advocates." His notion of an interlocking network of Jewish Holocaust professionals—an entire "Holocaust industry" that works to manipulate Holocaust memory—is foreshadowed by similar charges made by Stannard, Churchill, and Novick and finds its germ in Lopate's evocation of the Holocaust as a "corporation" headed up by Elie Wiesel. Finkelstein's excoriations of Elie Wiesel as the "high-priest" of a "mystery religion" come right out of Novick's critical remarks on Wiesel and finds an exact analogue in Michael Goldberg's mocking criticisms of Wiesel as the "High Priest" of a new religious "cult." Since, in Finkelstein's formulation, "Elie Wiesel *is* The Holocaust," an exposé of Wiesel's "moral corruptions" and compromised political posturing is a denunciation of the whole "bankrupt" project itself.[55] What makes such an attack imperative, in Finkelstein's view, is the "Zionist" underpinnings of the "Holocaust industry," for what is the Holocaust if not the "perfect weapon for deflecting criticism of Israel?" In seeing the development of Holocaust consciousness in these terms, as a strategy devised by American Jewish elites to support the power of the Jewish State and to "delegitimize all criticism of Jews," Finkelstein is echoing sentiments that are now commonplace among critics of Holocaust consciousness.[56] In addition, Finkelstein's notion that American Jews have a "newly acquired identity" as a result of their adoption of the Holocaust as their central symbol is in accord with the views of Peter Novick, who claims the Holocaust was "virtually the only common denominator of American Jewish identity" and the only thing that might save American Jewry from "demographic catastrophe."[57]

A review of these and other related themes should make clear that Finkelstein's book has its lineage in the writings of a number of earlier critics of Holocaust consciousness, all of whom stress the utilitarian and exploitative function of memory, as if Holocaust awareness were nothing but a means of enhancing ethnic identity and advancing political agendas of one kind or another. If they do not see a Jewish conspiracy as such behind the promotion of the Holocaust, these writers see at work the hand of "Jewish uniqueness advocates," or that of the "proponents of Jewish exclusivism," or, in the words of Peter Novick, the labor of "thousands of full-time Holocaust professionals dedicated to keeping [Holocaust] memory alive."[58] It is of little interest to these critics that thoughtful people might feel compelled to think about the Jewish catastrophe under Hitler for other, less functional reasons. Where some might point to compelling historical, religious, moral, or ethical claims on consciousness as legitimate prods to remember the Nazi crimes, Novick, Finkelstein, and others who share their point of view see mostly Jewish influence-peddling in the media and "massive investments by Jewish communal organizations in promoting 'Holocaust consciousness.'"[59] In these and other ways, it is claimed, the Holocaust has been "sold" to the broad public, which, in "buying" it, finds an easy way to keep from facing its moral and historical responsibility for crimes closer to home. Thus, Novick seriously questions the belief that Holocaust memory has an important ethical dimension because, in his view, feeling bad about what happened to the Jews of Europe only enables Americans to keep from feeling bad about "whatever the United States has done to blacks, Native Americans, Vietnamese, and others."[60] Far from making people more sensitive to past historical atrocities and more alert to present-day political oppression, Holocaust consciousness "trivializes crimes of lesser magnitude" and is, for most Americans, "virtually cost-free: a few cheap tears."[61] In the end, as Novick assesses the place of the Holocaust in American life, it has become not much more than a "sordid game."[62]

To the degree that remembrance of the Holocaust continues to be viewed in such terms, it will go the way of other sordid games—into a state of diminishment and decline. Even under the best of conditions, Holocaust memory, like all historical memories, is prone to attenuate over time. In addition, the enormity of the Nazi crimes against the Jews makes it notoriously difficult for the mind to assimilate such horror and make any sense of it. For these reasons as well, one can hardly be confident that, in the years to come, public awareness of the Holocaust will be widely and responsibly maintained. In light of these considerations, it is no wonder that writers like Primo Levi, Jean Améry, Elie Wiesel, and others who reflected deeply about the Nazi assault against the Jews often came close to despair when they contemplated the future of Holocaust memory, for they recognized how tenuous such memory is.

What even the best of these writers was unable to foresee is an invidious element that has come to accompany attacks on Holocaust consciousness and amounts almost to a mocking of the dead. The popularization of the flippant but oft-repeated expression—"There is no business like Shoah business"—is symptomatic of a now commonplace attitude of derision that calls into question the value of *any* serious ongoing engagement with the Holocaust. Add to this note of belittlement an inclination to reduce the catastrophe merely to an ideological construct of Jewish, or "Zionist," interests, and the story of Jewish fate under Hitler is further devalued. Finally, the integrity of Holocaust memory is weakened still more by those who object to its so-called "centrality" on political grounds and link their critique of Holocaust consciousness to a critique of Jewish "power," especially as such power is exercised in the State of Israel.

The accumulated force of these tendencies over time may, indeed, bring about the "end of Auschwitz." But carried to its logical conclusion, what does "the end of Auschwitz" signify if not the end of any meaningful memory of the victims of Auschwitz and the other Nazi camps, ghettos, and killing fields? What does it mean if not the devaluation, and ultimately the nullification, of the testimony of the survivors of those places? None of that is about to happen anytime soon, but the wish to see it happen is finding a more audible voice than had been detectable in the past. As such voices emerge more prominently within mainstream culture, Imre Kertész's contention that "nothing has happened since Auschwitz that [can] reverse or refute Auschwitz" is called into question. The *fact* of Auschwitz may not be reversible, but its memory can and is being altered, appropriated, distorted, denied, and turned against its victims. If such developments continue apace, the fulfillment of the wish to see "the end of Auschwitz" will not be the return of the Jewish people to a higher ethical calling, as some of the critics I have cited here claim, but their return to the kind of vulnerability that preceded Auschwitz and helped to bring it about.

Epilogue:
A "Second Holocaust"?

The use of even one nuclear bomb inside Israel will destroy
everything. . . . It is not irrational to contemplate such an
eventuality.

—FORMER IRANIAN PRESIDENT HASHEMI RAFSANJANI

The second Holocaust. It's a phrase we may have to begin
thinking about. A possibility we may have to contemplate. A
reality we may have to witness.　　　　—RON ROSENBAUM

Shortly before the end of the last century, the political scientist
Walter Truett Anderson published a brief article calling attention
to a spate of books that struck him as constituting a new subgenre
of literature. These works were all about "the end of" something—
history, affluence, the nation-state, education, work, ideology, etc.
Spotting over nine hundred titles that began with those porten-
tous three words, Anderson realized that, with the approaching
end of the twentieth century, a trend was in the making. In part,
he decried it, labeling the easy recourse to the rhetoric of termination "promiscuous" and little more than a "literary device." At the
same time, he acknowledged that the emergence of a voluminous
literature projecting "the end of" so much that was familiar and
valued needed to be taken seriously. Were we moving not only

into a new century but a profoundly different world, marked by a "final shutdown of some piece of life as we have known it to be or hoped for it to become?"[1] Anderson suspected we were.

I share some of his suspicions, even as I realize that the present volume contributes still one more title to the growing corpus of books that concerned him. In the spirit of Anderson's skeptical inquiry, one might properly ask if we are, in fact, witnessing a series of cultural and intellectual transformations of such reach that, if continued, they might lead to "the end of the Holocaust?" I maintain that we are. As I have sought to show, the course of change with respect to Holocaust representation and memory is widespread and accelerating. In writing *The End of the Holocaust*, I have aimed to chart some of the more salient dimensions and consequences of such change. Certain aspects of it are inevitable, for they are part of the natural processes that Jean Améry called the "silently erosive and transformative effects of time."[2] Change is also a function of national priorities and cultural pressures that lead to the reshaping of Holocaust history to satisfy a variety of present-day goals. These goals spring from circumstances that are vastly different from those that led to the Nazi program of genocide against the Jews, yet rooted as they are in the social needs and aspirations of particular groups of people, such appropriations of the Holocaust are also probably inevitable.

But if Améry and others featured in these pages turned deeply pessimistic about the future prospects of Holocaust memory, it was because they were alert not only to these but also to more disturbing sources of transformation, which are neither natural nor inevitable. What especially troubled them were the uses and misuses of the past for clearly iniquitous ends, ranging from malign efforts to intentionally distort and diminish the Holocaust to expressions of Holocaust resentment, rejection, and denial. To Améry, these manipulations of the past were immoral, and he denounced them as such. What he and most other Holocaust writers of the twentieth century did not foresee, or caught only early glimpses of, is a development still more extreme: the emergence of voices that publicly *affirm* the Nazi slaughter of the Jews and promote it as a powerful and useful precedent. To regard the Holocaust in these terms, not as admonishment and warning but as encouragement and incitement, moves our subject beyond the inevitability of "endings" to the desirability of replications.

Those who follow events in the Middle East know that fears of a Second Holocaust have shadowed the State of Israel ever since its beginning and became especially acute at the time of the Six-Day War in 1967 and the Yom Kippur War of 1973. Exhortations to "drive the Jews into the sea" were common then and, understandably, were not readily dismissed as merely extravagant examples of Arab political rhetoric. The military means to destroy the Jewish State may have been lacking, but the openly declared desire to put an end to Israel's Jews, as voiced by Egypt's Gamal Abdel Nasser and others, was taken at face value.[3] Not surprisingly, in the aftermath of the Nazi catastrophe, Jews have become literalists. Hence, when they encounter anti-Jewish genocidal fantasies enshrined as part of state ideology, as in today's Iran, they are apt to take such declarations seriously. And Iran is not a lone example. Shouts of "Jews to the ovens" and "back to Auschwitz," which accompanied street demonstrations against Israel following the Gaza war of January 2009, are understood to mean just what they say. The same holds true for posters on display in New York City as recently as May 2010, depicting a mushroom cloud rising above the Israeli flag and carrying the slogan "Allah Is Gathering All The Zionists For The 'FINAL SOLUTION.'" As in these instances, appeals to Holocaust memory as prod or inspiration have emerged prominently in recent years and are both a symptom of and contributor to a resurgence of antisemitism on a global scale. In response to these troubling developments, it is not surprising that a number of contemporary writers have been moved to reflect on the possibilities of "the next Holocaust," or a "Second Holocaust."

One would prefer to view such nightmarish scenarios as un-thinkable, but reputable authors argue otherwise. Ron Rosen-baum, the author of *Explaining Hitler* and other well-regarded books, maintains that "the time has come to think about the Second Holocaust. It's coming sooner or later; it's not 'whether,' but *when*." Rosenbaum's fearsome prognostication was stimu-lated by his reading of Philip Roth's novel *Operation Shylock*, in which one of the characters, stealing the name "Philip Roth" and speaking from Israel, muses on the catastrophe-to-come in these terms:

> The meanings of the Holocaust . . . are for us to determine, but one thing is sure—its meaning will be no less tragic than it is now if there is a second Holocaust and the offspring of the European Jews who evacuated Europe for a seemingly safer haven should meet collective annihilation in the Mid-dle East. A second Holocaust is *not* going to occur on the continent of Europe, *because* it was the site of the first. But a second Holocaust could happen here all too easily, and, if the conflict between Arab and Jew escalates much longer, it will—*it must*. The destruction of Israel in a nuclear exchange is a possibility much less farfetched today than was the Holo-caust itself fifty years ago.[4]

Rosenbaum remarks, "Re-examining Mr. Roth's use of the phrase 'Second Holocaust' less than a decade later, even his darkest imaginings seem *optimistic* now. Especially when examined by the glare of burning synagogues in France."[5]

Roth's novel appeared in 1993, following the first Palestin-ian intifada and new outbreaks of violence against Israel that accompanied it. Rosenbaum's essay, "'Second Holocaust'? Roth's Phrase Isn't Necessarily Novelistic Fantasy Anymore," was written in early 2002, following massive terror strikes against America and Israel, including Al Qaeda's horrific assaults against New York and Washington, on September 11, 2001, and a rash of murderous Palestinian suicide bombings against Israeli civilians. At the same time, and carrying on over many months, hundreds of antisemitic attacks were directed against Jews and Jewish institutions in the cities of Europe, South America, and elsewhere. Far from being a metaphorical or historical allusion, Rosenbaum's disturbing reference to "the burning synagogues" suddenly had contemporary application. Moreover, it pointed not only to events in France, for throughout much of Europe, antisemitism had returned in open and often brutal ways. The words and images of the Holocaust were frequently invoked in the public rhetoric of these years, but this time they often targeted the Jews, especially the Jews of Israel, and were not issued in support of them. While individual Jews and Jewish schools, synagogues, cemeteries, community centers, and Holocaust memorials were being attacked, the victims of these aggressive actions, often portrayed in Nazi terms, were being perversely blamed for the violence directed against them. On the posters that accompanied street demonstrations that went on for many weeks across European cities, Israel's Ariel Sharon was commonly equated with Hitler, and the Jewish Star of David was crudely but ubiquitously intermingled with the swastika. This radical inversion of tropes was dumbfounding, but it caught on and revealed much about a newly awakened attitude of hostility toward Jews. As an explanation of its causes, Paul Berman's clarification seems accurate: "Palestinian terror [became] the measure of Israeli guilt. The more grotesque the terror, the deeper the guilt." To place the ultimate brand of condemnation on the now-criminalized Jews, "Israel became, in the rhetoric of its accusers, a Nazi entity—a state so utterly devoted to evil, so far beyond the bounds of human decency as to make suicide murder a comprehensible reaction on the part of its victims."[6]

These vilifications are now frequently heard in Europe and have become standard fare in many parts of the Muslim world, where defamation of Jews and Israel often goes hand in hand with unrestrained expressions of Holocaust denial. No public figure exemplifies the extremity of such anti-Jewish animus as passionately and consistently as Iran's Mahmoud Ahmadinejad, whose followers ardently declaim "Death to the Jews" and cheer on their president's calls for the end of the Jewish State. In a bizarre but now-familiar two-step, Ahmadinejad mocks the sufferings of the Jews during the Nazi years, as he ostentatiously did in his infamous Holocaust cartoon contest (February 6, 2006), and also casts doubt on the veracity of such sufferings, as he tried to do in his sordid Holocaust deniers' conference (December 12, 2006). At the same time, Ahmadinejad's repeated public excoriations of Israel and prophecies of the country's imminent demise have strategically positioned him as the leading advocate of the next Holocaust. Versatile in the spewing of hatred, the president of Iran fulfills the double role of being both a Holocaust denier and a Holocaust promoter. Matthias Küntzel, one of his most perceptive critics, sums up Ahmadinejad's thinking with exacting precision: Ahmadinejad "denies the Holocaust" not so much "to revise the past" as "to shape the future: to prepare the way for the next Holocaust. . . . Auschwitz is delegitimized in order to legitimize the elimination of Israel. . . . Israel must vanish."[7]

The endpoint of such thinking is clear: a "Second Holocaust," should it come to pass, will find its epicenter in Israel. Once again singled out for genocide, the Jews, according to this apocalyptic vision, are to be murdered en masse. While the instruments used to destroy them will vary from those of the Nazi period, the goal is fully and recognizably Hitlerian. Here is the Israeli historian Benny Morris's projection of Ahmadinejad's catastrophe-in-the-making:

> The Nazis . . . industrialized mass murder. But still, the perpetrators had one-on-one contact with the victims. They . . . had to round up the men, women and children from their houses

and drag and beat them through the streets and mow them down in nearby woods or push and pack them on cattle cars and transport them to the camps, where 'Work makes Free', separate the able-bodied from the completely useless and lure them into 'shower' halls and pour in the gas and then take out, or oversee the extraction of, the bodies and prepare the 'showers' for the next batch.

The second Holocaust will be quite different. One bright morning, in five or ten years' time, perhaps during a regional crisis, perhaps out of the blue, a day or a year or five years after Iran's acquisition of the Bomb, the mullahs in Qom will convene in secret session, under a portrait of the steely-eyed Ayatollah Khomeini, and give President Ahmedinejad, by then in his second or third term, the go ahead. The orders will go out and the Shihab III and IV missiles will take off for Tel Aviv, Beersheba, Haifa, and Jerusalem, and probably some military sites, including Israel's half dozen air and (reported) nuclear missile bases. Some of the Shihabs will be nuclear-tipped, perhaps even with multiple warheads. Others will be dupes, packed merely with biological or chemical agents, or old newspapers, to draw off or confuse Israel's anti-missile batteries and Home Guard units.

With a country the size and shape of Israel (an elongated 8,000 square miles), probably four or five hits will suffice: No more Israel. A million or more Israelis, in the greater Tel Aviv, Haifa and Jerusalem areas, will die immediately. Millions will be seriously irradiated. Israel has about seven million inhabitants. No Iranian will see or touch an Israeli. It will be quite impersonal.[8]

The post-Auschwitz future was not supposed to turn out this way. In response to the Nazi destruction of European Jewry, the resolute conviction "never again" has been widely voiced and, presumably, also widely adopted. Based on the assumption that the memory of the dead would serve to protect the living, this formula has been devised as a shield against future genocides. As the previously mentioned character in Philip Roth's *Operation Shylock* puts it, "Whatever hatred of Jews may be present in Europe . . . there are ranged against this residual anti-Semitism powerful currents of enlightenment and morality that are sustained by memory of the Holocaust, a horror that operates now as a bulwark *against* European anti-Semitism, however virulent" (pp. 44–45).

Most of the writers studied in the chapters of this book no doubt would have endorsed this notion in the early stages of their careers. Indeed, a large part of what prompted them to write in the first place was the belief that accurate, irrefutable evidence of the atrocities they witnessed might help to safeguard against a repeat. With the progressive dilution, distortion, and denial of the historical record of Nazi crimes against the Jews, however, the hope that Holocaust memory might stand as a "bulwark" against the return of Jew-hatred has given way to a sense of futility, and, in some cases, despair. Far from being merely "residual," antisemitism has become resurgent in Europe over the past decade. Moreover, repeated evocations of the Holocaust, instead of acting to retard hostility to Jews, have been used as incitement against them. The incentives for this aggressive turn are complex and varied and encompass motives that are political, psychological, social, and cultural. Among these, a "secondary antisemitism," prompted by negative reactions to reminders of the victimization of the Jews, can bring on a backlash against them.[9] As the Berlin-based writer Henryk Broder has put it, "The Germans will never forgive the Jews for Auschwitz."[10]

As these instances indicate, Holocaust memory, far from being prophylactic, is evidently capable of provoking new forms of anti-Jewish hostility, which, at their most extreme, summon up the Nazi death camps as precedent. Hence, Imre Kertész's observation that "the anti-Semite of our age no longer loathes Jews;

he wants Auschwitz."[11] And hence, as well, the projections of a "next Holocaust" or "Second Holocaust" found in the writings of Philip Roth, Ron Rosenbaum, Benny Morris, Matthias Küntzel, Nat Hentoff, Hillel Halkin, Robert Wistrich, and numerous others.

No one has described the dynamic that defines this new and potentially genocidal strain of antisemitism more clearly than Kertész:

> The expression has been so often repeated that it has become almost a cliché: it is necessary to preserve memory of the Holocaust so that it can never again come to pass. But since Auschwitz, nothing has happened that makes a new Auschwitz impossible. On the contrary. Before Auschwitz, Auschwitz was unimaginable. That is no longer so today. Because Auschwitz in fact occurred, it has now been established in our imaginations as a firm possibility. What we are able to imagine, especially because it once was, can be again.[12]

In less overwrought times, one might regard these insights as perceptive but perhaps of more theoretical than practical interest. We are not living in such times. Unsubtly and unashamedly, the language of mass murder is once again being broadly disseminated, and those who hear in it the preparatory rhetoric of a "Second Holocaust" may be hearing correctly. When the former Iranian president Hashemi Rafsanjani boasted, in December 2001, that "the use of even one nuclear bomb inside Israel will destroy everything," the centrifuges in his country's nuclear plants were far fewer and had not yet begun to spin so rapidly. Today they are working overtime. So is the murderous imagination of the current Iranian president Mahmoud Ahmadinejad, who seems never to tire of pronouncing death sentences on the State of Israel: "The Zionist regime will be wiped out, and humanity will be liberated."[13] Substitute "Jews" for "Zionists," and the proclamation to liberate the world by destroying the Jews will ring all too familiar to students of the Nazi period.

Few people took Hitler at his word when he voiced such sentiments. The result was Auschwitz, a warning from the past and, to some, a coveted possibility for the future.

NOTES

INTRODUCTION

1. Yosef Hayim Yerushalmi, *Zakhor: Jewish History and Jewish Memory* (Seattle: University of Washington Press, 1982), p. 98.

2. Raul Hilberg, *The Politics of Memory: The Journey of a Holocaust Historian* (Chicago: Ivan Dee, 1996), p. 83.

3. Imre Kertész, "Who Owns Auschwitz?" *The Yale Journal of Criticism* 14, no. 1 (2001): p. 268.

4. Raul Hilberg, *Perpetrators Victims Bystanders: The Jewish Catastrophe, 1933–1945* (New York: Harper Collins, 1992), p. xi.

5. Primo Levi, *The Reawakening*, trans. Stuart Woolf (New York: Collier Books, 1993), p. 207.

6. Shai Oster, "Shoah Business: Humour and the 'Second Generation,'" *The Jewish Quarterly* (Autumn 1998): pp. 13–18.

7. "Imre Kertész, "Language in Exile" [unpublished English translation of a Hungarian essay, courtesy of the author.]

8. Jean Améry, *Radical Humanism: Selected Essays*, trans. Sidney Rosenfeld and Stella P. Rosenfeld (Bloomington: Indiana University Press, 1984), pp. 64–65.

1. POPULAR CULTURE AND THE POLITICS OF MEMORY

The epigraph is from Milan Kundera, *The Joke* (New York: Harper & Row, 1982), p. 245.

1. John Bodnar, author of *Remaking America: Public Memory, Commemoration, and Patriotism*, as quoted in "A Belated Place in U.S. History," *New York Times*, March 6, 1997.

2. *Newsweek*, April 29, 1985, p. 14.

3. *New York Times*, March 22, 1985.

4. Ibid., March 22, 1985; April 22, 1985.

5. Ibid., April 19, 1985.

6. Ibid., May 6, 1985.

7. Ibid.

8. *Indiana Daily Student*, May 1, 1985, and *The Notre Dame Observer*, April 24, 1985.

9. See Alvin H. Rosenfeld, *Imagining Hitler* (Bloomington: Indiana University Press, 1985), pp. 13–25.

10. For a review of *Love Letters to Adolf Hitler*, which first was staged in Berlin in 1996 and, in an expanded version, opened in New York in January 1997, see "Even Hitler Had His Groupies," *New York Times*, January 11, 1997.

11. Gordon Craig, *The Germans* (New York: G. P. Putnam's Sons, 1982), p. 80.

12. Norman Spinrad, *The Iron Dream* (New York: Avon Books, 1972), p. 9. For a comprehensive study of allohistorical fictions about Nazi Germany, including numerous such works about Hitler, see Gavriel Rosenfeld, *The World Hitler Never Made: Alternate History and the Memory of Nazism* (Cambridge: Cambridge University Press, 2005).

13. Cited in *Philadelphia Jewish Exponent*, June 28, 1985.

14. "The Hitler Business," *Life*, July 1983, pp. 83–88.

15. Robert G. L. Waite, *The Psychopathic God: Adolf Hitler* (New York: Basic Books, 1977), p. xi.

16. See Geoffrey Hartman, ed., *Bitburg in Moral and Political Perspective* (Bloomington: Indiana University Press, 1986), pp. 262–273.

2. THE RHETORIC OF VICTIMIZATION

1. Christopher Lasch, *The Minimal Self: Psychic Survival in Troubled Times* (New York: W. W. Norton & Company, 1984), p. 64. The words quoted as an epigraph to this chapter are taken from pages 111 and 129 of this same book.

2. *New York Times Sunday Magazine*, December 15, 1996, p. 21.

3. *Los Angeles Times*, October 1, 1995.

4. See Joseph A. Amato, *Victims and Values: A History and a Theory of Suffering* (Westport, Conn.: Greenwood Press, 1990), pp. 159–160. For astute commentary on the "black holocaust," see Eric J. Sundquist, *Strangers in the Land: Blacks, Jews, Post-Holocaust America* (Cambridge, Mass.: The Belknap Press of Harvard University Press, 2005).

5. The quotation, from "The Eighteenth Brumaire of Louis Bonaparte," can be found in *The Marx-Engels Reader*, ed. Robert C. Tucker (New York: W. W. Norton & Co., 1978), p. 594.

6. "Using Nazi Images to Hit Political Opponents Now a Common Tack," *New York Times*, October 23, 1995.

7. Elie Wiesel, "Some Questions that Remain Open," in *Comprehending the Holocaust*, ed. Asher Cohen, Joav Gelber, and Charlotte Wardi (Frankfurt am Main: Verlag Peter Lang, 1988), p. 11.

8. Edward Alexander, *The Jewish Idea and Its Enemies* (New Brunswick, N.J.: Transaction Books, 1988), 99–109.

9. Zlata Filipović, *Zlata's Diary: A Child's Life in Sarajevo*, trans. Christina Pribichevich-Zoric (New York: Viking, 1994).

10. Cara Wilson, *Love, Otto: The Legacy of Anne Frank* (Kansas City: Andrews and McMeel, 1995), p. 96.

11. Louis Daniel Brodsky, *Gestapo Crows: Holocaust Poems* (St. Louis, Mo.: Time Being Books, 1992), p. 100.

12. Betty Friedan, *The Feminine Mystique* (New York: W. W. Norton & Company, 1963), pp. 305–307.

13. Amato, *Victims and Values*, pp. xvii, xxiii.

14. Tzvetan Todorov, "The Abuses of Memory," trans. Mei Lin Chang, *Common Knowledge* 5 (Spring 1996): p. 24.

3. THE AMERICANIZATION OF THE HOLOCAUST

1. These studies, the first of which appeared in 1993, have been published by the American Jewish Committee as a series of "Working Papers on Contemporary Anti-Semitism." Titles include: *What Do Americans Know about the Holocaust?* (1993), *What Do the British Know about the Holocaust?* (1993), *What Do the French Know about the Holocaust?* (1994), *What Do Australians Know about the Holocaust?* (1994), *Current German Attitudes toward Jews and other Minorities* (1994), and *Holocaust Denial: What the Survey Data Reveal* (1995); they are available from the American Jewish Committee, 165 East 56th Street, New York, NY 10022–2746.

2. Jennifer Golub and Renae Cohen, *What Do Americans Know about the Holocaust?* (New York: The American Jewish Committee, 1993), p. 13.

3. Ibid., pp. 38–40.

4. Tom W. Smith, *Holocaust Denial: What the Survey Data Reveal* (New York: The American Jewish Committee, 1995), p. 31.

5. For an excellent study of this subject, see Gavriel D. Rosenfeld, "The Reception of William L. Shirer's *The Rise and Fall of the Third Reich* in the United States and West Germany, 1960–62," *Journal of Contemporary History* 29 (1994): pp. 95–128.

6. The exact number of Jews killed is not known and probably never will be known precisely. Raul Hilberg has placed the figure at 5.1 million; Lucy Dawidowicz estimated it at 5,933,900; Martin Gilbert, at 5.75 million; the *Encyclopedia of the Holocaust* states a minimum figure of 5,596,000 and a maximum of 5,860,000; and Wolfgang Benz sets the minimum at 5,290,000 and a maximum of over six million. As previously unavailable archival materials in the former Soviet Union are made known to scholars, these figures are likely to be revised and, from early indications, probably upwards. Some of these figures and an informed explanation of how they have been reached can be found in Franciszek Piper, "The Number of Victims," in *Anatomy of the Auschwitz Death Camp*, ed. Yisrael Gutman and Michael Berenbaum, pp. 61–76 (Bloomington: Indiana University Press, 1994).

7. In Yehuda Bauer's view, the Wiesenthal position is seriously flawed historically as well as conceptually: "It is apparently no less a man than Simon Wiesenthal . . . who has invented the '11 million' formula that is a key slogan in the denial of the uniqueness of the Jewish experience. Wiesenthal is going around campuses and Jewish congregations saying that the Holocaust was the murder of 11 million people–the six million Jews and five million non-Jews who were killed in the Nazi camps. In purely historical terms this is sheer nonsense. The total number of people who died in concentration camps during the war period–excepting Jews and Gypsies– was about half a million, perhaps a little more. On the other hand, the total number of non-Jewish civilian casualties during the war caused by Nazi brutality cannot be less than 20–25 million. . . . Probably some 2.5 million Soviet POWs died in special camps that were not part of the concentration camp system (though some thousands were shipped to concentration camps and murdered there)." Yehuda Bauer, "Whose Holocaust?," *Midstream* 26, no. 9 (November, 1980): p. 43.

8. For a convenient summary of these arguments, see A. Dirk Moses, "The Holocaust and Genocide," in *The Historiography of the Holocaust*, ed. Dan Stone (New York: Palgrave Macmillian, 2004), pp. 533–555; see also Dan Stone, *History, Memory,*

and Mass Atrocity: Essays on the Holocaust and Genocide (London: Vallentine Michell, 2006) and, by the same author, *Constructing the Holocaust: A Study in Historiography* (London: Valentine Mitchell, 2003), chapter 5.

9. See Gavriel D. Rosenfeld, "The Politics of Uniqueness: Reflections on the Recent Polemical Turn in Holocaust and Genocide Scholarship," *Holocaust and Genocide Studies* 13, no. 1 (1999): pp. 28–61.

10. See *Auschwitz: A History in Photographs*, ed. Jonathan Webber, Teresa Swiebocka, and Connie Wilsack (Bloomington: Indiana University Press, 1993); the essays printed in this volume reflect a significant change in Polish thinking about Auschwitz.

11. A large body of scholarly literature now exists on the construction of national memories of World War II and the Holocaust. Among other works, see Peter Baldwin, ed., *Reworking the Past: Hitler, the Holocaust, and the Historians' Debate* (Boston: Beacon Press, 1990); Saul Friedländer, *Memory, History, and the Extermination of the Jews of Europe* (Bloomington: Indiana University Press, 1993); Charles S. Maier, *The Unmasterable Past: History, Holocaust, and German National Identity* (Cambridge, MA: Harvard University Press, 1988); Judith Miller, *One, By One, By One: Facing the Holocaust* (New York: Simon and Schuster, 1990); Henry Rousso, *The Vichy Syndrome: History and Memory in France since 1944* (Cambridge, Mass.: Harvard University Press, 1991); Gavriel D. Rosenfeld, *Munich and Memory: Architecture, Monuments, and the Legacy of the Third Reich* (Berkeley: University of California Press, 2000); Michael C. Steinlauf, *Bondage to the Dead: Poland and the Memory of the Holocaust* (Syracuse: Syracuse University Press, 1997); Jeffrey Herf, *Divided Memory: The Nazi Past in the Two Germanys* (Cambridge, Mass.: Harvard University Press, 1997).

12. For an early but still useful study of terminological origins and changes, see Gerd Korman, "The Holocaust in American Historical Writing," *Societas* 2, no. 3 (Summer, 1972): pp. 251–270; see also Zev Garber and Bruce Zuckerman, "Why Do We Call the Holocaust 'The Holocaust?' An Inquiry into the Psychology of Labels," *Modern Judaism* 9, no. 2 (May 1989): pp. 197–212.

13. Zev Garber and Bruce Zuckerman advocate a broader conception of what the "Holocaust" was and are open to the same historical criticism that Bauer levels at Simon Wiesenthal: "[The Holocaust] becomes a warning of what too easily can happen at any time, at any place, with anyone in the role of victim or victimizer. This is the way 'The Holocaust' should be characterized and especially how it should be taught. . . . The 'six million' figure, often invoked in characterizations of 'The Holocaust,' points up the problem of stressing uniqueness and chosenness over commonality. The truth is that eleven million people were killed by the Nazis in the concentration camps. Nearly half of these are excluded in most characterizations of 'The Holocaust,' and this seems to imply that Gentile deaths are not as significant as Jewish deaths" ("Why Do We Call the Holocaust 'the Holocaust?,'" p. 208). The authors cite no sources to corroborate their reference to "eleven million" people killed in the concentration camps and probably look to Wiesenthal as their authority on this matter.

14. See "Address by President Jimmy Carter," printed in "President's Commission on the Holocaust," September 27, 1979.

15. Daniel Levy and Natan Sznaider, *The Holocaust and Memory in the Global Age* (Philadelphia: Temple University Press, 2006), p. 195.

16. Bauer, "Whose Holocaust?" p. 42.

17. Ilan Avisar, *Screening the Holocaust: Cinema's Images of the Unimaginable*

(Bloomington: Indiana University Press, 1988), pp. 96–97; see also Lawrence Baron, "The First Wave of American 'Holocaust' Films," *American Historical Review* 115 (Feb. 2010): pp. 90–113.

18. Ibid., p. 116.

19. Frances Goodrich and Albert Hackett, *The Diary of Anne Frank* (New York: Random House, 1956), p. 174.

20. Undated, four-page letter of solicitation by Miles Lerman, Chairman, United States Holocaust Memorial Museum.

21. Estelle Gilson, "Americanizing the Holocaust," *Congress Monthly*, September/ October, 1993, p. 6.

22. See *New York Times* article, "Photographs of Balkans Draw Fire: Serb Groups Fault Holocaust Museum," September 24, 1994; see also Alfred Lipson, "Anger at a Holocaust Museum Exhibit," *Midstream* 40, no. 9 (December, 1994), pp. 26–27.

23. Michael Berenbaum, *After Tragedy and Triumph: Essays in Modern Jewish Thought and the American Experience* (Cambridge: Cambridge University Press, 1990), p. 22.

24. Ibid., p. 20.

25. See *New York Times* article, "Crowds Strain U.S. Museum on Holocaust," December 23, 1993.

26. These aims are set forth in a Simon Wiesenthal Center–Museum of Tolerance promotional brochure.

27. Judy Chicago, *Holocaust Project: From Darkness into Light*, with photography by Donald Woodman (New York: Penguin Books, 1993).

28. Ibid., p. 36.

29. Ibid., p. 37; italics and brackets in the original text.

30. Ibid., pp. 9–10.

31. Ibid., p. 19; italics in the original text.

32. Ibid., p. 62; italics in the original text.

33. Ibid., pp. 27, 31.

34. Ibid., p. 90.

35. Ibid., p. 138.

36. Ibid., P. 139.

37. Ibid., p. 132.

38. Quoted in an article, "ADL Hits Christian Fundamentalists," in the *Forward*, June 10, 1994.

39. The American Jewish Committee studies referred to in footnote # 1 indicate that Americans acquire their information about World War II and the Holocaust chiefly from television programs. On occasion, popular television and radio talk shows "debate" the reality of the Holocaust by featuring a "revisionist" and a "survivor" presenting what is commonly understood to be their respective "views." These programs reach large audiences, who seem drawn by the sensational and the controversial, but to what effect, we do not know. Inasmuch as these popular "debates" pit neo-Nazi "deniers" against Jewish "survivor/witnesses," they recapitulate the fundamental aggression of the Holocaust itself. In this respect, the television talk shows might be considered a continuation of the war against the Jews by other means.

40. For a detailed study of postwar responses to the Holocaust within American Jewish communities, see Hasia Diner, *We Remember with Reverence and Love: American Jews and the Myth of Silence after the Holocaust, 1945–1962* (New York: New York University Press, 2009).

41. William Helmreich, *Against All Odds: Holocaust Survivors and the Successful Lives They Made in America* (New York: Simon & Schuster, 1992), p. 38.

42. The Fortunoff Video Archives for Holocaust Testimonies at Yale University has been engaged in filming the testimonies of Holocaust survivors for a number of years now and is a major resource of its kind. At least two books have already been produced on the basis of these archival holdings: Lawrence Langer's *Holocaust Testimonies: The Ruins of Memory* (New Haven, Conn.: Yale University Press, 1991) and *Testimony: Crises of Witnessing in Literature, Psychoanalysis, and History,* by Shoshana Felman and Dori Laub (New York: Routledge, 1992). In addition, the USC Shoah Foundation, which has taken over and expanded the work of Steven Spielberg's Foundation, has recorded and videotaped the testimonies of more than fifty-two thousand Holocaust survivors.

43. Leon Uris, foreword to Ernst Michel, *Promises to Keep* (New York: Barricade Books, 1994), p. xiii.

44. For more on the Bitburg affair, see Geoffrey Hartman, ed., *Bitburg in Moral and Political Perspective* (Bloomington: Indiana University Press, 1986).

45. With assistance provided by some of these institutes, much work has been done over the years in introducing the Holocaust into the curricula of American secondary schools, and a number of states now mandate that such study be required of all of their students. In Michigan alone, for instance, over one hundred schools have adopted a well-regarded text on the Holocaust produced by Sidney Bolkosky and others, *Life Unworthy of Life: A Holocaust Curriculum.* Other states employ other texts, not all of which stand up as well to critical scrutiny. In this regard, see Lucy Dawidowicz's "How They Teach the Holocaust," *Commentary,* December 1990, pp. 25–32.

46. Stephen Schiff, "Seriously Spielberg," *The New Yorker,* March 21, 1994; Terrence Rafferty, "A Man of Transactions," *The New Yorker,* December 20, 1993; the Katzenberg encomium is quoted in the Schiff article above.

47. James Bowman, "Lost and Profound," *The American Spectator,* February, 1994; J. Hoberman, "Spielberg's Oskar," *Village Voice,* December 21, 1993; Donald Kuspit, "Director's Guilt," *Artforum,* February, 1994; and Claude Lanzmann, "The Twisted Truth of *Schindler's List,*" London *Evening Standard,* February 10, 1994.

48. Since the appearance of the film, Oskar Schindler's grave in the Latin Cemetery of Jerusalem has become a popular religious site for pilgrims visiting Israel. In addition, tourists can visit Poland on monthly tours called "Oskar Schindler's Poland." See Jack Schneidler, "The Ghosts of Poland's Past," *St. Petersburg Times,* October 9, 1994.

49. Michael André Bernstein, "The *Schindler's List* Effect," *The American Scholar* 63, no. 3 (Summer 1994): pp. 429–432.

50. Eva Fogelman, *Conscience and Courage: Rescue of Jews during the Holocaust* (New York: Anchor Books Doubleday, 1994), pp. xix, 3.

51. In addition to Fogelman's *Conscience and Courage,* notable titles include Gay Block and Malka Drucker's *Rescuers: Portraits of Moral Courage in the Holocaust* (1992); Peter Hellman's *Avenue of the Righteous: Portraits in Uncommon Courage of Christians and the Jews They Saved from Hitler* (1980); Douglas K. Huneke's *The Moses of Rovno: The Stirring Story of Fritz Graebe, A German Christian Who Risked His Life to Lead Hundreds of Jews to Safety during the Holocaust* (1985); Samuel P. Oliner and Pearl Oliner's *The Altruistic Personality: Rescuers of Jews in Nazi Europe* (1988); Mordecai Paldiel's *The Path of the Righteous: Gentile Rescuers of Jews during the Holocaust* (1993); Eric Silver's *The Book of the Just: The Unsung Heroes Who Rescued Jews from Hitler* (1992); Nechama Tec's *When Light Pierced the Darkness:*

Christian Rescue of Jews in Nazi-Occupied Poland (1986); Hillel Levine's *In Search of Sugihara* (1996); and many others of a similar kind.

A lengthy and critically perceptive review of much of the literature on "rescuers" that has appeared to date is David Gushee's "Many Paths to Righteousness: An Assessment of Research on Why Righteous Gentiles Helped Jews," *Holocaust and Genocide Studies* 7, no. 3 (Winter 1993): pp. 372–401.

52. See, for instance, Elinor J. Brecher, *Schindler's Legacy: True Stories of the List Survivors* (New York: Penguin Books, 1994).

53. Fogelman, *Conscience and Courage*, p. xix.

54. Yosef Abramowitz, "Is Elie Wiesel Happy?" *Moment*, February 1994, pp. 32–37, 78. The article is accompanied by photographs of Wiesel kissing his wife, bantering with a friend, and, to really make its point in unambiguously American fashion, posing with a baseball. It includes lines like these: "Elie Wiesel has not merely survived, he has triumphed. And if he would pause long enough to consider it, he might even say he's happy" (p. 32). Anyone who has read Wiesel's brooding and deeply melancholy novel, *The Forgotten* (1992), will have a hard time imagining its author as the same person profiled as "happy" in Abramowitz's article.

55. See Dennis Klein, "The Exceptional Intervention," *Dimensions* 3, no. 3 (1988): p. 3.

56. Fogelman, *Conscience and Courage*, p. 301.

57. Harold M. Schulweis, "The Bias against Man," *Dimensions* 3, no. 3 (1988): pp. 4, 5.

58. Harold M. Schulweis, *For Those Who Can't Believe* (New York: HarperCollins, 1994), p. 150.

59. Schulweis, "The Bias against Man," p. 5.

60. Ibid., pp. 4, 6, 8.

61. Schulweis, *For Those Who Can't Believe*, pp. 148–149.

62. André Schwarz-Bart, *The Last of the Just*, trans. Stephen Becker (New York: Atheneum, 1961), p. 374. For a brief but illuminating history of the Jewish folk legend of the "just man," see Gershom Scholem, "The Tradition of the Thirty-Six Hidden Just Men," in *The Messianic Idea in Judaism and other Essays on Jewish Spirituality* (New York: Schocken Books, 1971), pp. 251–256.

63. Schulweis, *For Those Who Can't Believe*, p. 157.

64. Fogelman, *Conscience and Courage*, p. 303.

65. The authors of *What Do Americans Know about the Holocaust?* and *Holocaust Denial: What the Survey Data Reveal* are in agreement about the knowledge level of Americans regarding the Holocaust and conclude that it is generally "shallow, incomplete, and imperfect." In their informed view, "Holocaust ignorance is widespread" (*Holocaust Denial*, pp. 3, 22).

66. Aharon Appelfeld, *Beyond Despair* (New York: Fromm Publishers, 1994), p. xiii.

67. I am indebted to Eric Sundquist, of UCLA, for sharing insights into this phenomenon with me.

68. Other notable books in this vein include Henry Feingold, *The Politics of Rescue: The Roosevelt Administration and the Holocaust, 1938–1945* (New York: Holocaust Library, 1980); Richard Breitman, *Official Secrets: What the Nazis Planned, What the British and Americans Knew* (New York: Hill and Wang, 1998); and Saul Friedman, *No Haven for the Oppressed: United States Policy toward Jewish Refugees, 1938–1945* (Detroit: Wayne State University Press, 1973).

69. Among other works on the American media, see Deborah Lipstadt, *Beyond*

Belief: The American Press and the Coming of the Holocaust, 1933–1945 (New York: The Free Press, 1986), and Laurel Leff, *Buried by the Times: The Holocaust and America's Most Important Newspaper* (Cambridge: Cambridge University Press, 2005).

70. As a counter-argument, see William D. Rubinstein, *The Myth of Rescue: Why the Democracies Could Not Have Saved More Jews from the Nazis* (New York: Routledge, 1997).

71. Father John A. O'Brien, foreword to Philip Friedman, *Their Brothers' Keepers* (New York: Holocaust Library, 1978; first published, 1957), pp. 7–8.

4. ANNE FRANK: THE POSTHUMOUS YEARS

The epigraph is from Dick Houwaart, *Anne in 't voorbijgaan: Emoties, gedachten en verwachtingen rondom het huis en het Dagboek van Anne Frank* (Amsterdam: Keesing Boeken, 1982), p. 20.

1. David Barnouw and Gerrold van der Stroom, eds., *The Diary of Anne Frank: The Critical Edition*, trans. Arnold J. Pomerans and B. M. Mooyaart-Doubleday (New York: Doubleday, 1989).

2. Karen Shawn, *The End of Innocence: Anne Frank and the Holocaust* (New York: International Center for Holocaust Studies, Anti-Defamation League of B'nai B'rith, 1989).

3. *Legacy: The Newsletter of the Anne Frank Center* (June 2, 1989).

4. Louis de Jong, "The Girl Who Was Anne Frank," *The Reader's Digest*, October 1957, p. 118.

5. Jan Romein's essay is reprinted in Anna G. Steenmeijer, ed., *A Tribute to Anne Frank* (Garden City, NY: Doubleday & Company, 1971), p. 21; in a slightly altered translation, it also appears in *The Diary of Anne Frank: The Critical Editon*, pp. 67–68; the citations here are to the version in *A Tribute to Anne Frank*.

6. *The Diary of Anne Frank: The Critical Edition*, p. 71.

7. The text of the play was published as *The Diary of Anne Frank*, by Frances Goodrich and Albert Hackett (New York: Random House, 1956).

8. Introduction to *Anne Frank: The Diary of a Young Girl* (New York: Pocket Books, 1953), p. ix.

9. *Newsweek*, June 16, 1952.

10. *Saturday Review*, July 19, 1952, p. 20.

11. *New York Times Book Review*, June 15, 1952, pp. 1, 22.

12. Introduction to *The Works of Anne Frank* (Garden City, N.Y.: Doubleday & Company, 1959); the Birstein-Kazin essay is also printed as the introduction to *Tales from the House Behind* (New York: Bantam Books, 1966).

13. *Herald Tribune*, October 23, 1955.

14. *New York Post*, October 8, 1955.

15. Lawrence Langer, "The Americanization of the Holocaust on Stage and Screen," in *From Hester Street to Hollywood*, ed. Sarah Blacher Cohen (Bloomington: Indiana University Press, 1983), p. 216.

16. *New York Times*, October 2, 1955.

17. *Herald Tribune*, October 2, 1955.

18. *Newsweek*, June 25, 1979.

19. *Variety*, October 6, 1955.

20. *Daily News*, October 6, 1955.

21. *B'nai B'rith Messenger*, February 3, 1956; *Congress Weekly*, December 19, 1952.

22. Langer, "The Americanization of the Holocaust on Stage and Screen," pp. 214–215.

23. Ibid., pp. 34–35.

24. Ibid.

25. Ibid., pp. 186–187.

26. Goodrich and Hackett, *The Diary of Anne Frank*, p. 168.

27. Lawrence Graver, *An Obsession with Anne Frank* (Berkeley: University of California Press, 1995), p. 89.

28. Ibid., pp. 172–173.

29. Ibid., pp. 170, 174.

30. This letter is quoted in Lawrence Graver, *An Obsession with Anne Frank*, p. 54.

31. *The Diary of Anne Frank: The Critical Edition*, p. 74.

32. Ernst Schnabel, *Anne Frank: A Portrait in Courage*, trans. Richard and Clara Winston (New York: Harcourt, Brace and World, 1958), p. 16.

33. Ibid., p. 167.

34. Ibid., p. 185.

35. President Reagan's address at Bergen-Belsen is collected in *Bitburg in Moral and Political Perspective*, ed. Geoffrey Hartman (Bloomington: Indiana University Press, 1986), pp. 253–255.

36. Ibid., p. 255.

37. The figures were given to me in a private communication by Gabriele Shettle, an assistant to Monika Schoeller, the head publisher of Fischer Verlag, in Frankfurt (March 12, 2010).

38. Cited in "In the Hearts of Men: The Progress of Anne Frank's 'Diary,'" *The Wiener Library* 12 (1958): p. 45.

39. Cited in Emanuel Litvinoff, "Berlin's High Noon," *Jewish Observer* and *Middle East Review*, February 8, 1957, p. 13.

40. *Theater der Zeit*, June 1957.

41. Norbert Muhlen, "The Return of Anne Frank," *ADL Bulletin*, June 1957, p. 2.

42. Passing reference to changes in the diary was made in an article that appeared in *Der Spiegel*, April 1, 1959; a fuller account is given in *The Diary of Anne Frank: The Critical Edition*, pp. 72–73. Readers who wish to trace the changes described and analyzed in this chapter can consult the German critical edition, *Die Tagebücher der Anne Frank* (Frankfurt am Main: S. Fischer Verlag, 1988). *Anne Frank: Tagebuch*, newly translated by Mirjam Pressler (Frankfurt am Main: S. Fischer Verlag, 1991), is a significant improvement upon the earlier German edition of Anne Frank's diary and corrects the kinds of problems pointed to in this chapter.

43. Hannah Arendt, "Letter to the Editor," *Midstream* (September 1962): pp. 84–85.

44. Bruno Bettelheim, "The Ignored Lesson of Anne Frank," *Harper's*, November 1960, p. 46.

45. "The Return of Anne Frank," *ADL Bulletin*, June 1957, p. 8.

46. Martin Dworkin, "The Vanishing Diary of Anne Frank," *Jewish Frontier* (April 1960): pp. 9, 10.

47. Algeine Ballif, "Anne Frank on Broadway," *Commentary*, November 1955, pp. 466–467.

48. Ludwig Lewisohn, "A Glory and A Doom," *Saturday Review*, July 19, 1952, p. 20.

49. Meyer Levin, "A Classic Human Document," *Congress Weekly,* June 16, 1952.

50. Meyer Levin, "At Long Last We Have A Real Story of Jews Under Nazism," *National Jewish Post,* June 20, 1952.

51. Lewisohn, "A Glory and A Doom."

52. Bettelheim, "The Ignored Lesson of Anne Frank," p. 46.

53. Bettelheim, "Freedom from Ghetto Thinking," *Midstream* (Spring 1962): pp. 16–25.

54. Hannah Arendt, *Eichmann in Jerusalem: A Report on the Banality of Evil* (New York: Viking, 1963).

55. Bettelheim, "Freedom from Ghetto Thinking," p. 16.

56. Otto Frank, "The Living Legacy of Anne Frank: The Memory Behind Today's Headlines," *Ladies Home Journal,* September 1967, p. 87.

57. "The 'Diary' in Israel," *New York Times,* February 17, 1957.

58. The text of the play is available under the title *The Diary of Anne Frank* by Frances Goodrich and Albert Hackett, newly adapted by Wendy Kesselman. Definitive Edition (New York: Dramatists Play Service, Inc., 2009).

59. For Albrecht Goes, see "Vorwort," *Das Tagebuch der Anne Frank* (Frankfurt am Main: Fischer Bücherei); for Daniel Rops, see "Préface," *Journal de Anne Frank* (Paris: Calmann-Lévy); for Storm Jameson, see foreword to *Anne Frank's Diary* (London: Valentine, Mitchell).

60. G. Boogaard, "Poem on May 5," collected in *A Tribute to Anne Frank,* ed. Anna G. Steenmeijer (Garden City, N.Y.: Doubleday & Company, 1971), p. 53.

5. THE ANNE FRANK WE REMEMBER/THE ANNE FRANK WE FORGET

The first epigraph is from Dick Houwaart, *Anne in't voorbijgaan: Emoties, gedachten en verwachtingenrondom het huis en het Dagboek van Anne Frank* (Amsterdam: Keesing Boeken, 1982), p. 114. The second epigraph is from an interview with Rachel van Amerongen-Frankfoorder, in Willy Lindwer, *The Last Seven Months of Anne Frank* (New York: Pantheon, 1991), p. 110.

1. Judith Miller, *One, by One, by One: Facing the Holocaust* (New York: Simon and Schuster, 1990), p. 287.

2. Primo Levi, *The Drowned and the Saved* (New York: Summit Books, 1988), p. 157.

3. Ibid., 56.

4. Willy Lindwer, *The Last Seven Months of Anne Frank* (New York: Pantheon Books, 1991), pp. 103–104.

5. In David Rosenberg, ed., *Testimony: Contemporary Writers Make the Holocaust Personal* (New York: Random House, 1989), pp. 101–103. For a fuller and more mature response to Anne Frank's diary, see Francine Prose, *Anne Frank: The Book, The Life, The Afterlife* (New York: Harper, 2009).

6. *Testimony,* pp. 27–28.

7. For an account of right-wing attacks on the authenticity of Anne Frank's diary, see *The Diary of Anne Frank: The Critical Edition,* pp. 84–101. For a fuller, more detailed account of the work of the Holocaust deniers, see Deborah Lipstadt, *Denying the Holocaust* (New York, The Free Press, 1993).

8. Frances A. Koestler, "The House on the Prince Canal," *The National Jewish Monthly* (February, 1969): p. 20.

9. Alvin H. Rosenfeld, "Anne Frank and the Future of Holocaust Memory," Joseph and Rebecca Meyerhoff Annual Lecture. Center for Advanced Holocaust Studies, United States Holocaust Memorial Museum (Washington, D.C.), October 14, 2004.

10. Cnaan Liphshiz, "Dutch Jewish group slams card of Anne Frank wearing kaffi-yeh," *Ha'aretz*, January 27, 2008, http://www.haaretz.com/hasen/spages/948514.html.

11. Sebastiaan Gottlieb, "Controversial Anne Frank post card won't be withdrawn," Expatica.com, January 29, 2008, http://www.expatica.com/nl/life_in/feature/Contro-versial-Anne-Frank-post-card-won_t-be-withdrawn.html.

12. Liphshiz, "Dutch Jewish group slams card of Anne Frank wearing kaffiyeh."

13. Quotation in Damien McElroy, "Anne Frank Diary Used to Portray Bush as Nazi," *Telegraph* (London), March 8, 2004.

14. David Little, "Could a Little Girl Be the Key to Stopping the Violence in Iraq and Palestine?" *Al-Jazeerah*, June 13, 2004.

15. Quotation in Rodney Carmichael, "Jewish Studies Class Draws Fire from Some Local Jews," *WACO Tribune-Herald*, April 28, 2001.

16. Ghada Karmi, *In Search of Fatima: A Palestinian Story* (London: Verso, 2004).

17. Muhammad Khan, "Voices of a People Living in Exile," www.muslimnews .co.uk/paper/index.php?article'1582 (accessed July 20, 2004).

18. Quotation in Yusuf Agha, "The Anne Franks of Palestine," Yellowtimes.org, June 20, 2002, www.yellowtimes.org/article.php?sid'410 (accessed July 20, 2004).

19. Quotation in Edna Yaghi, "My Humanity on Hold," www.hejleh.com/edna _yaghi/suad.html (accessed July 20, 2004).

20. *Legacy: The Newsletter of the Anne Frank Center USA* 3, no.1 (November 1992): p. 5.

21. *Testimony*, pp. 195–196.

6. JEAN AMÉRY: THE ANGUISH OF THE WITNESS

The epigraph comes from Jean Améry, *At the Mind's Limits: Contemplations by a Survivor on Auschwitz and Its Realities*, trans. Sidney Rosenfeld and Stella P. Rosen-feld (Bloomington: Indiana University Press, 1980), p. 94.

1. Lawrence Langer, *Using and Abusing the Holocaust* (Bloomington: Indiana University Press, 2006), p. xii. Levi's words, spoken to Ian Thomson, are cited by Langer.

2. Elie Wiesel, *The Accident* (New York: Hill & Wang, 1962), p. 77.

3. See William Helmreich, *Against All Odds: Holocaust Survivors and the Suc-cessful Lives They Made in America* (New York: Simon & Schuster, 1992).

4. Abraham I. Katsh, ed., *The Warsaw Diary of Chaim A. Kaplan* (New York: Col-lier Books, 1973), p. 30.

5. The words are Himmler's, addressed to a group of SS officers on October 4, 1943; quoted in Lucy Dawidowicz, *A Holocaust Reader* (New York: Behrman House, 1976), p. 133.

6. Alvin H. Rosenfeld and Irving Greenberg, eds., *Confronting the Holocaust: The Impact of Elie Wiesel* (Bloomington: Indiana University Press, 1979), p. 206.

7. Jean Améry, *At the Mind's Limits: Contemplations by a Survivor on Auschwitz and Its Realities*, trans. Sidney Rosenfeld and Stella P. Rosenfeld (Bloomington: Indiana University Press, 1980); all references to this book are to this edition and are cited by page number within the body of the chapter.

8. In addition to *At the Mind's Limits*, three of Améry's other books are available in English translation: *Radical Humanism: Selected Essays*, trans. Sidney Rosenfeld and Stella P. Rosenfeld (Bloomington: Indiana University Press, 1984); *On Aging: Revolt and Resignation*, trans. John D. Barlow (Bloomington: Indiana University Press, 1994); and *On Suicide: A Discourse on Voluntary Death*, trans. John D. Barlow (Bloomington, Indiana University Press, 1999). Among the author's untranslated works are *Unmeisterliche Wanderjahre* (1973), a work of autobiographical reflection that is largely a self-study of the growth of an intellectual; and *Widersprüche*, a collection of essays. Améry also wrote two novels, *Lefeu oder der Abbruch* (1974) and *Charles Bovary, Landarzt* (1978). Three volumes of essays appeared posthumously: *Örtlichkeiten* (1980), *Bücher aus der Jugend unseres Jahrhunderts* (1981), and *Weiterleben--aber wie?* (1982).

9. Améry, *Radical Humanism*, p. 65.

10. Ibid., 64–65.

7. PRIMO LEVI: THE SURVIVOR AS VICTIM

The epigraph comes from Elie Wiesel, "Why I Write," in *Confronting the Holocaust: The Impact of Elie Wiesel*, ed. Alvin H. Rosenfeld and Irving Greenberg (Bloomington: Indiana University Press, 1978), p. 205.

1. Primo Levi, *The Drowned and the Saved*, trans. Raymond Rosenthal (New York: Summit Books, 1988), p. 136.

2. Primo Levi, "Jean Améry, Philosopher and Suicide," originally published in *La Stampa*, December 7, 1978, collected in *The Black Hole of Auschwitz*, ed. Marco Belpoliti, trans. Sharon Wood (Cambridge: Polity Press, 2005), pp. 48, 50.

3. Ibid., p. 50.

4. Ibid., p. 49.

5. Readers interested in reviewing reports of Levi's death and various interpretations of it will find pertinent material in Myriam Anissimov, *Primo Levi: Tragedy of an Optimist*, trans. Steve Cox (Woodstock, N.Y.: The Overlook Press, 1999); Carole Angier, *The Double Bond: Primo Levi, A Biography* (New York: Farrar, Straus and Giroux, 2002); and Ian Thomson, *Primo Levi: A Life* (New York: Metropolitan Books, 2002). See also Jared Stark, "Suicide after Auschwitz," *The Yale Journal of Criticism* 14, no. 1 (2001): pp. 91–114.

6. Primo Levi, "Afterword: The Author's Answers to His Readers' Questions," *Survival in Auschwitz and the Reawakening: Two Memoirs* (New York: Summit Books, 1986), p. 276.

7. Quoted in Primo Levi, *The Drowned and the Saved*, pp. 11–12.

8. Améry, *At the Mind's Limits*, p. 3.

9. *The Drowned and the Saved*, pp. 24, 25.

10. Ibid.

11. *Self-Portrait of a Holocaust Survivor* (Jefferson, N.C.: McFarland and Company, 1985), p. 10.

12. *The Drowned and the Saved*, pp. 135, 136.

13. Cynthia Ozick, "Primo Levi's Suicide Note," in *Metaphor and Memory* (New York: Alfred A. Knopf, 1989), pp. 47–48.

14. *The Drowned and the Saved*, p. 137.

15. Ibid., pp. 137–138.

16. Ibid., p. 128.

17. *Self-Portrait of a Holocaust Survivor*, p. 82.

18. Ferdinando Camon, *Conversations with Primo Levi* (Marlboro, V.T.: The Marlboro Press, 1989), p. 61.

19. Ibid., p. 37.

20. *Survival in Auschwitz*, p. 26.

21. Ibid., pp. 105–106.

22. Ibid., pp. 107–108.

23. Primo Levi, "Aus einem Brief Primo Levis an den Übersetzer," in *Ist das ein Mensch? Erinnerungen an Auschwitz* (Frankfurt am Main: Fischer Taschenbuch Verlag, 1979), pp. 8–9.

24. Primo Levi, *The Periodic Table* (New York: Schocken Books, 1984), p. 223.

25. Afterword to *Survival in Auschwitz*, p. 381.

26. *The Drowned and the Saved*, pp. 19–20.

27. *The Reawakening*, pp. 370–371.

28. Ibid., p. 203.

29. Primo Levi, "Questions and Answers at Indiana University," *Midstream* 32 (April 1986): pp. 26–28.

30. Primo Levi, "The Dispute among the Historians," in *The Mirror Maker* (New York: Schocken Books, 1989), pp. 163–166.

31. Ibid., p. 168.

32. Ibid., p. 76.

33. "Pliny," in Primo Levi, *Collected Poems*, trans. Ruth Feldman and Brian Swann (London: Faber and Faber, 1988), p. 33.

34. Primo Levi, "Westward," in *The Sixth Day and Other Tales* (New York: Summit Books, 1990), p. 128.

35. Ibid., p. 129.

36. Ibid., p. 132.

37. Ibid., p. 135.

38. Primo Levi, *Moments of Reprieve* (New York: Summit Books, 1986), pp. 159–160.

39. Levi uses this Yiddish proverb as an inscription to *The Periodic Table* and also quotes it elsewhere.

40. Afterword to *Survival in Auschwitz*, p. 375.

41. *Survival in Auschwitz*, p. 87.

42. *The Drowned and the Saved*, p. 36.

43. Ibid., pp. 23, 24, 34.

44. Primo Levi, "Beyond Survival," *Prooftexts* 4 (January 1984): p. 13.

45. *The Reawakening*, p. 373.

46. *The Drowned and the Saved*, p. 19.

47. Ibid., p. 68.

48. Ibid., p. 69.

49. Ibid., pp. 78–79.

50. Ibid., p. 75.

51. Ibid., pp. 76–78.

52. Ibid., pp. 81–82.

53. Ibid., pp. 82–84.

54. Ibid., pp. 83–84.

55. "A Romantic Grows Up," an interview with Dan Vittorio Segre, *Jerusalem Post International Edition*, September 5, 1987.

56. Primo Levi, *The Monkey's Wrench* (New York: Penguin Books, 1987), pp. 118–119.

8. SURVIVING SURVIVAL: ELIE WIESEL AND IMRE KERTÉSZ

The epigraph is from Elie Wiesel, *The Accident,* trans. Anne Borchardt (New York: Hill and Wang, 1962), p. 105.

1. Eva Fleischner, ed., *Auschwitz: Beginning of a New Era?* (New York: Ktav, 1977), p. 409.
2. Rosenfeld and Greenberg, *Confronting the Holocaust,* p. 201.
3. Elie Wiesel, *Memoirs: All Rivers Run to the Sea* (New York: Alfred A. Knopf, 1995), p. 320.
4. Elie Wiesel, *One Generation After,* trans. Lily Edelman and Elie Wiesel (New York, Random House), p. 9.
5. *One Generation After,* pp. 9–10.
6. Elie Wiesel, *The Testament,* trans. Marion Wiesel (New York: Summit Books, 1981), p. 30.
7. *One Generation After,* p. 174.
8. *At the Mind's Limits,* p. 82.
9. Ibid., p. 16.
10. *One Generation After,* p. 231.
11. Ibid., pp. 166, 165.
12. *At the Mind's Limits,* p. 34.
13. "Why I Write," in *Confronting the Holocaust,* p. 205.
14. Ibid., p. 205.
15. Elie Wiesel, *And the Sea Is Never Full: Memoirs, 1969–,* trans. Marion Wiesel (New York: Alfred A. Knopf, 1999), p. 59.
16. *Memoirs: All Rivers Run to the Sea,* p. 321.
17. *One Generation After,* p. 19.
18. *And the Sea Is Never Full,* p. 347.
19. Elie Wiesel, *The Forgotten,* trans. Stephen Becker (New York: Summit Books, 1992); page numbers referencing citations from this novel will be given in parentheses in the body of the chapter.
20. Elie Wiesel, *From the Kingdom of Memory: Reminiscences* (New York: Summit Books, 1990), p. 9.
21. Elie Wiesel, *A Mad Desire to Dance,* trans. Catherine Temerson (New York: Alfred A. Knopf, 2009).
22. *And the Sea Is Never Full,* p. 355.
23. *One Generation After,* pp. 9–10.
24. Imre Kertész, "Language in Exile" (unpublished English translation of a Hungarian essay, courtesy of the author).
25. Ibid., p. 5.
26. John Freeman, "Finding a Reason to Live," *Jerusalem Post,* January 16, 2005.
27. Imre Kertész, "The Language of Exile," trans. Ivan Sanders, *The Guardian,* October 19, 2002.
28. Imre Kertész, "The Holocaust as Culture," trans. Tünde Vajda, *Szombat,* August 1998, p. 8.
29. "The Language of Exile."
30. "The Holocaust as Culture," p. 8.
31. Imre Kertész, "Heureka!." *Szombat,* May, 2004, p. 8.
32. "The Holocaust as Culture," p. 9.
33. Ibid.

9. THE END OF THE HOLOCAUST

1. Werner Weinberg, *Self-Portrait of a Holocaust Survivor* (Jefferson, N.C.: McFarland & Company, 1985), pp. 14–15.

2. "Heureka!," p. 8.

3. Manfred Gerstenfeld, *The Abuse of Holocaust Memory: Distortions and Responses* (Jerusalem: Jerusalem Center for Public Affairs, 2009).

4. "Polish bishop says Jews exploiting Holocaust," http://jta.org/news/article/2010/01/25/101319/polish-bishop-says-jews-exp

5. See Deborah Lipstadt, *Denying the Holocaust: The Growing Assault on Truth and Memory* (New York: Penguin, 1993); also, Michael Shermer and Alex Grobman, *Denying History: Who Says the Holocaust Never Happened and Why Do They Say It?* (Berkeley: University of California Press, 2000).

6. Elhanan Yakira, *Post-Zionism, Post-Holocaust: Three Essays on Denial, Forgetting, and the Delegitimation of Israel*, trans. Michael Swirsky (Cambridge: Cambridge University Press, 2010), pp. 41, 21.

7. Matthias Küntzel, "Iran's Obsession with the Jews," *The Weekly Standard*, February 19, 2007.

8. *Attitudes toward Jews in Seven European Countries*, Anti-Defamation Report 2009.

9. *European Conditions: Findings of a Study on Group-focused Enmity in Europe*, available at www.amadeu-antonio-stiftung.de.

10. "Holocaust scholars slam EU for backing Nazi-Communist comparison," http://www.haaretz.com/hasen/spages/1145183.html

11. Yehuda Bauer, "Remembering accurately on International Holocaust Remembrance Day," *The Jerusalem Post*, February 4, 2010.

12. Dovid Katz, "On Three Definitions: Genocide; Holocaust Denial; Holocaust Obfuscation," in *A Litmus Case Test of Modernity: Examining Modern Sensibilities and the Public Domain in the Baltic States at the Turn of the Century*, Interdisciplinary Studies on Central and Eastern Europe 5, ed. Leonidas Donskis (Bern: Peter Lang, 2009), pp. 259–277; many of the documents relevant to this discussion, including the Prague declaration and responses to it, are available on Dovid Katz's website.

13. Donskis, "The Inflation of Genocide," July 24, 2009, EuropeanVoice.com.

14. These goals are taken from the missions statements of various institutions listed in the 2010 *Directory of the Association of Holocaust Organizations* (Houston, Tex.: Holocaust Museum Houston, 2010).

15. Quoted from Professor David Leonard's electronically-circulated "CALL FOR PAPERS," November, 2002.

16. Walter Benn Michaels, *The Trouble with Diversity* (New York: Metropolitan Books, 2006), pp. 53, 55.

17. *Teaching the Representation of the Holocaust* (Modern Language Association, 2004), p. 10. Weitz, who teaches history at the University of Minnesota, is deeply ambivalent about these matters. On the one hand, he acknowledges that the "Holocaust was an atrocity of monumental proportions and the greatest tragedy in Jewish history." He also makes clear that he is "not suggesting that we abandon courses and research on the Holocaust and on Nazi Germany." At the same time, he admits that he personally has "never taught a Holocaust course" and finds "unconvincing and unsatisfying the sheer unwillingness to move beyond the German national frame and the fate of the Jews under the Third Reich" (*Teaching the Representation of the Holocaust*, pp. 136, 138).

18. See Jeffrey Alexander, *Remembering the Holocaust: A Debate* (New York: Oxford University Press, 2009); this volume includes Alexander's essay and six responses

to it by other scholars; Michael Rothberg, *Multidirectional Memory: Remembering the Holocaust in the Age of Decolonization* (Stanford, Calif.: Stanford University Press, 2009); and Daniel Levy and Natan Sznaider, *Holocaust and Memory in the Global Age* (Philadelphia: Temple University Press, 2005).

19. *Remembering the Holocaust*, p. 3.

20. Ibid., p. 176; Alexander is here citing the words of a German scholar, Dirk Rupnow.

21. Rüdiger Lautmann, "The Pink Triangle: Homosexuals as 'Enemies of the State,'" in *The Holocaust and History: The Known, the Unknown, the Disputed, and the Reexamined*, ed. Michael Berenbaum and Abraham J. Peck (Bloomington, Indiana University Press, 1998), p. 345.

22. The critic is Nathan Glazer; see *Remembering the Holocaust*, p. 146.

23. Elihu Katz and Ruth Katz, in *Remembering the Holocaust*, p. 160.

24. Norman Finkelstein, *The Holocaust Industry: Reflections on the Exploitation of Jewish Suffering* (London: Verso, 2000), pp. 7–8.

25. Peter Novick, *The Holocaust in American Life* (Boston: Houghton Mifflin Company, 1999), p. 6.

26. Michael Goldberg, *Why Should Jews Survive?: Looking Past the Holocaust toward a Jewish Future* (New York: Oxford University Press, 1995), pp. 5, 41, 59, 175.

27. Philip Lopate, "Resistance to the Holocaust," in *Testimony: Contemporary Writers Make the Holocaust Personal*, ed. David Rosenberg (New York: Random House, 1989), pp. 307, 287, 289, 300, 293, 299, 286; an earlier version of this essay appeared in *Tikkun* 4, no. 3 (May/June 1989), with critical replies by Yehuda Bauer and Deborah Lipstadt, pp. 55–70.

28. See Hasia Diner, *We Remember with Reverence and Love: American Jews and the Myth of Silence after the Holocaust, 1945–1962* (New York: New York University Press, 2009).

29. Tim Cole, *Selling the Holocaust: From Auschwitz to Schindler: How History Is Bought, Packaged, and Sold* (New York: Routledge, 1999), p. 1.

30. Novick, p. 10.

31. Lopate, p. 307.

32. David Stannard, "Preface" to *A Little Matter of Genocide*, by Ward Churchill (San Francisco: City Lights Books, 1997), p. xvii.

33. David Stannard, "Uniqueness as Denial: The Politics of Genocide Scholarship," in *Is the Holocaust Unique?: Perspectives on Comparative Genocide*, ed. Alan S. Rosenbaum (Boulder, Colo.: Westview Press, 1996), pp. 192, 198, 168, 167, 194, 167. For a critical review of Stannard's work and the whole question of "uniqueness" in Holocaust scholarship, see Gavriel D. Rosenfeld, "The Politics of Uniqueness: Reflections on the Recent Polemical Turn in Holocaust and Genocide Scholarship," *Holocaust and Genocide Studies* 13, no. 1 (Spring 1999): pp. 28–61.

34. Churchill, *Little Matter of Genocide*, pp. 7, 73–74.

35. Stannard, "The Politics of Genocide Scholarship," in *Is the Holocaust Unique?*, p. 198.

36. Churchill, *Little Matter of Genocide*, pp. 9, 50, 36.

37. Stannard, "Uniqueness as Denial," pp. 198–199.

38. Thomas Friedman, *From Beirut to Jerusalem* (New York: Farrar, Straus and Giroux, 1989), p. 281.

39. Zygmunt Bauman, *Modernity and the Holocaust* (Ithaca, N.Y.: Cornell University Press, 1989), p. ix.

40. Marc H. Ellis, *Beyond Innocence and Redemption: Confronting the Holocaust and Israeli Power* (San Francisco: Harper & Row, 1990), p. 187.

41. Marc H. Ellis, *Ending Auschwitz: The Future of Jewish and Christian Life* (Louisville, Ky.: Westminster/John Knox Press, 1994), pp. 40, 42, 43.

42. Ibid., p. 39.

43. Avishai Margalit, "The Kitsch of Israel," *New York Review of Books*, March 9, 2000, p. 19.

44. Novick is on record as a critic of Finkelstein's work and has written a sharply negative review of *The Holocaust Industry*; see "A charge into darkness that sheds no light," *Jewish Chronicle*, July 28, 2000, p. 28. For Finkelstein on Novick, see "Uses of the Holocaust," in *London Review of Books* 22, no. 1 (January 6, 2000).

45. Novick, pp. 6, 168, 208, 12.

46. Ibid., pp. 186–188, 269, 207, 12, 201, 110, 195.

47. Norman Finkelstein, *A Nation on Trial: The Goldhagen Thesis and Historical Truth* (New York: Henry Holt and Company, 1998), p. 94.

48. *The Holocaust Industry*, pp. 4, 5, 130, 150.

49. Ibid., 38, 8, 81.

50. Lorenz Jaeger, "Necessary Hyperbole," *Frankfurter Allgemeine Zeitung* (August 14, 2000).

51. Benjamin Weinthal, "Pandering to subtle German Antisemitism," *The Jerusalem Post*, February 21, 2010. Piper Verlag, the book's German publisher, notes that 200,000 copies of the German translation of Finkelstein's book have been sold to date (private communication from Piper Verlag, February 22, 2010).

52. *Der Spiegel*, July 2000, p. 224.

53. Arnold Jacob Wolf, "The Holocaust as Temptation," *Sh'ma*, November 2, 1979, p. 162; see also Wolf, "The Centrality of the Holocaust is a Mistake," *National Jewish Monthly*, October 1980, p. 8.

54. *The Holocaust Industry*, p. 47.

55. Ibid., pp. 55, 3.

56. Ibid., pp. 55, 3, 30, 37.

57. Novick, p. 7.

58. Ibid., p. 277.

59. Ibid., p. 152.

60. Ibid., p. 15.

61. Ibid., pp. 14, 15.

62. Ibid., p. 10.

EPILOGUE

The first epigraph by Rafsanjani was spoken on World Al Quds (Jerusalem) Day, in Teheran, on December 14, 2001, cited in Matthias Küntzel, "Iran's Obsession with the Jews," *The Weekly Standard*, February 19, 2007. For astute analysis of the religious and ideological dimensions of the thinking of Rafsanjani, Ahmadinejad, and Khomeini, see Robert Wistrich, *A Lethal Obsession: Antisemitism from Antiquity to the Global Jihad* (New York: Random House, 2010), pp. 830–927.

The second epigraph is from Ron Rosenbaum, ed., *Those Who Forget the Past: The Question of Anti-Semitism* (New York: Random House, 2004), p. 170.

1. Walter Truett Anderson, "Let's Put an End to 'The End of' Books," *Pacific News Service*, March 4, 1996, http://www.pacificnews.org/jinn/stories/2.05/960304 -end-of.html

2. Améry, *Radical Humanism*, p. 64.

3. The place of the Holocaust in Israeli consciousness and public life has been studied by a number of scholars. For a detailed, reliable account of this complex subject, see Dina Porat, *Israeli Society, The Holocaust, and Its Survivors* (London: Vallentine Mitchell, 2008).

4. Philip Roth, *Operation Shylock* (New York: Simon & Schuster, 1993), p. 43.

5. Rosenbaum, p. 171.

6. Paul Berman, *Terror and Liberalism* (New York: W. W. Norton & Company, 2003), pp. 134, 135–136.

7. Küntzel, "Iran's Obsession with the Jews." For the diffusion of Nazi ideology within parts of the Muslim world, see also, by the same author, "Iranian Antisemitism: Stepchild of German National Socialism," *Israel Journal of Foreign Affairs* 4, no. 1 (2010), and *Die Deutschen und der Iran* (Berlin: WJS Verlag, 2009); and Jeffrey Herf, *Nazi Propaganda for the Arab World* (New Haven, Conn.: Yale University Press, 2009).

8. Benny Morris, "The Second Holocaust Will Not Be Like the First," originally published in German, in *Die Welt* (January 6, 2007), available in English translation on numerous websites, including http://groups.yahoo.com/group/eejh/message/63915.

9. See Roland Imhoff and Rainer Banse, "Ongoing Victim Suffering Increases Prejudice: The Case of Secondary Antisemitism," *Psychological Science* 3, no. 1 (2009); also, Yves Pallade, "Delegitimizing Jews and the Jewish State: Antisemitism and Anti-Zionism after Auschwitz," *The Israel Journal of Foreign Affairs* 3, no. 1 (2009), pp. 63–69.

10. Henryk Broder, *Der ewige Antisemit* (Frankfurt am Main: Fischer Taschenbuch Verlag, 1986), p. 125; Broder may be adapting an earlier formulation coined by the Israeli psychoanalyst, Zvi Rix.

11. Imre Kertész, "The Holocaust as Culture," *Szombat* (August, 1998), p. 8.

12. Imre Kertész, "über den neuen europäischen Antisemitismus," http://print.perlentaucher.de/artikel/3312.html; the translation is mine.

13. "Iran's Obsession with the Jews," *The Weekly Standard*, February 19, 2007.

INDEX

ALVIN H. ROSENFELD holds the Irving M. Glazer Chair in Jewish Studies and is Professor of English at Indiana University Bloomington, where he is also founder and former director of the Borns Jewish Studies Program. He is author of *A Double Dying: Reflections on Holocaust Literature* (1980) and *Imagining Hitler* (1985), and editor of *Thinking about the Holocaust: After Half a Century* (1997) and *The Writer Uprooted: Contemporary Jewish Exile Literature* (2009), all published by Indiana University Press. Rosenfeld held a presidential appointment on the United States Holocaust Memorial Council from 2002 to 2007. He currently serves on the Executive Committee of the United States Holocaust Memorial Museum and is chair of the Academic Committee of the Museum's Center for Advanced Holocaust Studies. He is Director of the Indiana University Institute for the Study of Contemporary Antisemitism.